Elton, *my* Elton

Elton,

my Elton

Gary Clarke

SMITH GRYPHON
PUBLISHERS

First published in Great Britain in 1995 by
SMITH GRYPHON LIMITED
Swallow House, 11–21 Northdown Street
London N1 9BN

A CIP catalogue for this book
is available from the British Library

ISBN 1 85685 093 5

Typeset by Computerset, Harmondsworth
Printed and bound in Great Britain by Butler & Tanner, Frome

Contents

I dedicate this book to all those showbiz legends still standing
who have had the courage to confront their abyss . . .
especially Elton John

Acknowledgements

I would like to acknowledge Tim Fiske, who helped me sustain my belief that I wrote this book for all the right reasons.

Also: Anita, Linton, Peter, Ross and Shaun, for all their encouragement, Brian Littlechild and Eric Harding for research, Helen Armitage for her fine editing and my family for learning to understand.

1. Blue Eyes

'We're the last two people in the world that should be introducing this record,' Elton winked when asked to introduce the song 'I Wanna Be Straight', before adding, 'Some chance!'

BAM! THE STAGE lights burst the darkness. Melbourne's Festival Hall is on its feet. Five thousand people call for Elton. Ear-splitting screams and cheers. Urgent stamping of feet. The welcome builds to a deafening roar. From the stage, fog machines and sound effects create the familiar *whoosh!* opening of 'Funeral for a Friend'. Then, there he is! In striped blazer, thumping on piano, dry ice hissing into a light-striped cloud of swirling mist. Elton's eyes stare intently at the keys as the song's ponderous overture builds to a crescendo.

Elton circles the stage, giving the baying crowd his traditional thumbs-up gesture. Yeah! The Bitch is Back! He bounces back to his stool for 'Candle in the Wind'. Lights flicker in silent salute to Marilyn Monroe. Elton is having a great time. During 'Benny and the Jets' he leaps on the piano, throwing the stool across the stage and grins. Road crew scatter. Sprinting across to his lead guitarist, Davey Johnstone, Elton mimics Davey's movements.

It is April 1982. Elton is on the Australian leg of his *Jump Up!* world tour. The stint in the wilderness in the late 70s is over. His break in 1976 with writer and long-time partner, Bernie Taupin, had seemingly broken the magic. Elton's records, which once came crashing straight into the charts at No. 1, were barely scraping the lower end of the Top 20 in America and Britain. Albums like *A Single Man* and *Victim of Love* were receiving lukewarm reviews, at best.

But as the 80s dawned, Elton returned recharged. He had become the first rock star to tour behind the so-called Iron Curtain. 'Little Jeannie' was a runaway hit, rocketing to No. 3 Stateside. At the end of his US tour in 1980, a free concert at New York's Central Park drew a crowd of 400,000 – his largest-ever audience, with Elton making an appearance in a Donald Duck costume. In September 1980 he left MCA Records and signed with a new label, Geffen. His debut album for the label, *The Fox*, was acclaimed as his best collection of songs in a long time, a resurgence compounded by *Jump Up!* going gold status, and it yielded two Top 20 hits, 'Blue Eyes' and 'Empty Garden'.

For the 1982 *Jump Up!* world tour, he had assembled his band from the glory days – Davey Johnstone, Dee Murray and Nigel Olsson. He was also excited about reviving his relationship with lyricist Bernie Taupin in Montserrat, later in the year.

Australia had gone through its punk and New Wave phases, and fans had younger, more flamboyant heroes erupting from the burgeoning dance/pop culture and the glitz-glossiness of MTV's latest creations. But Australian audiences had remained loyal to Elton, and the energy circuiting the auditorium tonight is awesome. Sweating boys in blue singlets thrust fists into the air, feet pounding in a relentless chorus. Girls sing and scream; the more daring leap on to the stage, enjoying their brief flicker of glory before burly roadies drag them into the cold autumn night air. Sartorial statements dot the crowd – a sweat-stained black Zeppelin T-shirt, cut-down army fatigues, grey Italian suit, nose ring and Birkenstock sandals. The bridge between fashion tastes testify to Elton's astonishingly wide appeal.

The star stares into the darkness broken by occasional sparklers cascading white light. 'This one's for GC,' Elton announces. The band moves into 'Blue Eyes'. Who is this GC? It's my precious secret. The fans go wild around me, responding to the familiar riff of a song that's been thrashed on the radio, but I am hardly aware for I'm on a different planet. I am feeling blissfully special. A song for GC? Elton had written it for me – ME! Warhol's 15 minutes of fame, right! Elton had not said 'Blue Eyes' was specifically about me, but much later when I had met Gary Osborne, who had penned the lyrics at Elton's suggestion, Osborne, who is not gay, had looked closely at my face and turned to Elton and said, 'Yeah, he *has* got lovely blue eyes.' Later, on tour, the entourage knew it was my song – more so than 'Crystal', which was another of his pet names for me.

I was aware Elton had felt something special for me when we had first met two years before in Queensland at a TV studio and later at a party in the Melbourne home of a mutual friend, Ian (Molly) Meldrum. Molly was the self-styled guru of the Australian pop scene and also one of its most powerful and influential figures. He hosted the national rock show, *Countdown*, which Elton sometimes co-hosted when in Australia. On this visit, things were starting to hot up between Elton and me. One of the world's biggest superstars had called me at work to invite me to the show . . . to meet him in his dressing room trailer prior to the show . . . to come back to his hotel room after the concert.

'GARY!' Huh? I'm engrossed in Elton's charismatic performance. He is already racing into his second encore, kneeling on the floor, head back and banging the keyboards. The crowd's unbridled enthusiasm clearly indicates that a third encore is in order. 'GARY!' It is Elton's Australian publicist, Patti Mostyn. When Elton is in Australia, Patti's role extends to more than co-ordinating promotion and deciding which media person receives complimentary review tickets. Patti, who sat next to me during the show, was obediently seeking my attention. 'I've got to go now. Don't forget Elton wants you to come back to the hotel,' she yelled over the din.

What takes place over the next few hours turns my life around for ever.

• • •

I first met Elton in late 1980, on Friday, 5 December, three days before his close friend John Lennon was assassinated. My life at the time was uncomplicated and fun-filled, if a mite mundane by international jet-setting standards. But for a nondescript kid who'd dropped out of high school, I was doing all right. I was pleased that I had recently gained a promotion at the State Law Department, where I worked as a law clerk.

I was also proud that I had obtained my student pilot's licence: I had applied to join the Royal Australian Air Force but had been offered a career in tools rather than electricals. I was a law clerk instead, but it remained a dream to become a pilot for one of the Australian commercial airlines. At this point I had neither the academic qualifications nor the $20,000 (£10,000) to do the course. Nevertheless every weekend I would traipse off to Moorabbin Airport to do an hour of flying. It cost $65 (£33) an hour, which ate deeply into my weekly wage. My father had been in the RAF in Britain, and I had obviously inherited his love of flying, but, to me, it wasn't so much the excitement of being in the air, as the majestic thrill of the control one had in such powerful, refined machinery. As a kid, I'd always been fascinated with electronic gadgets and mod cons, and an aircraft is the ultimate gadget.

At this time, my low-profile social life was starting to gain momentum. Occasional all-night parties and gay club rages. I was coming to terms with my sexuality and the insecurity that went with it. It had been quite a few years since I'd realized I preferred males. At 13 I'd had this niggling desire, a strong attraction to boys. I hoped it was a passing phase that everyone goes through. But, by 15, panic set in. This passing phase was slowly but surely becoming my only phase, my sexual reality. A reality that I was too scared to share.

Melbourne, like most of urban Australia, was slowly lumbering out of entrenched conservatism after decades of rule by the Liberal Party. The election of Whitlam's Labour Party and its socialist ideologies challenged the imperial indoctrination that Australians and Australian culture were somehow inferior. Under

Labour, there was a greater tolerance of multi-culturalism, female rights, sexual preferences, Aboriginal land demands, marijuana smoking and even porn. Australian art and literature flourished, a national identity was re-forming. The rebellious seeds of Republicanism were sown, and the ruling class was under siege. This was the Australia of my teens – an improving environment for young homosexuals.

But these were early days, and there was still little tolerance of minority groups. I had to make sure I continued to give the 'right' signals so no one at school – and, heavens, at home! – would suspect my homosexuality. Other boys suspected of being less than fully red-blooded Anzacs had been victimized with catcalls, and they took home the occasional black eye. I wasn't the muscular member of the football team whose interest in life went no further than brawling, drinking, hot rodding and screwing girls *en masse*. I was tiny, slim, had translucent skin, a love for motorbikes and minimal interest in contact sports. I was definitely no brawler, but I had no intention of being a victim. I would have preferred to have been straight, but I reasoned that as my gayness was something over which I had no control, I had to accept it, albeit grudgingly.

But, at 16, the Big Secret came tumbling out. An older man who had tried to molest me had become enraged when I refused sex. He turned mean and had a woman friend, posing as a distraught mother, phone my Mum. The woman lied to Mum, stating that I'd been sleeping with her teenage son. No son existed. Pandemonium! The sky dropped on Chicken Little! My father was an ex-cop, a distant man who had found it difficult to convey affection for his only son. Dad could not cope. I was out of school and out of home, and my father refused to speak to me for two years. When I was eventually made welcome in the family home, it was clear that my parents had done some reading about homosexuality and realized it was neither an evil sickness nor anything of their doing. However, my gayness was something that we never discussed again, much like a terminal illness, about which nothing could be done.

In those formative teenage years, my only choice was to hang out with my own kind on the fringes of the gay scene. I was young, naive, overly protected and painfully shy. The gay scene in Melbourne in the mid-70s was still very much a well-hidden and carefully disguised sub-culture. But there were the little known, almost secret, gay clubs that offered warmth and fun. Scores of homosexual men who had spent the week hiding their sexuality from their workmates and college friends would flock to these clubs. Everyone would dance to the Village People, Donna Summer and Tramps, the hot sweaty disco music helping to build the intensity and sexuality within the safe haven of the club walls.

In hindsight, it was unusual for a young man to be with older company most of the time, but the acquaintances of my age were impossibly straight and I hadn't met many young gays. The few I came to know were excessively and overtly effeminate, and this wasn't my style. The growing use of designer drugs and dope in these places and the bitchy mind games that scorned lovers played on each other were beyond me. I had come from a middle class family that was, to use the Australian slang, 'straight as a die', and had never come into contact with sleazy queens and their vicious ways. But even though the clubs were populated by many of these types, I still felt most comfortable in these fun places. So the illicit, underground playpens became my refuge, a place to build my network of older friends and to delight in the eccentricity of its inhabitants.

As well as the camaraderie of the club scene, there was something sinister and vulture-like that also pervaded the atmosphere. The vulnerable and innocent would be used and rejected, and it knocked around the fragile self-esteem of many a young man. I was particularly vulnerable because I had no home: I had moved house twenty times in four years. Inevitably some older man would promise to look after me, then become bored because I was reluctant to fulfil his sexual wishes. Out into the street I'd go! This search for willing young flesh seemed eternal: the older the man, the more desperate the quest. Life seemed pretty tough for I felt that I had been thrust into that kind of life through no fault of mine. Life for attractive homosexual boys of my age was a rat-trap – and we were the cheese.

By the end of 1979 yet another older queen had decided I'd become a pain to have around. Foolishly, but inevitably, I had once again thought we'd be able to 'just be friends'. Obviously an irrational hope, but I wanted to think otherwise. A host of disasters of my own making didn't help the situation either! At that point, I met Ross, who worked as the catering manager of the famous Melbourne Arts Centre – and he asked me to move into his house on Albert Road, South Melbourne, a distinguished address. Ross was quiet, liked to stay at home tinkering with his cars and never pressured me to sleep with him. I, on the other hand, loved clubbing, partying and zipping around on my new Yamaha motorbike. We were total opposites, but I was comfortable and secure with him, and I felt I had found a home and a friend.

I was also now hanging out with Molly Meldrum, the rock-show guru, who, while indignantly denying his homosexuality in public, would haunt the gay clubs, scotch and coke in hand. Through his high-rating weekly TV rock show, *Countdown*, radio spots and weekly column in the high-circulation magazine, *TV Week*, Molly could make or break careers. He'd been a beach bum in the 60s, and by getting to know big pop bands he'd scored himself a job as reporter on the country's biggest industry paper at the time, *Go-Set*. His real name was Ian, but he'd gained his nickname from the phrase 'band moll', Australian slang for groupie. Molly also danced while miming on a pop show called *Kommotion* and produced hits for other stars.

Through his contacts, Molly made his way to the top. Other journalists cringed at his bumbling celebrity interviews, but it was this unique style that appealed to his young TV audience. They identified with someone who had trouble putting a sentence together or remembering the last question. Molly would constantly 'um' and 'arr', and many years later, the Australian housewife superstar comedienne, Dame Edna Everidge, suggested that it was Ian that put the '*um* in Meldr*um*'.

Despite Molly's apparent inept and unprofessional manner, there was no one in the industry in Britain or America who had his influence, persistence or personality. He had to be admired for his resolve. 'Scotch and Coke' Meldrum (another affectionate nickname, derived from his favourite drink) was, and still is, a fixture at the gay clubs that played the best and hippest dance music. He often deliberately dropped a sly reference on TV to his sexuality and on one occasion appeared on *Countdown* in drag. Molly was more than a little extrovert and had a car number plate which read MM-069. But for all this he managed to keep his private life concealed from public view.

I first met Molly while working weekends at an American-style ice-cream parlour. When Molly came in, I was so ga-ga over the fact that I was serving a real, live celebrity that I gave him three large tubs of ice-cream instead of the three cones he ordered. He didn't raise a fuss, just paid for what he hadn't asked for and left. But he did make a point of coming back, and soon we were visiting each other. Before long Molly was inviting me to view the taping of *Countdown* or to the Croxton Park disco, where he DJ'd at nights. I became part of his circle: Molly had a group of young blond things who invariably ate and drank him out of house and home, but he loved the view. The boys formed a sycophantic club, serving as his chauffeur–protectors, and bitching and sniping as they scrambled to get closest to Molly. Being in Molly's entourage meant constant adventure and a 24-hour party, but it also meant constant trauma and mind games.

I could see how fame gave one a sense of privilege. Once, on a whim, we jumped into his Rolls-Royce and screamed up the Hume Highway to Sydney, doing 140 km per hour. I was driving. There was a 100 km speed limit on one stretch of the road, and soon the police were giving chase, blue lights flashing. The cop caught up with us, and angrily stomped over but as soon as he saw Molly his attitude changed, and he chatted about music before asking Molly for an autograph for his daughter. We left with a warning.

Being a member of Molly's entourage opened doors, and occasionally I met a passing celebrity. I enjoyed tea at the Hilton hotel with singer Sheena Easton, who had a big hit with '9 to 5 (Morning Train)'. She was charming although it mystified me how someone who sang so clearly could still speak with a barely comprehensible Scots accent. I also attended a lunch at the high-class Sardis restaurant with Bette Midler, who took delight in urging me to try Eggs Benedict for the first time. But these outings were unusual events and, generally speaking, Meldrum's boyfriends were 'obscene but not heard'.

These were my early days with Molly, and no one could have predicted what was to come. One day, quite out of the blue, Molly's assistant, Jeannie, rang me at the Law Department: 'Molly's going to Brisbane [in Queensland] to tape *Countdown* and was wondering if you would like to go.'

'Why Queensland?'

'Elton John's touring and is co-hosting *Countdown*.'

'When?' I said, trying to contain my excitement.

'It'll be Friday.'

I gave her my phone number and couldn't wait for Friday to arrive.

As Elton continually polled as the country's most popular international male performer, a top-rating show like *Countdown* was prepared to accept the expense of going to Elton John. To give you an idea of the importance of *Countdown* to visiting celebs, keen on appealing to the kids, even Prince Charles, when he was in Australia, made an appearance. Molly outdid himself that day when he inadvertently placed his hand on Charles's thigh during taping and asked him: 'How's your mum?'

Charles responded in an offended royal tone: 'You mean, Her Majesty?' Poor Molly cringed.

The Friday flight to see Elton was booked, and as soon as we arrived at the airport, people fell over themselves to attend to Molly or attract his attention. Fans sought autographs; taxi drivers and waiters offered opinions on new records. It was quipped that Molly was a bigger star than some of the people he interviewed. He wasn't a performer like McCartney or Jagger, but he was a star by association. Molly's access to the superstars was what his audience envied. But if I had known what was to come over the next decade, I would have gladly told Molly's secretary to cancel my booking.

Camera cranes careered around the ABC Brisbane studios; lights and reflectors were being tested; people stepped gingerly over thick grey cables. An assistant called for silence on the set as someone's kids ran giggling along the white tile corridors. Amid the chaos, Molly and Elton clowned around. They had been close friends since the early 70s, when Molly had championed the unknown singer/songwriter through the pages of *Go-Set* and helped break his first hit 'Your Song' in Australia.

At one stage Elton and Molly began reminiscing about Elton's infamous shopping binges. Elton recalled the time when he, Bernie Taupin and Maxine (Bernie's then-wife) rented a house in Malibu for a month's holiday. Bernie was still living in England then. They went shopping every day and ended up with 67 cases. Elton laughed, 'Can you believe it? *67 cases!* And half of them came from the same shop! We just bought everything.

'I went crazy and bought hundreds of records. In the end we had a Greyhound bus take all the things to the airport. Incredibly, we only had to pay £100 at customs. Fancy that! Just £100 for thousands and thousands of dollars-worth of records and books. Crazy! I go back to England every time from a tour with at least eight more suitcases than I started with. And I never know where to put the bloody stuff when I get home anyway!'

At the time I thought it was an amusing story of extravagance. It was only later that I understood that this mad craze for shopping was another form of bingeing – which some years later would manifest itself in bulimia. Elton needed to acquire material things and people, to search for fulfilment everywhere but inside himself.

But on that day I was innocent of all these complications. All

I knew of Elton was what I could see. He was dressed in a black jacket with colourful embroidery, cowboy boots and a Stetson. Physically and mentally he seemed at his prime, and to this day I think it was the best he ever looked. I loved the accent. He was amiable and down to earth. There was a whiff of attractive arrogance from a man whose earnings were then estimated at US$7 million a year, and whose social circle included members of the British Royal Family, the cream of British pop and sporting champions such as tennis stars Billy Jean King and Martina Navratilova and footballer Rodney Marsh.

You could tell by his demeanour that Elton was pleased to be back in Australia. He liked its weather, the fact that its people didn't suffer from stress and paranoia like many Americans and especially the knowledge that he could walk around Australian streets without being hassled. But, however much other countries appealed, Elton was very much the English patriot, refusing to desert the Mother Country despite its huge income tax demands. Another attraction Australia held for Elton was that it was virtually the opposite end of the earth to Britain, both in distance and attitude. Here he could, for a time, escape the blinkered vision and narcissistic snobbishness of its class structure, its horrendous weather and the viciousness of its tabloid press, which by this time had really found its niche in English society.

As the cameras rolled during the taping of the *Countdown* episode, it was obvious Elton and Molly were close friends. Molly admitted on camera it was the first time he'd allowed anyone else to co-host his gossip segment, Humdrum. Molly praised Elton for continuing his Sydney concert when drummer Nigel Olsson had fainted onstage, and he giggled uncontrollably when Elton was cheekily reviewing records. But the highlight was when Molly asked the artist to introduce Ian Dury's hit at the time, 'I Wanna Be Straight'.

Elton peered into the camera and quipped, 'I think they're putting this on on purpose for us. I mean, we're the last two people in the world that should be introducing this record . . . but, however, Ian Dury, "I Wanna Be Straight" . . . some chance!'

He turned to Molly with a querulous sly look, Molly acted horrified, and the lads collapsed in giggles.

Elton's fooling indicated that another attraction Australia held for the star was that he felt very safe here. Unlike in the UK, there was no vicious tabloid circulation battle to cause reporters to dig deep into people's lives. In the early part of the 70s, Elton's sexual preference was kept under wraps. He often told the tale of the time he almost married a six-foot girl, Linda Woodrow, for whom he felt compassion. Apparently Linda was dating a violent midget who beat her severely. Elton and Linda solved the problem by moving into a flat together and had a miserable six months, during which time Elton almost had a nervous breakdown – even an attempt at suicide.

According to Elton, Linda became antagonistic to him, and Elton's mother, Sheila, said she would refuse to speak to him again should he marry her. Elton finally moved out. The song 'Someone Saved My Life Tonight' from the *Captain Fantastic* album is written about this incident and refers to advice that Elton received from his mentor, Long John Baldry, about marrying Linda. Linda was so annoyed at this story being mentioned in interview that she contacted her lawyer to see if she could sue Elton.

This affair was one of Elton's favourite stories, and it is interesting to note that it was one of the few that included his mother. Obviously both these women lurked deep in the shadows of his psyche, where, no doubt, both stood tall and kept close company. The unloved Stan, Elton's real father, also lingers in those shadowy recesses waiting patiently to be encountered and embraced. But it was not yet to be: Elton's 1992 album *The One* includes a song lamenting the sadness of not making friends with one's father before death intervenes.

Fame inevitably brings public interest in any star's sexual encounters. Part of the androgynous enigma of the 70s, Elton attracted more than his share of smirking interviewers. Obviously journalists were aware of the gossip about his preference for male companions that circulated the music industry, but nothing specific ever reached print. Elton's populist image was that of a decent bloke who did a lot of charity work and had connections with the then sacred Royal Family. His English publicists were two former top rock journalists, themselves well acquainted with the media's quest for scoops and exclusives and aware of the sneaky, treacherous ways they gathered information. John Reid, Elton's manager, also kept a strict eye on how any interviews were conducted. As early as 1974, magazines such as *Playboy* and *Melody Maker* alluded to Elton's homosexuality, but he managed to avoid the tricky questions.

All that changed during the 1976 American tour. Elton had a drag queen as part of his stage show, camped it up during a celebrity guest stint on a New York radio show, and accompanied gay star, Divine, to a New York gay disco called Crisco Disco. Crisco was a frying oil used as a lubricant during anal intercourse.

Around this time David Bowie broadcast that while he had been honest about his bisexuality, other stars hadn't – and he then mentioned Elton by name. That must have rankled, for the media were just starting to hammer away at Elton. Right after this Bowie comment Elton was quizzed by *Rolling Stone* magazine about whether he received love and affection at home, and Elton honestly replied that the only love he received was from his huge collection of records. But he added that one day he wanted to settle down with someone – of either sex. It was a confession that came out of the blue, and his publicists and management over in England must have freaked; Elton would later claim that the *Rolling Stone* journalist was so flabbergasted by his scoop that he asked if Elton wanted to edit that statement. Elton actually seemed relieved after confessing an interest in both sexes.

Twenty years later, he'd admit that it would have been more correct to have admitted to being a homosexual, rather than a bisexual. 'I was probably scared,' he told *Q* magazine. 'It was easier to say. I suppose it was a cop-out, but at the time I thought, Well, let's be diplomatic about it.'

In that interview he said as a youngster he had gone out with girls, probably felt the odd opportune breast in the back seats of a cinema, 'but I didn't get any great satisfaction from it.' Instead, when he had his first gay experience at 23, he realized which way his path was going. He'd already known he was gay and was quite comfortable with it when he made the revelation in *Rolling Stone in 1976*. 'I thought everybody knew anyway.'

Nevertheless, admitting to being bisexual in 1976 was a real revelation. In America, some radio stations stopped playing his records for a time, and some people reportedly burnt his records in the streets. The confession would not make the English papers until a few years later. The first Elton heard of the story reaching his home turf was when he was in a hotel in Manchester, to watch Watford play against Rochdale. Sheila had asked him if he'd read the morning's *Daily Mirror*. He hadn't. 'Well, I'd better warn you,' she said.

When he went to the game, the then-manager of Watford took him aside and told him the players had seen the morning's newspaper and weren't bothered by what they had read. Generally, the British media of the time didn't indulge in the hysteria and moralizing that was to greet later Elton scandals. The only negative reaction, it seemed, came when the *Sun* was accused of dumping plans to give away 50 copies of Elton's *Blue Moves* album as prizes because its cover sleeve – a painting by Patrick Proktor called *The Guardian Readers* – featured all young men.

As was to be expected, there was a rush to re-examine earlier Elton songs and LP sleeves to see if there were any hints of his sexuality. 'Daniel' was cited to be about a gay lover, but it was obvious that Bernie Taupin's lyrics were about an embittered war veteran. The 'To David' tribute on the cover of *Tumbleweed Connection* was not to any ex-lover but to singer/songwriter David Ackles whom Elton admired. Elton performed a benefit show for the National Youth Theatre not because he'd been turned on by a play they did called *Good Lads At Heart,* about a Borstal reform school, but because his solicitor was the theatre company's chairman. 'Song for Guy' was supposedly about a lover who'd ridden in a motorbike gang. In fact, Guy Burchett was a messenger boy who worked for Elton's Rocket Records, and Elton hardly knew him. Elton had finished the piece of music on a Sunday and heard about the boy's death in a motorbike accident the next morning. He rang Burchett's mother to offer his condolences and asked if he could use her son's name in his new song. Such touches reveal that despite his sometimes callous behaviour, there is a lot of heart in Elton John.

Well, that's how it all started. I had embarked on a gay life: fun, excitement, anecdotes about the stars. So naive and innocent. Yet, what appears as a random series of events, on reflection, is part of a jigsaw. My puzzle was in an early stage of development. It had the corners completed, but the essential Elton was yet to be revealed.

2. Where to Now St Peter?

The evening after I told Elton I'd leave Australia to be with him in England, I came home to 100 white roses on my doorstep.

O N THE EVENING after the Brisbane *Countdown* taping, I returned to my room at the Park Royal Hotel for a quick nap. Going clubbing with Molly usually meant we wouldn't be home until dawn. It was 8.30 pm, and the phone jangled next

It was Molly: 'Come up to Patti's room, we're eating with Elton.'

It was, I later discovered, typical of Elton. He would book the most expensive and luxuriously equipped suite in the hotel, yet seldom stay in it. He'd either be hanging out with his personal assistant, Bob Halley, or, as in this case, inhabiting Patti Mostyn's room. I came to learn that wherever Elton lived, he kept shrines in homage to his image, rooms like the Hilton's presidential suite, but he preferred to live elsewhere.

When I wandered into the suite, Molly, Patti and a soft-spoken man called Kevin Ritchie, the tour promoter, were sitting around waiting for Elton to finish his shower. I knelt on the floor. Ten minutes later, Elton swept in wearing a white terry-towelling dressing robe, and plonked himself on the chair opposite me, legs casually open, pelvis forward, his draped robe accentuating his bulge. Everyone sat in a semi-circle around Elton, but there was a respectful distance between the star and his friends. Then Elton turned to me and said: 'Molly tells me you're learning to fly.' It registered with a thump – Elton is actually talking to me! He continued on, and I heard him say: 'I've always wanted to drive a plane!'

'You don't drive a plane, you fly one,' I curtly replied.

Good grief! I sounded so abrupt! Where was that brittle haughtiness in my voice coming from? Maybe it was because I'd never met a real live superstar before. Or maybe I suffered from this notion that real gods, like Elton, did not make mistakes – and Elton stuffed it after only a few words.

Mind you, at the time, Elton was only a minor god to me. You see, as far as I was concerned, someone like Molly was a bigger star than Elton. My musical tastes were more for sexy disco acts like Donna Summer and Village People. These were the stars I'd have loved to have met. It was coincidental that the first single I owned was an Elton track: my Mum had heard me singing 'Philadelphia Freedom' around the house and bought me a copy for my birthday.

Thankfully Elton laughed at my snotty answer. There was no further scintillating chat from me, and the conversation drifted off to showbiz chatter, an area in which I was presumed ignorant. Elton recounted how he'd recently paid US$8000 to a former BBC producer for a collection of 30,000 singles. 'Every single released in the UK for the last 15 years!' he cackled happily.

I plucked up courage. 'So what is your most prized possession?' I said, smiling. A safe question.

'Oh, that's easy,' Elton said, 'I've got a drawing of me and Groucho Marx. He signed it "Marx Groucho" because he said my name was back to front. A very funny man. I'm in awe of legends like that. The first time I met Mae West I was so tongue-tied I just couldn't speak.' I didn't have that problem. I just corrected the star's grammar.

The topic of the Beatles slipped into the conversation. In 1968 Molly had worked for the Beatles' Apple company and had, in

fact, scooped the world. Molly was interviewing John Lennon for
Go-Set, and John let slip that he was so tired of the Fab Four that
he wanted to leave. This was an astonishing statement, considering how omnipotent the Beatles were at the time. Molly was so
overawed at being in John's presence that he didn't realize what
John had said, and it was only when Molly sent the interview tape
back to the Melbourne editor that they realized what a hot story
they had in hand. Molly gained quite a reputation around the
world for breaking what had to be the rock 'n' roll story of the
year.

'The Beatles! Don't let's start on them!' Elton groaned, but his
voice held affection, 'I've always said that if I ever made an album
as good as *Abbey Road*, I'd retire.' Elton was godfather to John's
second son, Sean, so he must have known the Lennons well. And
he spoke fondly of John:

'John was the first superstar I fell in love with. He was doing
a Phil Spector session in LA, about 1973. Usually it takes me ages
to get close to someone, at least about seven or eight meetings
because I can be quite introverted. John's so down to earth and
friendly. I remember one time I arrived at LA airport, and
suddenly I heard this screech, "Oh, my God, it's Elton. Elton!
Aaaaah!" It was John, and he pretended to faint at my feet right
there on the floor among the masses of travellers. Of course
everybody stared.

'Anyway that night of the Spector session, John said, "Do you
want to go and see this great band called the Dramatics, they're
playing at the Roxy." We went past the Roxy, and all these beautifully dressed black people were waiting outside to go in, and
John put his head out of the sun roof of this hired Mercedes
yelling out, "Right on! right on!" The place was so jam-packed we
couldn't get in.' I became aware that whenever Elton spoke to
me, his stare was intense. I'd seen that look in older gays when
they chatted me up in clubs.

Patti Mostyn called for sandwiches to be brought to the room,
and we munched on those. About 20 minutes later, Elton went
off. The conversation turned to how uptight Elton seemed to be

and whether sex would help the situation. 'How would you like a spend a few minutes with Elton?' Patti said jokingly. 'Er, no thanks!' I mumbled, eliciting more laughter from her.

Although I wasn't a big fan of Elton's music, that was to change dramatically. The next night I experienced his charisma as a stage performer for the first time at his concert at Brisbane Festival Hall. Molly watched from the side of the stage. So did I. It was such a buzz to hear the songs that had blared from the radio so many times actually being sung by the man in person, just a few feet away. I remember thinking to myself: this is someone I'd love to get to know better. Not because he was wealthy or famous but because he seemed such an extraordinary human being. There were lots of pluses about Elton: I was impressed by the way he treated people with courtesy and put them at ease, and the effort he put into his performance, making sure he never short-changed his fans. Elton made his paying public feel part of the event, as if he had flown from the other end of the world just to play for them.

Molly and I moved into the audience midway through, just to experience the show from out front. Molly, in between shaking hands with kids in the crowd, was making his way to the mixing desk when he spotted a small, rotund, bright-eyed guy with short dark hair, and an older curly-haired woman in a black jumper and pants. We were introduced. The man was Elton's manager, John Reid, and the woman was Elton's mother, Sheila. Reid grinned and then went off to check the sound from different parts of the hall. I felt Sheila was a warm-natured and pleasant person.

Any comprehensible conversation was obviously impossible: one had to yell over the amplified noise coming from the stage, so Molly and I screamed our goodbyes and returned to the wings. After the third encore, Elton rushed through the off-stage door and straight into his limo. With a screech of tyres, he was gone, well and truly, before any of the fans had time to run through the front door and around to the back.

The next day, when Molly and I were returning to Melbourne, we stopped over in Sydney where I witnessed my first scene of big-time drug indulgence. Molly took me along when he met with a high-profile manager of an American superstar band, who was visiting Australia to check out the possibilities of touring. The guy was very New York – hyper, lots of buzz words and very aware of his power. He and his flunkies were snorting cocaine in their hotel suite, so much in fact that the white powder was smeared around their snouts like talc on a baby's bottom. I sat on the side watching quietly while Mr New York put the heat on Molly to play more of his band's videos on *Countdown*. During the conversation, the manager kicked open the door to his bedroom. A young rent boy was lying naked on the bed, face down, obviously out of his head on various substances, literally drug-fucked.

'Go for it, Molly,' the New Yorker insisted, swishing his arms towards the sad mess inside.

Molly looked outraged. 'No, I've got to go now,' he said curtly. He turned to me and said, 'You can stay if you want to, Gary.'

'Thanks, Molly!' I fumed. Did he really think I'd have a good time partying with these creeps? No way! We took off out the door.

I wasn't to see Elton again for another few weeks. This time it was when Molly threw his annual Christmas bash at his Alfred Street flat for his showbiz friends. Molly's parties were legendary: the music was loud, the drinks were plentiful, his guests were extravagant, and you invariably woke up the next morning to discover people passed out on the couch, the stairs, under the table and even in the bathtub. This party was just as raucous.

It was a very hot night and stifling inside, so I made my way up a ladder to the roof. Another guest had the same idea, and we exchanged pleasantries. He told me he was Michael Hewitson, a member of Elton John's entourage. We got into a rave about his travels with the superstar, and about 20 minutes later, when I went back into the house for an orange juice, I noticed Elton wearing a hat, a light blue jacket over a T-shirt and black pants. He was standing by himself, gazing enviously at a framed copy of the Beatles' *White Album*, autographed by all four Fabs – a legacy from Molly's days at Apple.

We exchanged cordial hellos, and I was genuinely pleased to see E. As we spoke Elton gave me 'that lecherous look', but, of course, there were too many people about for it to go any further. In any case, there was always someone wanting to talk to him; he was as charming as ever, graciously thanking people when they congratulated him on his concerts and music.

After an hour or so, I noticed Elton leave. He'd had enough and returned to his hotel in the limo waiting outside. I later discovered that when Michael Hewitson, the guy from the roof, had gone back to his hotel room, Elton had pumped him endlessly for information about me – what had I said? what had I been up to?

By 1982 I'd become one of Elton's biggest fans. I bought all his records, virtually knew every song by heart and eagerly scanned the showbiz magazines for any tit-bits about him. 'Blue Eyes' became another big hit for him in Australia. The first time I heard it was on the radio while at work at the Law Department, and everyone in my section crowded around and declared it one of his great songs.

When Elton announced his March 1982 tour, most of my workmates, including my boss, decided to go to one of his shows in a group. We seldom saw each other outside office hours, except for the occasional lunch or theatre show at night, and they knew very little about my personal life. But we were all Elton fans. Elton was playing an entire week in Melbourne, and we decided to go for the Thursday night's concert. I bought two tickets: the other one was for Cameron, a straight boy with whom I'd recently fallen in love. Cameron was a good-looking plumber's apprentice, and we had come to know each other after being abused by the same older man. We did explore some sexual barriers, but a long-term love affair was never a possibility. Being part of a Victim's Club is one way to meet people, I guess!

A future member in the club that I would relate to in her pain was Elton's wife, for we both had our hearts broken by the Piano Man.

On the Friday night before Elton's run of concerts in Melbourne, Molly rang: 'Elton's back in town, and he wants you to come to dinner.' Elton, a curry buff, had booked us into an Indian restaurant, where piped sitar music, dim lighting and Indian art gave the place an intimate, sensual setting.

Molly and I arrived fashionably late. Elton, already installed, was wearing an expensive leather jacket with shoulder pads that made him look like a rugby player, and a black hat with black pants. Patti Mostyn was at his side, dripping with diamond earrings, bangles, rings and loops of all kinds. Sitting opposite Elton was Bob Halley, who was utterly devoted to Elton. Everyone was exquisitely dressed, and I felt plain in my jeans and sneakers, although now I know youthful naivety is quite a turn-on for older gays.

That night, the imperious Elton held court, keeping his guests entertained with his anecdotes of the rich and famous. How at Prince Andrew's 21st, he had danced with the Queen to Bill Haley's 'Rock Around the Clock' with her handbag still dangling from Her Majesty's wrist. About Liberace and how his autograph wasn't just a scrawl like most peoples, but an elaborate flourish with a drawing of a piano. About Keith Moon, who, when he earned his first million dollars, rushed out and bought four houses, a hotel, eight cars, expensive furniture – and in six weeks had spent the lot. About David Bowie, who apparently at one stage wanted to be Judy Garland.

Elton spoke in a quiet, confident manner, and unlike many lesser celebs didn't seek public attention. But you could tell by the way the waiters eagerly hovered around, and from the constant stares and whispers of other diners, that having Elton John in their midst was a thrill.

Elton loved his Indian food, the spicier the better. He ordered like an expert, and the smiling waiter congratulated him on his correct pronunciation of Indian words. This was my first experience of Elton as a host, and he was a delight. He didn't flash his wealth but ensured that his guests knew he wanted them to have the best of everything – and plenty of it. I noticed it again the next day when Molly and I went to Bob's suite at the Hilton to watch tennis on TV. Elton is a more than adept player and was quite excited that Australia's Wendy Turnbull was winning. When Molly and I arrived, he immediately rose and mixed drinks at the bar, personally replenishing our glasses throughout the visit. Not once did he ask someone else to fetch and carry for him. His manner as he moved was precise, almost fussy.

Someone asked him about his supposed affair with Billie Jean King, and Elton laughed loudly: 'We hung out together, that's all. She's such a lot of fun. We're very much alike as people – both determined to win at all costs. Before I met her I'd read all these stories about her, what a moody bitch she was, and she's absolutely nothing like that.'

With the tennis over, the television was silenced and we made plans for dinner. Nothing of note happened that night.

Two days later, on Tuesday morning, while I was flicking through some papers at work, the switchboard operator buzzed me: it was Patti Mostyn. The artiste wanted to talk. The familiar clipped English accent then came on, exuding joviality: 'How about a hot date?'

'Er, no thanks,' I replied.

The tone changed immediately: 'No, no, I didn't mean it like that. I'd really like you to come to the concert tonight.'

Elton's instructions were simple: come to the rear of the Festival Hall about an hour before show-time. He would make sure someone would take care of me. I was thrilled. This was big time. Leaving work early, I bought myself a stylish but inexpensive jacket especially for the occasion. On arriving at the Festival Hall on my motorbike, I had to weave through the antic-ipated thronging crowd, but I had assumed there would be no one around the back. My heart sank. There were hundreds of fans milling about, hoping to catch a glimpse of those famous features, and the police and security guards were holding them at bay. I edged my way through the crowd wondering what I was going to say: 'Er, Mr Elton John personally asked me to come and see him before the show.' You can imagine the response: 'Oh, sure, sonny! And I'm Mickey Mouse, now get lost.'

Oh God, what was I going to say to the security guard? He certainly didn't look the friendly type. Gee, should I have hired a limo to arrive in? Should I have asked for a letter signed by Elton authorizing my admittance to the dressing-room area? Mild panic set in. But unknown to me, Elton had a member of his entourage in wait. On sighting me, roadies were sent to clear a path to Elton's caravan. Boy, did I feel a big shot. Some fans gave me the sort of envious looks that suggested they could have strung me up right then and there.

The caravan was full of music-industry people, but as soon as I entered, Elton announced: 'Right, everyone out!' We were left alone. Elton said affectionately: 'I'm so glad you came.' As we chatted, Elton's designer, Bob Stacey, knocked on the door and entered to dress the star for the show. It was something else to see a star strip down to his underwear. Elton was as unlikely a sex symbol as you could ever find – and he would agree. He was pudgy, and I was fascinated by the amount of hair on his body. After dressing, Elton called for Patti to take me to my seat, his final words being: 'Don't forget, whatever you do, make sure you come back to the hotel after the show!' This show was to be the first time he dedicated 'Blue Eyes' to me.

The post-gig party was for no more than 20 close friends, who dropped in to congratulate Elton briefly, have a drink or two and chat. Elton had showered as soon as he returned and now chatted quietly with his guests, still wearing his bathrobe. His guests knew he was tired, obviously, and after half an hour started to leave. Elton indicated that he wanted me to stay, and when he shut the door on the final guest he turned and said quickly: 'I'd like you to come on the rest of the tour with me . . . then I want you to come and stay at my house in England.' I was stunned, of course, and who wouldn't be? But without hesitation I shook my head. No! 'Will you think about it?' Elton pleaded. He was starting to sound anxious. 'No, I don't think so,' I said.

Disappointed, Elton still managed a smile, and we chatted pleasantly for another quarter of an hour, and then I excused myself, saying I had to work the next morning. Riding my bike home was exhilarating in Melbourne's crisp autumn air. My thoughts started to clear. I sadly shook my head in resignation. This was getting out of hand. I was beginning to think I would go. Did I want to leave Melbourne? To live in England, of all places. I'd been born there, but when I was six my father had decided to follow the trail of thousands of British working men – the trail to sunny paradise where everyone had a car, an indoor toilet and the promise of a swimming pool.

Dad had brought my mother and my two younger sisters, Deborah and Susan, to settle in Melbourne for keeps, but by the time I was 14 he had become disenchanted with Australia and homesick. It hadn't been the glorious paradise he'd hoped for, and his work as a salesman had been far from satisfying. Letters from relatives in England reinforced his desire to leave. Finally, much to my annoyance, he dragged the family back to Britain. But a ruder shock was to greet him there. London had changed. It was more crowded, dirty and dilapidated than he remembered. Within a year, we picked up our bundles and returned to Melbourne.

The question kept playing on my mind: Did I really want to live with Elton in England? I had trouble sleeping and tossed over Elton's unexpected and enticing proposal. I was very confused, and I had no one to talk to – no one who would understand what all this meant to me. Would I be able to cope with a rock star's entourage? Was I sophisticated enough? And what of leaving Australia and my job? Aside from the family's return trip to London and the occasional sojourn to Sydney and Brisbane, I had hardly travelled. Now here was this exceptional man asking me to forgo everything and live with him in an England that held no allure for me.

But, hang on! Think of the glamour, the travel, the high-class living. Surely I could cope with that! Couldn't I? Could I? Listen,

Gary, there's more to life than just material security, isn't there? Yes, there was. No, there wasn't. Fibber! Yes, there was! Who are you fooling? Let's face it, life with Elton John was going to be a lot more exciting and comfortable. My childhood in Melbourne was outside the lap of luxury, for father's salesman's wage had to support three growing kids, and there wasn't a lot left over to splash around. Elton had offered me a weekly wage that was a lot more than I'd been offered at jobs I'd done since leaving home. Besides, I thought to myself, what's here for you in Melbourne? I wasn't in love with Ross, although he was a wonderful person. I was in love with Cameron, but he could never reciprocate, so there was certainly no future there. It was 4.30 am before I drifted into sleep.

The next morning, as I sat bleary-eyed at work, miserably looking at the files on my desk, Elton rang. This time he dialled the number himself: 'Will you come to the show tonight?'

'Well, I've got tickets for Thursday night.'

'Yeah, but come tonight too. How are you feeling?'

'OK, why?'

'I was wondering if you'd thought about what I said last night.'

'No . . . well, I'm still not sure yet.' Oh dear, I could detect a waiver in my voice. Sheepishly I had to admit it to myself: I was falling for him.

For the Thursday show, I borrowed a car so I could pick up Cameron, who lived almost an hour out of town. On the way to the Festival Hall I told him: 'Elton wants us to go back to his hotel after the show, what do you think?'

'Sure, why not?' Cameron shrugged, playing it cool. Like a true Aussie, he was not about to get over excited about meeting 'tall poppies'. Cameron knew that I'd met Elton two years earlier and had spent time with him on the recent weekend. I suspect, though, he wondered how much of my claim was actually true. But when we were ushered into Elton's presence in his caravan, and he found himself pumping hands with the Great Man, the full realization hit.

We rejoined my work mates at our seats, and they were asking in excited whispers what had happened. Before I could tell them, the house lights dimmed, and the hall erupted. Midway through the concert, Elton again stared out into the crowd just before 'Blue Eyes', this time announcing: 'For all the people with blue eyes . . . especially for GC.' I remember turning around to glance at my boss, whose initials were also GC and, from the look in his eye, I knew he had latched on to the relationship between his employee and the man on stage. Oh shit, I thought, now everybody at work will know I'm gay. It was not the sort of thing I'd chatted about over biscuits at morning tea break. But, to be honest, I didn't care any more.

Friday was a night off for Elton, and he rang and invited me to dinner. We were going to a restaurant, but when I entered his suite I found a young couple called Jonathan and Janie visiting with their baby, James. Jonathan was an extremely good-looking fellow who had met Elton while working as a bartender in London. Earlier that evening, Elton had agreed to be their son's godfather, and everyone was in high spirits. Elton was also excited about the green tram recently purchased in Melbourne that was to be shipped back to his estate in England, chattering about it like a kid with a new toy. Jonathan and Janie were earnest suburbanites, and I suspect Elton tired of them after an hour. So we had dinner in the room, and after they left Elton asked me to stay the night. 'Look, we don't have to do anything if you don't want,' he coaxed. 'Just sleep in the same bed as me.'

I wasn't quite sure about this because I wasn't physically attracted to him. But taking him at his word, I climbed the staircase to his bedroom. He went to one side of the bed, and I sat on the edge, kicked off my shoes and my trousers, leaving on my T-shirt and jocks. As soon as I put my head on the pillow, Elton started to caress me, giving me a peck on the lips; he had soon whipped off the rest of my clothes. I froze. His hands moved awkwardly over my rigid body. 'Oh, my God,' he murmured, 'I can't believe what soft skin you have, Gary.'

'I can't believe you're so hairy!' I blurted out honestly but not wisely.

Not the most romantic of replies, I'll admit, but typical of my lack of thought about these things. Elton just laughed: 'Yeah, but it's in the wrong places, I wish I could keep more on my head.' I couldn't distract him. He had one thing in mind, and me in hand. Panic set in! Despite his efforts, I wasn't aroused. He wasn't fazed: 'It's all right, Gary, just relax, it's OK.'

I closed my eyes and thought of Cameron and quickly hardened. What scared me most was, what did this man want in bed? There had been instances with other men where, once having impressed me with a ride in their Rolls-Royce, a cruise on their yacht and drinks in their penthouse, hands would start to wander. They were never tender. Grabbing, pulling out their bottles of vaseline and grunting, 'Roll over!' If you said no, the chances were they would get rough. It was a form of rape: but to whom could you complain to? Elton, though, was gentle. When his head went down between my legs, it was obvious he was experienced. He gave great head. Elton had been drinking, so he was relaxed, but I wasn't. Instead, I started the night rigid and stayed rigid – as a board. Staring out at the skies through the huge windows, I concentrated on the physical sensation, and after a deal of encouragement, I came in his mouth. Thank God that was over!

That was it. No more demands and we both went off to sleep; in the morning, when I awoke, I felt Elton stirring next to me and pretended to be asleep in case he wanted another session. Soon I could hear him padding around downstairs, so I quickly dressed, and as I descended the stairs there was Elton smiling like a Cheshire cat, waiting with a Polaroid camera, snapping photos as I emerged from his lair. At that point, I was unaware that Elton liked to have Polaroid photos of his conquests, and, compared to the future, these snaps were to be the most innocent. As we breakfasted on bacon and eggs, Elton continued to photograph me at the table: 'I'm going to have these framed,' he crowed, as he crouched in different positions clicking away madly.

I took a deep breath: 'You know I don't know what my feelings are for you.'

'Does that matter?'

'Well, I'm 23. Don't you want someone younger?'

'Well, I'm 35, so I'll always be older than you!' Elton laughed, but he noted his quip wasn't getting the same response from me. 'Look, I can't see that it matters, why should you?'

There was a knock at the door. It was Bob Halley. 'I hear you're coming with us to England,' Bob said by way of greeting.

'I'm not sure, yet,' I said, glancing at Elton, who was studying the letters Bob delivered.

'Oh, you will!' Bob said with a big and knowing smirk growing from ear to ear.

That morning the tour was moving to Adelaide, its second last stop in Australia before ending in Perth, and Elton had to meet schedules. We walked down to the lobby, and as we passed the jeweller's shop, Elton stopped to buy his guitarist a Cartier watch: 'It's his birthday,' the magnanimous boss explained.

Elton and I said goodbye inside the hotel, and through the revolving doors we could see fans gathered outside. Elton's limo was waiting to take him to the airport, and some of his band members were gathering in the lobby before boarding the tour bus. 'Think about what I've said,' Elton murmured, giving me a hug. I hopped on my motorbike and roared off, glancing back once to see this lonely figure waving madly away through the huge windows, and even before I reached the end of the street, I had started to miss him. I knew then that despite the confused signals I was giving out, I'd already made my decision. 'I'll ring you,' he'd promised as we parted. Hmmm, I'd thought, how many times have I heard that line before? I was also scared that once having seduced me, Elton would discard me as a one night stand. But, true to his word, he rang me first thing the next day.

'I've just resigned,' I told him. 'I've given a fortnight's notice.' That evening when I returned home, there was a bouquet of 100 white roses on the door step. 'To Gary, from EJ.', said the accompanying note. I was overwhelmed by the romantic gesture. As I whisked around the house, jamming roses in every jar I could find, I started to worry. Now, how do I tell Ross? Er, goodbye, I'm going to live in England with a man I've only met half a dozen times and who'll be true and faithful even though he can probably win over anyone he wants? And what do I do with my things? When I told Elton I would be joining him, he immediately asked if I wanted any money to tide me over while I was winding up my affairs. I said no. I wanted to do it all by myself. To accept money was too close to prostitution for me.

That Thursday another call came from Adelaide. Elton again: he wanted me to join him. This was all certainly new for me. People looking after me, concerned about my comfort, caring in a different way to those who had used me in the past.

Bob and Patti were waiting for me outside the Arrivals Lounge at Perth airport. For a few seconds I was disappointed that Elton wasn't there. Then my eye was caught by someone standing by the far wall, a cap covering his face, trying to look as un-Elton as possible. Feeling self-important, I joined the others in a gleaming black BMW limo – wow, this is what a limo looks like! – with a bar and a TV set, and we drove straight back to the Parmelia Hotel. As with all his suites, Elton had a powerful stereo set installed, and we spent the evening chatting enthusiastically, playing music and watching TV. Elton had just bought a swag of latest Australian cassettes, which he had methodically arranged in a row on the window ledge. He had bought me a Walkman and presented me with an autographed copy of the *Jump Up!* cassette, which had my 'Blue Eyes' on it. But we didn't have the time all to ourselves, of course. There were always callers and problems that had to get a final 'yeah' or 'nay' from him. But he liked me just being there. There was a lot of hand touching and eye contact, and we both felt good being around each other, being in the same room together.

The Australian cricket team came around before the show to meet Elton and it was mutual respect. That last show in Perth was the best of the entire Australian leg of the tour. Everyone agreed.

The audience had been in Elton's palm the minute he sauntered on to stage: throughout the entire performance, you could hear them sing along like a football crowd, afterwards dragging him back for encore after encore. Elton was so exhausted when it was all over that he sank into a chair in his dressing room, unable to speak for a few minutes. The band members were ecstatic, celebrating the end of the tour. Well, I thought, Elton would want to finish on a high, wouldn't he? But Bob Halley said to me: 'He's in a great mood these days. You should have seen him just before we came to Australia. Talk about bad moods! When he's on an up, he plays so well. It's you!'

In the hotel room, while a couple of us sat around chatting, a fan found his way into the suite via the fire escape, having skirted the security men, and he barged in screaming: 'You're fantastic! I love your music, man!'

Elton had become paranoid about psycho fans since John Lennon's assassination. He went red in the face and started to scream: 'Get him out of here! Get him the fuck out of here!'

Bob was already on his feet, grabbing the kid roughly by his arm and shoving him out the room. Even as he was being escorted down the hallway, you could hear the intruder yelling: 'Elton, I think you're fantastic!'

There was a stunned silence for a minute then Elton's face relaxed. He was furious, but he was determined not to let the incident sour our fun. 'Crazy!' he said, pretending to shrug it off and reaching for another glass of champagne. Like most rock stars, Elton suffered the stress of fearing for his safety.

True, we mere mortals aren't always safe on the streets and in our houses, but big stars have to cope with fans who find it difficult to distinguish between adulation and possession. They are stalked, harassed on the phone, receive letters threatening suicide if their 'love' is not returned, get attacked by jealous boyfriends or girlfriends, have people creeping into their beds and fans jumping onstage in the excitement of the concert. Anyone of them could have a gun or a knife. What a tragic loss John Lennon's assassination was: the killer was so obsessed that he thought *he* was Lennon, which meant that the 'pretender' had to be blown away.

My Perth stay with Elton soon came to an end. The rest of the entourage were bustling about, doing last-minute shopping, saying goodbye to new-found friends and packing their bags. I was to catch Sunday's midnight flight from Perth to Melbourne – known as 'The Redeye' – on which you flew back into time zones. My flight was to leave two hours after Elton's departure. Elton accompanied me to the airport and gave me a quick cuddle in the VIP lounge. He whispered: 'See you in a couple of weeks.' An emotional hug, and he left.

Now that I'd moved closer to Elton, I was already learning quickly about fame. Suddenly people I didn't know were being especially nice to me. I felt that destiny had penned me into a Shakespearian farce set in the Royal Court of Sheila's boy, Elton, complete with scheming advisors, ghostly fathers, wicked queens, foppish sons, wilting lovers and doting subjects. Which was to be my role? The trickster king appeared to be short one jester. If the king was not smiling, the court would look around for heads to roll, so it's best the jester be happily tolerated. We in the colonies would eventually learn how the empire was ruled. It is called 'favour', royal favour, and I was the favourite. There was something about Elton's family that had a touch of history and destiny about it, which led me to a quick search of family name origins. This is what I found for Reginald Dwight – alias Elton John: **Dwight** (*m*) *English* – surname from medieval Greek god, *Dionysios*, whose orgiastic cult originated in Persia. The myth of this god encourages impulse, ecstasy and the irresistible irrational. **Reginald** (*m*) *English* – of Norman origin, influenced by Latin word for queen, *regina*.

On reflection the origins bode the future. When it was time for me to depart to England, the best farewell present came from my father. Dad wrote me an encouraging letter saying he was pleased that I had wangled a job with Elton's entourage – the official story. He also said that he was proud of me. We'd had our differences in the past, and the wounds were deep, but it was Dad who drove me to the airport and presented me with a pen set – which I still treasure – just as I boarded my flight to London to start my new life.

3. Honky Château

As I sat in his luxurious gold-inlaid bathtub easing my jetlag, Elton slipped into the room and started to soap me.

BY THE TIME I flew into London in late April 1982, Elton and I had been separated for two weeks, and I was still feeling very confused about my decision to accept his hospitality. I knew I was fond of him, sure, and excited about the prospect of moving in with an international superstar. However, I was forsaking my job, my family, my friends and whatever possessions I had – everything – to live in another country with someone I'd only just met. He loves me, he loves me not. It was a big risk for a young man.

Elton had called every night during the previous fortnight, from wherever he was in the world, exhibiting typical royal disregard for time in other parts of his empire. This imperious disdane for the ordinary man rankled with my housemate Ross who, at two in the morning, would sleepily stumble to answer Elton's call and then wake me. 'It's that bloody Elton!' Ross would say indignantly, trying to look agitated but spoiling it by bursting into laughter.

Telling Ross I was going had been painful, for even though our relationship had been platonic, and I'd never felt there was any future in it, my leaving to join someone I hardly knew must have been a slap in his face. I had the guilts. Ross had been very kind and had never forced me to do anything against my wishes; he was the last person that I wanted to hurt. As always, Ross, a nurturing soul, was concerned about my well-being, and he was worried I might be rushing into something that was beyond me. As it turned out, he wasn't far wrong. Thankfully, despite Ross's opinion of Elton's intentions, the two men remained cordial on the phone.

Each call generally lasted 15 minutes, chatty stuff, about what Elton was doing. For instance, he'd been invited to the White House to meet President Reagan and the first lady, and he was quite chuffed about it. He would tell me how much he missed me and how he was longing to see me again. Given the time of morning it wasn't surprising that conversations were usually one-sided, but there was more to it than that: I was thrilled to hear from Elton but I couldn't help being passive, to just listen and hope I wouldn't say anything that would offend him. It nagged me that I was slipping easily into a role where he was virtually in command, and I was later to find out that in sex and all matters Elton felt he had to be in control, to give rather than receive. His constant prattle meant no one had the opportunity to question him closely. Conversely, when on a downer, he uses withdrawal to hold control, taking solace in drugs and booze. No doubt the late calls were part of that control technique, a means of checking that I was home and preparing to leave, to fend off any last-minute doubts and to monitor my progress. He was also letting me know that his anticipation was building.

As flight QF4 circled London, I grabbed for a pullover with kangaroo motifs. How kitsch! And I even wondered if Elton would be there to greet me. If he wasn't, what was I going to do? I had changed my entire life, he was merely adding to his. Stumbling into customs at the ungodly hour of 7.30 am on Friday 23 April, and feeling like shit, I heard Elton's voice, a loud yell from above, reverberating through the lounge. He was on the public gallery balcony, shades and large cap covering most of his face, and he called down to me: 'Wait right there, Gary! Bob's coming to get you.'

Elton was ecstatic to see me. Beaming. He embraced me in a bear hug and quickly ushered me to his waiting Bentley. Bob was left to attend to the luggage. Naive as I was, I was momentarily disappointed: Oh, what an old car, I thought, expecting to see a shining new Rolls-Royce. Later I realized that the Bentley was far more prestigious and expensive than the modern flash that I had wistfully admired in car magazines. I began to appreciate that our age and experience differences were reflected in our tastes. Sitting in the rear of the car, I was most impressed by the fold-down bar and seductive aroma of old leather. Halley drove, and Elton sat in the front passenger seat frequently looking back at me as he spoke and laughed. Luscious green fields and trees flashed past as the Bentley cruised majestically down the motorway, then veered off on the winding country roads to Old Windsor, the Berkshire village near Elton's 37-acre Woodside estate.

During the 25-minute journey, the stoic Bob kept his eyes on the road and remained silent. He was, as ever, distantly polite and no more. I felt uncomfortable when Elton casually let it drop that Bob, as his 24-hour aide, would be sharing Woodside with us.

Bob came from a poor background and liked his new-found first-class trappings. I also later realized that one of Bob's roles was to be the buffer between Elton and the world and that Bob would diplomatically re-route friends and associates according to his boss's whims. Elton would suddenly decide he didn't want to entertain or talk to someone that day. Bob would have to invent a charming excuse. To do his job effectively, he had to keep his distance; and as Bob saw his life's work as serving Elton's every desire, limiting the star's personal circle of friends was all in a day's work.

Old Windsor is a quaint village, which looks as if it has been lifted from a postcard. Windsor Castle dominates the landscape, and occasionally one can see Her Majesty riding horses in the nearby park. The four million tourists who come annually to spot a royal head, or watch the changing of the guards, would sometimes suss out that a superstar of another kind lived around here as well. Occasionally they would mill about, peeping through the fence or taking photos of themselves in front of Woodside's electronic gates. Very few would try to sneak in: the large warning sign ELECTRIC FENCE – KEEP OUT! was an effective deterrent. Certainly the English fans understood an Englishman's home is his castle and respect that Woodside is no tourist haven. In more ways than one, Gracelands and Woodside are worlds apart.

Bob slipped his key into the slot to activate the gates, which were set about 200 metres from the road. The Bentley crunched along the gravel-lined driveway that led to Elton's fairyland, and I viewed the scene before me in wonder. Immediately inside the gates on the left was The Orangery, comprising two self-contained living areas, one of which housed Elton's 87-year-old gran Ivy. The other was reserved for Elton's mother and stepfather if they chose to stay overnight; usually, however, they lived about one-and-a-half hours away in a red-brick house in an upper-class part of Sussex, a home that Elton had bought for them, and a place where he housed many of his mementos.

The Bentley rolled under a brick archway and came to a stop opposite the stables, where I could see a long row of garages housing about 18 cars, including a number of Bentleys, a green Rolls-Royce Corniche convertible, a black Porsche, a yellow Aston Martin Vantage and a Range Rover, which Elton had re-sprayed whenever a new colour took his fancy. Elton, a smile on his face, leant over and tapped me on the shoulder, pointing in the direction of the front of the house, and exclaimed: 'That's for your benefit, Chook!'

He was referring to the flagpole that stood in the front court. From Woodside he could see the Union Jack hoisted to mark Her Majesty's presence at Windsor Castle. Not to be outdone, Elton had started a practice of hoisting the Watford Football Club flag to let people know that *this* queen was in residence. Today the Australian flag was fluttering in the English spring breeze. My flag. The flat I had presented to Elton as a keepsake.

'So, what do you think of Woodside, Chook?' Elton said,

slipping into the nickname he gave me when we were in Perth.

'It's fantastic, I've never been in a place like this before!' I gushed.

Elton started mimicking the Queen: 'Oh, it's rather small, isn't it . . . and over there . . .,' he laughed, pointing to the stables, 'that's your bedroom.' How apt, a roll in the hay! I thought how amused his fans would be to see their idol goofing about like this, for despite his outrageous performance costumes, Elton projected the dour public persona of a serious artist. No one would believe it if they heard him slip into his falsetto dowager accents or saw him play his impish practical jokes.

It was time to unload and as Bob took my two suitcases – containing my earthly belongings – I thought: 'Gee, Elton, I bet it'd take more than two suitcases if the roles were reversed, and you had to sell up to live with me.'

Elton was in an expansive mood that day and took me on a guided tour of Woodside, with the first port of call being the kennels to make friends with his boisterous German Shepherds, Bruce and Duncan. Then it was off to the kitchen: 'Come and meet Ollie!' he exclaimed, striding out in advance. I was expecting Ollie to be the housekeeper. It turned out to be a madcap cockatoo that mimicked Gladys, an elderly lady who came to help with the daily chores. With little encouragement Ollie would gleefully recite a litany of swear words from a perch in the kitchen, and, when overexcited, the bird would flap furiously, triggering the alarm system.

The housekeeper, Jenny, lived on the estate with her husband, John, in a cottage sandwiched between the garages. I liked this couple immediately: down to earth and warm, they stood no nonsense. John was in charge of maintaining the estate, and Jenny's tasks were to cook, look after the pets and help Gladys keep the house as impeccably neat as the fastidious Elton desired. This tidiness greatly appealed to me. Woodside, a red-brick Queen Anne-style three-storey house, looked impressive from the outside and reeked of wealth. Inside it was neat and dust-free with expensive antiques and paintings, their beauty enhanced by lighting, setting and use of space.

When it came time to visit the boudoirs Elton was brimming with excitement. 'Come along to your *real* bedroom,' he called, leading the way. We passed walls decorated with framed gold records, climbed a wide staircase and continued the grand tour down yet another opulently furnished hallway. This was storybook stuff: I was an Alice in Elton's Wonderland. As we approached a door guarded by a huge stuffed cheetah, Elton confided: 'I thought it might be a good idea if you had your own room, Chook. It is important that you have your own personal space.' Should I be insulted or relieved? With a dramatic flourish, Elton flung open the door to reveal a magnificent sight. Hundreds of red roses spectacularly arranged in expensive vases filled the room.

I was still taking it all in when Elton proudly said: 'See the bed, it used to belong to a king!' I must admit I was more impressed with his next comment: 'Rod Stewart slept in this bed.'

I was curious about the bathroom. Australians tend to sneer at the English because they don't bathe as much as the Aussies, and there is an old joke based on this myth: Q. 'Where would you hide money from an Englishman?' A. 'Under the soap.' As someone who bathed at least twice a day, I was anxious that the joke should not apply to me. Thankfully the en-suite had a shower and a bath. Elton then pointed out the TV set and stereo system, and a gift-wrapped package lying on the bed. It was a pictorial, *A Day in the life of Australia*, in which he had inscribed: 'Dear Gary, a little reminder of Australia – Love always – Elton.' Then he approached me, gently encircling me with his arms and cooed: 'I knew you'd be homesick.' After years of never belonging, of being shunted from place to place, Woodside already showed signs of becoming a secure, accepting and love-filled place for me. A home. Where I was loved – at last.

We marched down to the kitchen, where Jenny bustled about preparing Elton's favourite breakfast of bacon, sausages and eggs. Elton immediately immersed himself in his daily ritual of wallowing in the morning newspapers, while I tried to teach Ollie some Australian slang. Elton's favourite papers were the *Sun* and *Daily Mirror.*

About midday I heard a car screech into the driveway, and a few minutes later Sheila Farebrother walked in followed by Elton's stepfather, Fred, whom everybody refers to as Derf. Derf is Fred spelt backwards. It's a nickname bestowed upon him by Elton in his early teens. Elton had already told his Mum that I was a very special person in his life, and she responded accordingly. In time I would see that Sheila is the major influence on Elton's personal life and experience how she ran the household's affairs with tough discipline. However, she went out of her way to make me feel welcome, and I was comforted by that – and grateful.

'I've already met you, I was with Molly backstage at one of the Australian concerts,' I gushed.

'Did you?' She had a most dignified voice and a smile that matched. 'Oh yes, of course, I remember you,' she fibbed politely, but I knew we would become good friends.

Derf was a tall, distinguished, stolid character, with very thick glasses and a tattoo on his arm, who preferred to remain in the background. Elton never hid the fact that Derf was his stepdad, and Derf was everything his real father, Stan Dwight, had never been. There was, however, more than a little of the cantankerous and impetuous Stan in Elton. Sheila and Stan had divorced when Elton was about 15. I, too, had lost contact with my father in my teens, although for a different reason. Apparently Stan had been a fun-loving guy when he and Sheila had first married, and his love for music and soccer flowed in Elton's veins. At one stage Stan played trumpet in a dance band called Bob Miller & the Millermen, and Stan's brother was a highly skilled professional footballer. Entertainment, in one way or another, was in the genes.

But, as Elton told it, joining the Royal Air Force changed his father for ever. Having risen in the world, Stan became attuned to the class snobbery, social climbing and apparent sophistication of his colleagues. The rift began to show when Sheila's down-to-earth manner, including rejection of the cocktail set, became a source of growing irritation. Stan's resentment of his surroundings was reinforced when his job took him away from home for long periods of time. Returning to the modest working-class council home, the unwanted reminder of his lowly beginnings made him sullen and depressed. Things were gloomy, and Stan projected his anger on to his son, applying a rigid military discipline to the household. Elton was yelled at if he did something as trivial as slurp his soup or kick the football too close to the house. Stan Dwight didn't like being put out, and Elton's presence exacerbated the problem. The child was far from impressed by his father's surly behaviour, and he spoke of it in later years.

'He's still a miserable sod,' Elton said when interviewed by Michael Parkinson in Australia. 'I don't talk about him much . . . but I remember I had a big inferiority complex as a child because I was so scared of him.'

As Elton approached his teenage years, the Dwights' marriage was over in everything bar name, and by this time both spouses had found romantic diversions. But when the crunch came, and Stan filed for divorce, it was Sheila who was accused of alleged adultery. Fred Farebrother, a local painter and decorator, was named as the other party.

Elton was very much his mother's son and protector, and he was pleased that Derf, who treated him like a son, would be a permanent addition to the household. But the resentment Elton felt about his mother's victimization and public humiliation during the divorce turned to rage and a sense of betrayal when Stan remarried less than two years later. Even worse, Stan went on to have four more sons – having told all and sundry that he had only sired one child with Sheila because he 'hated children'. Perhaps Stan had matured after his divorce and saw his children as a privilege and not a duty, or maybe his new partner had engendered a more relaxed perspective. Whatever the reason for Stan's change in attitude, not unjustifiably, Elton felt rejected, and he remained distant from his father and step-brothers, harbouring a hostility he submerged, conveniently categorizing it as indifference.

Elton had not grown past the divorce and was probably grieving like most children of broken marriages – blaming himself for the split and wondering if his father was walking away from him and not Sheila. His unresolved grief still has an edge of vindictiveness, and he can easily reach down into its storehouse of anger. Years later this anger surfaced when a repenting Stan attempted reconciliation. Father and son might have sorted out their problems if Elton's superstardom and wealth had not taken control of his ego. Rightly or wrongly, Elton decided in a sudden rage, reminiscent of Stan's own early behaviour, that his real father and half-brothers were all after his money, so he dismissed them with a single hand-out.

Elton rarely spoke of Stan and his step-brothers to me, but, years later, on *The One* album, he sang about a son asking forgiveness from his father; he admitted to interviewers that he wished he had made peace with Stan. Elton's memories of living with his biological father are painful, yet he still resents Stan's decision to leave and the fact that Sheila was portrayed as the scarlet woman – although for divorce to proceed in those days, it was necessary for one spouse to be accused of infidelity.

The divorce, although not a matter of contention between his parents, continues to provide Elton with much of his emotional edge and will continue to do so until the paradox of the loved but hated father is resolved. Until then, Sheila remains the constant in his life – the one trustworthy human – and she holds a secret sway in all matters of heart, both dark and joyous. Elton is boxing with shadows. His audiences, however, will continue to be excited by the energy bubbling from this long-time grief for, in concert, it's his need to be loved that pulls at his audience.

Elton needs to give, and his audiences soak it up – there is no end to their capacity or their adulation. More is what they want, and he gives beyond his limits. His is an unconditional love begging to be reciprocated, and it is this that he identifies with in me. In this way, I am like him, and I came to realize that when he tired of himself, Elton tired of me.

In career terms, there is a sad side to this, for if you look

carefully you can see that the lacklustre records and performances come in those periods when Elton is emotionally secure
– when he is feeling loved, happy and comfortable. It's a paradox
that seems to be part of the price that many creative people pay
for their fame.

Looking back at his childhood, it is obvious that the Dwights'
seperation came when Elton was at a vulnerable age. It was Derf,
20 years Elton's senior, who replaced Stan as his father figure,
becoming a confidant and friend to the lonely youth. Derf
provided ample pocket money and encouraged young Reg to
listen to rock and roll, wear the gear that Stan had frowned upon
and be himself in all things. Derf bought Elton his first pushbike,
was supportive of his music and even landed the boy his first gig,
so that at age 15 he was playing piano at a local pub.

While Elton suffered childhood, Sheila, a contender for the
most devoted mother award, worked as a government clerk to
provide her only son with the best she could afford. Even when
Elton's singing career was launched in 1970 with 'Your Song', and
money started to roll in, Sheila refused to leave her job. And it
was only when he achieved superstar status and made his first
million that Sheila gave in to Elton's growing insistence that she
retire and help him run his household. In return for her assistance
Elton gave Sheila and Derf their own house and whatever they
wanted. They had done their best for him, and now he
considered it his pleasure and duty to do the same for them.

On my first morning at Woodside, I watched mother and son at
the breakfast table. Derf had disappeared to the Orangery – I
suspect he did not particularly like me and questioned my
motives and intentions. As they nibbled at cheese on toast, arm
in arm and exchanging jokes, there seemed to be a strong and
enduring affinity between the two. I would later discover that this
was not as constant a bonding as I had imagined – more of a
seasonal thing. And Sheila was in charge of the weather.

Conversation centred on Elton's European tour, set to start in four days' time in Stockholm – however, it stimulated Sheila to reminisce about Elton's first public gig. Apparently the rough Friday night pub crew hurled ashtrays and crumpled bags of crisps at Elton, the Billy Bunter bespectacled prodigy, and even poured beer into his piano. Even at this early age, Elton showed a courage and determination beyond his years – returning to conquer after a humiliating start. This ability to turn adversity into a positive, something he had cultivated during childhood, would lift him beyond the tribulations of a turbulent career.

Tired from my long journey, I went up to my room to sleep. Relaxed and satisfied, I drifted off for what seemed a few minutes and awoke to Elton's touch. Raising myself on one elbow, I looked across at the clock by the bed and was surprised to see that I had been sleeping for four hours.

'Don't rest for too long, Chook,' Elton warned, 'you'll have a devil of a time trying to get to sleep tonight. Dinner won't be ready for another hour. Why don't I run you a bath?' I hadn't showered since leaving Melbourne so the idea was most inviting. Before I could reply, Elton said: 'You can use my bathroom.'

On entering the star's en-suite my eyes boggled. The bathroom was enormous, and so was the tub. Everything in green, Elton's favourite colour, with a gold-leaf inlaid bath. The vast bench surrounding the side washbasin was covered with every shape and colour of cologne bottle. A kaleidoscope of aromas and textures, each to its own purpose. Relaxing into the sensuous bubble bath I closed my eyes, trying to recover from jetlag. Elton wandered in to chat. His voice filled the space, then it trailed off as he left the room for a moment. Then he slipped back, and without a word he started to lather me. Imagine it – I was uncomfortable enough when he was just talking to me in the nude, but when he started to sponge me, I was pleased that my privates were well hidden under the bubbles.

All of a sudden Elton left the room, and I heard him chatting with Sheila, then he returned holding a Christian Dior bright pink bathrobe and proudly handed it to me saying: 'I bought this in Paris last time I was there. You'd better put it on.' Poor Sheila could hardly control her giggles when I swanned into the kitchen in that pink robe, looking for all the world like Vivien Leigh descending the stairs in *Gone with the Wind*.

Dinner was Elton's favourite – sausages, mashed potatoes, peas and gravy with lots of HP sauce – and the conversation centred on Australia. 'Did you know that Gary has been learning to fly a plane, Mum?' Elton beamed, showing me off like a new toy. 'I think when we get through this tour, he might like to get his helicopter pilot's licence.'

We talked for some time about my love of flying before the topic of Watford hit the agenda. I was soon to discover that where Watford was concerned everything – including music and myself – took second place. When it came to football, Elton was a man possessed.

Sheila returned to the Orangery to join Derf, and Elton glanced at my drooping eyelids: 'You're still exhausted, Chook. Best you go to bed. We could both do with an early night.' As we climbed the stairs to the first floor, the silence was deafening. Here it comes, I thought to myself, crunch time! I had been nervous all evening about this moment. It wasn't the first time I'd spent the night with him, but now we were in his house. Just what was I expected to do in this man's bed?

Elton was very gentle with me: 'Don't worry, I know how tired you are.' His voice was reassuring, and although I had my own room Elton had made it clear that his bed was ours. Later I was to discover that when Elton needed his sanctuary, usually after coming down after a drugs binge, I was to keep to my own space. But not tonight.

Elton's foreplay was soft and gentle, massaging my neck, his lips brushing lightly across my cheek as he whispered in my ear: 'Just relax, Chook. Relax.'

I so wanted to please Elton but I couldn't relax in this unfamiliar room, what with his expectations so high and my concentration broken by his dog baying not far from our window. However, Elton was very focused as he moved sensually over my body, kissing me repeatedly in such a knowing way; it took me back to my first time, back to when I was a gawky teenager, when the exhilaration of intimacy overrode the fear of being ridiculed. Even then I thought love-making had to be more than a momentary spark. To me it was a seal of permanence. In the years since, sex hasn't turned out like that, but at that time I still had hopes. And on that night I wanted it to be perfect with Elton.

In the half-dark I could see and feel his hands roaming my body, the moonlight softly illuminating the ripple of his undulating palms. What was he thinking? Was he pleased? He stroked my penis, taking it in his mouth, but when I reached for him he restrained me, murmuring: 'No, it's OK.' In bed, as with the rest of his life, Elton seemed to enjoy giving pleasure more than receiving it. Perhaps he had been so hurt as a child that he was unable to risk surrendering himself to others. Maybe he could only do this from the safety of a stage – performance substituted for intimacy.

This night's passion came to an abrupt halt, for as soon as Elton had satisfied me, he rolled over and went to sleep. He seemed uncaring about his own fulfilment, and it was a pattern of behaviour that was often to be repeated. Halfway through that night, after I tiptoed back from my own bathroom toilet, Elton awoke. He seemed concerned that I had left the room. Slipping back into bed, I felt him reach over and stroke my hair: 'You're very attractive, Gary. I'm glad you're here.'

One glorious benefit of making a lot of money is that you have the power to create the world of your fantasy.

Elton had his own support team, who were particularly active on tour when Elton was most vulnerable; their job was to keep negative vibes at bay. At home, in his early years, Elton's reclusive behaviour and involvement with Watford kept his slate relatively clean, and, as a further precaution, his mother made sure his household was staffed with reliable, down-to-earth types. So Woodside ran in a quiet, almost well-mannered way. Despite this, it was still very much Elton's dream, the container of his fantasies, and it overcompensated for his impoverished past.

When he was a child, there had been very little money for toys. In fact, and not surprisingly, the major source of entertainment was the piano. Elton recalled: 'I remember sitting on my grandmother's knee and banging away at the piano.' He couldn't avoid music, and 40s and 50s pop was very much a part of his early life. Both his parents bought records; Stan was a big fan of danceband music and particularly loved Glen Miller and George Shearing. Sheila had a policy of buying a record every Friday. Elton clearly remembers the evening she came home with two records, excited because it was a 'new kind of music'. One was Elvis's 'Hound Dog'; the other Bill Haley's 'ABC Boogie'. Elton still remembers being turned on, as a young boy, by the excitement of rock and roll.

But he could never openly show his taste in music, nor express how it affected his attitudes – especially while Stan and his rigid discipline dominated the household. Being an only child, petted by his mother and grandmother, he was seldom encouraged to play physical games with local kids. And once his piano talents surfaced, his life stopped being his own, for as far as his family was concerned, Elton's *raison d'être* had been discovered. Nothing else mattered. Once identified as a musical prodigy, he acquired a special status at school, constantly being invited to play at school functions. He was such a find that the fact that he was scraping average marks for his other subjects did not unduly concern the school authorities. And the young Reg played the role of prodigy to the hilt. As a primary-school child he never misbehaved and was always anxiously polite. Elton explained it this way:

'The reason I became so outrageous with my clothes when I started to make records is because my parents were strict with me about the clothes I could wear. If my father had his way, I'd be wearing white slippers and white socks! They wouldn't even let me wear Hush Puppies, for Christ's sake – mods used to wear them so it was taboo. So when I got into my twenties, I guess I took my teenage repression with me. I was too portly to wear jeans, that's for sure.'

In the mid-60s, when Elton became friendly with Bernie Taupin, the boys took to the Carnaby Street look with a passion. Sheila was horrified when her son sported old army jackets. 'She refused to walk on the same side of the street as me,' Elton would chuckle affectionately, 'and if I ran behind her, then she'd run faster!'

If strict parents had him feeling like a nerd, his thick lens spectacles, which he would from then on spend most of his life pushing back from his nose, had him looking like one. And no one told him that black-rimmed glasses were a fashion joke. He figured, in his innocence, that if Buddy Holly and Hank B. Marvin of the Shadows sported them, they were the go.

While his class mates spent their after-school hours kicking footballs around, trying to get laid or experimenting with pills and reefers, Reginald Dwight was practising the piano at his home at 111 Potter Street, Pinner, or going to lessons on Saturday mornings at the Royal Academy of Music. He was already exhibiting signs of great talent by being able to reproduce complex melodies on the piano after hearing the music for a short time, and the Academy taught him how to expand on this, alas, however, no one taught him about himself.

Elton's friends were the people on his records. Sitting in his tiny bedroom he played their music repeatedly, lovingly handling the sleeves, fantasizing about the lives of the performers. Each record was catalogued and wrapped in protective brown paper so that even the sleeves would never be spoiled. Pop music gave him access to a world that promised fulfilled love and eternal beauty, where broken hearts were joined by the power of song.

To the lonely young man, the performers on the airbrushed record covers seemed to come from a distant, happy world, where everyone was smiling in groups of four or five. Brothers in arms, it seemed to him, with a common bond in music. He couldn't believe any of them could feel insecure or ever argue with each other. Elvis might have walked down the lonely road to Heartbreak Hotel or anguished over His Latest Flame, but it never seemed to bring him down. The handsome face that stared out from the record cover was strong, sullen and in full control. All those rock stars like Little Richard, Buddy Holly, Chuck Berry and Jerry Lee Lewis had looks that said to the world: 'Don't mess with me, no one's been able to put me down.'

As far as young Reg was concerned, although his father would not let him dress like a rocker, he could at least mimic a rock star by wearing heavy-looking glasses – just like Buddy Holly. Even at that early age, music was a passion. In his room, Elton also built on his love for football, championing the Watford team. It gave him his thrills and a sense of belonging, and he collected books on the sport, religiously charting club placings, which he adjusted every weekend.

The Elvis Presley and Bill Haley records that Sheila had around the house inspired Elton, but seeing flamboyant piano-showmen like Jerry Lee Lewis and Little Richard changed his life. He liked the way they kicked their piano around the stage and leapt on it, and to him they were everything good-mannered classical pianists were not. In his final years at Pinner County Grammar, he would play piano at the school assembly hall, astounding classmates with rollicking up-tempo numbers, his stubby fingers banging away just like Jerry Lee or Little Richard, imitating them right down to kicking his stool or banging the keys with his feet. The word got about and during lunch hours or end-of-term socials the hall would be packed with eager school kids. No longer was Elton the school's pudgy nerd, he was the school's pudgy nerd who could belt out rock and roll.

So rock and roll transformed him. No longer a nonentity, he had his first taste of stardom, and it coincided with his first spate of clashes with authority. Music teachers lamented the way the lad was spending his time. The Academy's golden boy was starting to truant. He still had impeccable manners, but the clothes were no longer nerdy. On a school excursion to France, Reg, mimicking Elvis Presley, was a hit with the French school-girls. His self-doubt came to the fore early in his life, but he had an innate sense of destiny – there are ways around everything: 'I used to stand in front of the mirror – I was very fat – and I'd mime to Jerry Lee Lewis records, thinking, I wish this could happen to me.' He recalled later: 'I always thought I'd be a star, since the age of four or five. But I never really thought I'd be a singer. Realistically I thought I'd probably be somebody like Ferrante & Teicher – that kind of middle-of-the-road flash pianist – and put out records like 'Bent Fabric'. Sort of an English version of the Ventures, only on the piano.

'Look, *anybody* can be a star if they put their minds to it. I mean, I don't look like a star at all, but that's what fascinates me about it. I've always looked like a bank clerk who freaked out. That's what makes rock 'n' roll so great; that someone like me can actually be a star. The whole rock thing for me is a game, but it's a game I love playing. And I'll always be playing it, even if it should ever get back to just me and the mirror.'

By his mid-teens, Elton had formed his first band, Bluesology. They started performing at scout huts and youth-club dances, backing soul names like Patti Labelle and Doris Troy and then Long John Baldry. And once stardom came, he quickly set about changing his life. The first was a name change. The decision came in the back of a transit van while returning from a gig with his band, tired and sweat-soaked. 'Elton' came from Elton Dean, a player with him in Bluesology, who later acquired fame in the jazz-rock fusion outfit Soft Machine. The 'John' came from Long John Baldry.

For the first three years after leaving school, Elton remained in Pinner at Sheila and Derf's home in Frome Court, playing in bands around London and throughout England. He finally moved out of home in 1968 when he and his first girlfriend Linda found a place to live together in London in Furlong Road, Islington. Also staying with them were Linda's two dogs and, for a time, Bernie Taupin.

Once his records began selling Elton decided to relocate, for his central London flat was no longer suited to his lifestyle: 'The flat was only five minutes from the Speakeasy [club], and I never got any sleep for years.' He searched for a place in the country in keeping with his rising rock-star status, somewhere he could relax in peace in an area that was large enough for him to indulge his whims. So Elton bid on a place called Charter's Farm but offended the owners by accidentally referring to it as Farter's Farm. Elton's bid was refused.

Hercules was to be his first big house, complete with all the rock-star luxuries – swimming pool, games room and mini-football pitch. It was in the same area as stars such as Keith Moon, Rod Stewart and Donovan. When Elton moved in, he threw a housewarming party and invited 250 celebrities, entertaining them with drag acts and strippers. But he quickly outgrew the place. It was soon chock-a-block with his ever increasing acquisitions, and it was also becoming a security nightmare: only a patch of grass separated the house from the road, and often he would be startled by red-eyed fans' faces pressed against his ground-floor windows.

In early 1976 Elton placed Hercules on the market with a price tag of £125,000, but had to drop it to £80,000. Six months later he came close to shelling out £800,000 for magnificent Wargrave Manor, a 78-acre property on the banks of the Thames. It came with a Georgian house, a farm, a couple of tenants and a herd of prize cattle. But the deal didn't go through, much to Elton's disappointment. At that time, Elton was scheduled to fly to America, so he left the task of finding a place to his mother, and the minute she came across Woodside, Sheila was ecstatic: it had everything she believed her millionaire rock-star son would want – three lakes, a private cinema and a disco large enough for a hundred people, an internal lift, swimming pool, squash courts, cottages for the hired help and numerous garages. Sheila managed to snap it up for a bargain price of £400,000, and she and Derf decorated the house in Elton's absence.

This was only my second day, and I had certainly learnt a lot about the place and the history of its owner. I spent a few hours exploring the estate and eventually sauntered into the kitchen, where I waited for Sheila and Derf to escort me to the football. The kitchen had a walk-in freezer, large pantry and a jukebox in one corner. Dangling over the jukebox was a cardboard fox head mobile, a promotional gimmick left over from *The Fox* album. The threatening animal stared hungrily. Would the bug-eyed predator see the end of this Little Red Riding Hood one day?

The basement contained a well-stocked wine cellar, although Elton would say he was no connoisseur. It also housed the controls to an elaborate alarm system, which was connected to the walk-in safe. This is where Elt stored his antiques and some of his jewellery, such as a jewel-encrusted £6000 Cartier watch, or a diamond and sapphire ring, which I'd often admire and which occasionally he'd pull off his finger for me to look after while he performed a show. I'd be nervous while it was in my possession, because Elton had told me how expensive it was. He scared me by telling me it was worth over £35,000. Naturally, the house was securely protected with a direct alarm line to the Old Windsor police station, and Elton never worried about being burgled. In fact, the safe was probably only installed to appease his insurance company who would otherwise have insisted that his valuables be placed in a bank vault. The one theft, of Elton's diamond-encrusted watch, was attributed in Court to a young boyfriend, although nothing was ever proved.

Woodside was the sort of place where a child could roam around imagining Enid Blyton-type secret passages and hiding places. A long hallway, filled with framed gold and platinum discs, led to Elton's renowned record library, hailed as one of the biggest personal record collections in the world. Rack upon rack of cassettes and vinyl albums vied for space. They were slotted in alphabetical order, but no one had got around to cataloguing them: I decided that would be one of my jobs.

What I found disturbing, though, was the way the house seemed to be fragmented and compartmentalized, and there was no consistency to the decor. Clashing design gave a feeling of disequilibrium and disjointed function, and many of the rooms seemed to belong in a museum rather than a home. The formal living-room – with wooden floorboards, imported rugs, antiques, red-leather lounge suites, a Wurlitzer jukebox and a black grand piano – was only used when special company, such as Freddie Mercury, Cliff Richard or Princess Margaret and her two children, arrived for dinner.

On the other hand, the squash court was well used. Elton liked the game and was a good player. He was very competitive and occasionally invited friends over for tournaments. Although while I was there he used the space as a storeroom, having run out of room in the house for his ever growing collections, he was known to have had many a tough and sweaty game on court. Business associates were usually taken to the library, with its beautifully crafted English-style bar and tournament-sized pool table. Here there were hundreds of books lining the walls, mostly collected when Elton was on tour; he was big on romantic fiction and autobiographies.

Elton loved any sort of competitive game, and when David Geffen, head of Geffen Records, visited with his boyfriend, Elton had a wide smile on his face when they departed around midnight, because he had thrashed Geffen at pool. Elton hated Geffen with a passion and often grumbled that he had to produce a number of records to fulfil his contract with the label.

The star appreciated the best, and this was evident in the artworks he purchased. Original Van Goghs, Rembrandts and Warhols were part of an extremely valuable collection. In this house, even the guests' toilet was lavish, with press cuttings about Elton on the wall. Bernie Taupin's LA home had clippings in the guests' toilet, too – a notable one was a framed headline that read: TAUPIN, THE ONE WHO WRITES THE WORDS FOR ELTON JOHN.

The upstairs rooms were jam-packed with clothes, squeezed into every square inch of wardrobe space. Some rooms were still full of suitcases that Elton had yet to unpack after his move from Hercules. This hoarding, and the star's legendary compulsive spending, seemed to pinpoint a deep-seated anxiety. Many of his acquisitions were white elephants. One was the green tram from

Melbourne, for which he paid £5000 totally on a whim. It cost him £10,000 to ship it over to England; when it finally arrived at Woodside, part of the estate walls had to be demolished so that it could be accommodated. Special tracks were laid to the back garden, where the tram eventually nestled among the roses. Another oddity was a pair of stone lions, each weighing a massive six tons, which Elton snapped up as part of a £50,000 shopping spree on a visit to China with the Watford team. Upstairs in one of the bedrooms was priceless Bugatti furniture, which was great to look at but uncomfortable, and guests, only too aware of the furniture's worth, could never relax on these art treasures.

Woodside's upper floors also housed the purple and black video room; an entire collection of Warhol prints of Marilyn Monroe filled one wall. Elton spent a fair amount of time here, lounging on the white couches watching either the TV set or the huge wall screen. He devoured current-affairs programmes or selected from his considerable collection of classic Hollywood movies and sex videos.

When Prince Andrew visited Woodside to meet Elton before the entertainer played at his twenty-first birthday party, Randy Andy was reportedly quite taken with Elton's video collection. The upstairs games room was home to a couple of pinball machines and the mammoth boots Elton had worn in *Tommy*. There was a series of bedrooms, each with en-suites, which close friends like John Reid or Rod and Alannah Stewart would occupy when they stayed over.

Bob Halley's room was diagonally opposite Elton's. You couldn't miss the master's room. It had E-L-T-O-N spelt out in huge neon lights above the door. The magnificent bathroom, spa and steam rooms were on the left. To the right was the living area with a couch bulging with stuffed animals. A spiral staircase led to his music room, a surprisingly gloomy area with an electric piano and a couple of guitars. It was here his salacious videos were stored, and it was in this room that Elton looked deep inside himself and enjoyed whatever he found. There was no need here for the trappings that he had acquired since adolescence.

The bedroom area was full of exquisite craftworks, the dressing-room contents neatly filed away for easy access. One drawer was full of his famous spectacles. Another contained dirty magazines and polaroids of naked young men. Elton was never one to mix business with pleasure. His private rooms were arranged so that he could isolate himself from the rest of the household. Everyone in the house worked to one rule: when the boss threw his tantrums, they would leave him alone until he cooled off. Woodside pivoted around Elton's fierce demand for privacy and space. It's interesting that even in adulthood, he could never bring himself to understand or forgive his real father's need for space and solitude. After all, like any child, Elton must have at times been intrusive, irritating, morose and even insolent. Yet he always remembered Stan's demands for peace and quiet with anger.

To limit contact with the outside world, only one telephone line was connected to Woodside. Only trusted people had Elton's phone number – his parents, his manager John Reid and John's secretary. Everyone else communicated by telex. This way Elton chose those who could interrupt his peace. In any case, although virtually every room had an inter-house phone, the only incoming line was in Bob's room. If Bob was out or downstairs when it rang, it would be left unanswered. Elton hated the phone for its ring signalled another intrusion into his private world.

Even the immediate family knew and respected Elton's peace. His grandmother Ivy lived on the grounds, but seldom, if ever, came up to the main house. However, Elton would visit her at the Orangery and always made it a point to pop in and say goodbye if he was going abroad. His uncle, Sheila's brother, was one of the three gardeners, but he would never presume to walk into the house unless summoned, although this did not appear to have anything to do with Elton.

Sheila once told me that Woodside's annual running costs came to £100,000, and that she kept a close eye on expenses. That never made her popular with the staff. Maybe it was also because while Elton had a carefree relationship with his hired help, I gained the impression that Sheila saw them as disposable employees and not friends. In any case, that was the way she wanted to run the household: if anyone had to be fired, Sheila wielded the axe.

Woodside reflected the paradox that is Elton's life. He surrounded himself with material wealth, yet the people closest to him were aware of his loneliness. In autumn 1979 Sheila told the *Daily Express* newspaper that in her opinion, 'If Elton had gone for a normal 9 to 5 job, he would never have turned gay, and dealing with the rock scene created his homosexuality.' She added, with a certain amount of justifiable pride, that: 'in an industry where image is all-important and the biggest queens never come out of the closet, my son at least possessed the character to go public.'

It seemed to me that Sheila was having trouble coping with her son's homosexuality, as my parents had with mine, but at least Elton had never been driven from home.

'Loneliness – that's what I worry about for him more than anything else,' Sheila told the newspaper. 'I think he's desperate. He's got all the possessions you could wish for, but that doesn't make him happy. He hasn't anyone to share it with, and that's what he needs. He says he'd like to have a family. Unfortunately his lifestyle doesn't allow him to meet anybody. And he won't allow himself to. It's as if he holds back all the time. I feel that he's got everything – but nothing.'

What seemed saddest of all, to me, was that Elton does not have himself. His past owns his soul and dictates his present. Certainly anyone who has been touched by Elton's love and generosity would agree with Sheila. But those closest to him would probably also argue that a lot of the loneliness was brought upon him by his own immaturity, his wilful refusal to take responsibility. If he wasn't hiding behind his lackeys or his cocaine, he would still manage to avoid confronting a crisis. He missed out on the emotional growth that comes with pain. Everything is done for a star. In any case, the drugs made him insensitive to those around him. He became unable to tune in to the feelings of others. At these times, selfishness was survival for Elton. He was a devout reader of celebrity biographies, and I imagined that he could have learnt how not to lead his life. But, of course, it doesn't work like that. You only learn by your own mistakes.

Despite his immaturity, or because of it, he was preoccupied with giving. Elton rarely forgot the birthdays of people that mattered, and his presents were often extravagant. Cousins were given cars as presents; one had a boutique given to him after merely mentioning it to Elton in passing. A family who were neighbours from the Hercules days, with whom he frequently socialized, were aghast when Elton insisted on buying one of their daughters expensive perfume and a Cartier watch – not an unreasonable reaction, as she was only six years old at the time.

Something is running very deep in Elton, and it often erupts through inappropriate channels.

It says a lot about Elton's priorities that, while he never once told me to stay in the background when showbiz luminaries were around, he was very careful about keeping our relationship from the public where Watford Football Club was concerned.

Elton was an obsessive Watford fan during his childhood, and it was natural that he was concerned that by the 70s, sloppy management had seen the working-class club drop to No. 8 position in the Third Division, with debts of more than £100,000. His interest in soccer was probably more deep-seated than merely an interest in a local club's performance. Elton's uncle, Roy Dwight, was an outstanding footballer in the late 50s, playing for Fulham in an FA Cup Semi-Final and for first-division team Nottingham Forest at the Cup Final in Wembley. Roy was lauded by the press and fans as a 'goal snatcher', and his interception and speed thrilled crowds. Elton, who was born on 25 March 1947, was ten years old during Roy's heyday, and his uncle showed Elton that it was possible to achieve fame despite social and financial barriers.

In 1974 Elton became one of Watford's directors, playing benefit shows alone or roping in big-name friends like Rod Stewart, and he poured in more than £1.5 million to save the club. Possibly fans saw his Watford interest as nothing more than a rich man's toy. Perhaps his close friends might have smirked that, like most gay men, Elton suffered a paranoia that he was not considered 'macho' enough by straights and therefore became obsessed with sports and sporting figures. But when he became Watford's chairman – an accolade he says gave him a greater high than any of his rock and roll achievements – he proved that his commitment to the club was genuine. He even flew back from a US tour to preside over the board's general meeting. Another time he actually promised to reduce his touring schedule so he could devote more time and energy to solving Watford's problems. He had a family at last, and the love wasn't conditional.

Elton really helped kick the club back into life and not only by donating money. He nagged at the well-respected football coach, Graham Taylor, until Graham agreed to come in as manager. The two men liked and respected each other immensely; Graham was a person whom Elton would never try to dominate, because he wasn't dazzled by Elton's celebrity status. Years later, when Graham decided to move on, Elton was aghast. But in their time at Watford together, they came up with some clever ideas. Elton paid good money for stars like Ray Train, Steve Sims and Tommy Walley. By refurbishing the club building, he encouraged parents and children in the area back to the game and swelled grass-root support. Together Elton and Graham watched Watford creep back up the divisional ladder, until in 1984 the once ridiculed Watford reached the grand final.

It wasn't difficult to see Elton's commitment. I noticed it in the clothes he wore when he attended the matches. He played down the flamboyance so he wouldn't be perceived as a rock star, but not too much in case supporters thought his presence at matches was just a casual dalliance. No doubt about it, he took football very seriously. When opposing supporters would taunt Watford by chanting, to the tune of 'My Old Man Said Follow the Van',

'Don't bend down/When Elton's around/Or you'll get a penis up your arse,' Elton never lost his sense of humour over it. The title track of his 1995 album *Made In England* has a line, 'You can still say homo/And everybody laughs', which is a reference to the realization that people generally still see gayness or campness as something comical. So why get upset by gay slurs or, indeed, ever feel threatened by them? Elton said, 'You can't sit there and get angry about 10,000 West Bromwich Albion supporters singing [that song]. It's no big deal for me.'

What annoyed Elton wasn't that he was being publicly humiliated, but that the status of football was diminished. To him football was mystical, almost spiritual, and above wealth and bigotry. In fact, above everything else.

By the time Sheila and Derf arrived to take me to my first Watford match against Sheffield Wednesday, it was late morning. Sheila drove us there in her BMW with a confidence and skill that Elton lacked. The first time he was to take me for a spin in the Aston Martin Vantage, he crunched the gears, the car lurched around bends, and we almost piled into a vehicle stacked with irate farmers.

When Sheila's party arrived at the Watford grounds, we found that Elton had made arrangements for us to park in the privileged section, and I followed his parents to our seats. I could see Elton whizzing between the players' rooms and the bar, where the rest of the Watford board was nervously assembled. It was interesting to note that in the grounds, Elton, the Rock Star, merited no second glance or requests for autographs. The game was all important.

Elton and I sat in the same row of seats, although no one would have guessed we knew each other. Bob sat behind, as did John Reid and a friend, Paul. I was sitting between Sheila and a girlfriend of Bob's. But football is a bore to me, and I could feel sleep welling in me, my eyelids drooping and my head occasionally lolling. With the grand final looming, and with Watford's rise through the years, there was a genuine excitement among the team's supporters. But it wasn't enough for me to stay bright and light. Waking with a start and looking around sheep-ishly, I could see that Elton had noticed, and he was responding with a wink and grin. It was sort of like sleeping in church.

After the final whistle, the Farebrothers departed without me, and I accompanied Elton and Bob to John Reid's house, where there were some good-looking boys in attendance. Reid's was a large white house in outer London, not as flash as Elton's, but tastefully decorated. No museum pieces here.

Sheila had warned me about John Reid, calling him a 'real terrier'. I'd heard stories about Reid but always found him a gentleman, until he heard I was writing this book. The boys were pleasant and quite taken by my Australian accent. One of the guys, who worked in a clothes store, came in with goodies for everyone and insisted on giving me a pair of polo socks. It all seemed to be part of the entertainment. After a casual dinner, I fell asleep on the couch and awoke to find Elton cuddling me. We returned to Woodside, where our sleeping arrangements had become routine: I'd use my room for the day but never at night.

The next day we lolled around the house listening to music and playing with the dogs. Suddenly Elton grabbed my shoulders: 'Chook! I almost forgot! I've got something to show you.' We headed for the garage, and I remembered that during one of our phone conversations, Elton had mentioned that he had a car for me, a Panther Lima. I didn't have a clue what it was, but its name suggested the type of flashy modern sports car I adored. As I walked towards the garages I kept thinking: Will it be as good looking as the Aston? As powerful as a Porsche?

You can imagine how crestfallen I was to find that the car in question was indeed a Panther Lima, but was a roadster style, hardly my idea of heaven. As Elton seemed so excited at handing over the keys, I put on a happy face. But in some things he had misjudged me. 'Come on, let's take her for a spin,' he yelled.

As we reversed out of the garage, Elton was called back into the house, so I went off on my own. It was a glorious feeling, tearing through the country lanes. Old Windsor is about as quaint as England can be and virtually untouched by progress. Thatched cottages glimpsed through the trees, broad shallow streams sparkling in the sun. After a while I began to feel a little out of my territory, so I headed back in the direction of Windsor Castle.

By now Woodside was in full swing, preparing for Elton's European tour. Bob was running in and out of the place, the telex machine clattered endlessly, and all anyone seemed to talk about was the upcoming event. One evening the tour programmes were sent around by courier. 'Look, right here,' Elton said, proudly showing me where my name was listed. I noticed I was eleventh in the entourage.

'Oh, they've misspelt my name – they've left the "e" out of the end of my surname,' I complained. It irks me when people spell my name incorrectly, usually the surname or sometimes getting it wrong all together by putting two rs in Gary.

'Ooh, the end of bloody civilization!' Elton said, affecting his regal voice and clutching his forehead, and we started to giggle. Before we left Elton gave me a lecture on the realities of touring:

'It's not glamorous, Chook. It's an emotional and physical drain. We have to leave here on time to catch the flight to Stockholm. We don't wait for anyone. You have to be ready.' Despite my excitement and best efforts, I was late. Touring was to turn out to be a real eye-opener for someone who'd never been on the road with a rock band before. And another side of Elton was to emerge. I thought I'd only meet the devil after death.

4. Jump Up! Jump Down!

'I'm not going to do the show tonight!' Elton screamed. 'I mean it! I'm going to cancel the rest of the tour!'

ONE THING YOU could say about Stockholm – it's neat. The train stations are tidy, the shop assistants impeccably attired, the streets are litter-free – and the only time you see a traffic jam is on Friday evenings when everyone tears out of the city. Tastefully decorated modern apartments abound. Every family appears to have a moped, and the country has more telephones and radios per capita than any other in the world except the USA.

But on the night of Friday, 30 April 1982, Elton John was oblivious to his surroundings. As the applause receded in the enormous cavern that is the Johanneseshovs Isstadion, Elton stormed from the hall, past the entourage waiting in the back area and into his limo without a word. On the drive back to the Sheraton Hotel, he glared out of the window, hunched in a corner. Opera houses and theatres flashed past unnoticed. He was fuming.

'It seemed to go all right,' I said, tactfully trying to break the silence, 'although "Blue Eyes" sounded different ... I was watching from the back.' That elicited a 'Hmmp!' and an even frostier silence. I didn't realize that after looking forward to the Stockholm show – as the first of his month-long European tour – Elton had felt let down by the sound. He was furious, and no doubt he would scream at John Reid to scream at whoever was responsible.

Once we reached the Sheraton, Elton stomped into the lobby, brushed past other guests who had politely acknowledged his presence with an 'Oh, Mr John, we really like your . . . .' Elton then had his customary after-show shower and went straight to bed. It was left to John and Bob to suggest that if anyone felt like having a drink with the star in his suite, it might not be a good idea.

John cornered me in the corridor outside our suite. 'Gary it looks as though Elton's a bit upset about the sound tonight . . . make sure you stay with him. OK?'

Looking back, it was presumptuous of Reid to instruct me on my personal relationship with his boss. However, I merely commented on the performance: 'Upset? I thought the crowd seemed to have a good time.'

Reid was prepared to make excuses for Elton's prima-donna truculence: 'Well, he's probably just a bit uptight, this being the first few shows and all. Don't worry, he'll be OK in the morning.' With that, Reid left. No doubt he knew that with me to calm down the star, this manager would probably be saved from a savage blast in the morning. Bob obviously knew the routine for he was already waiting in the lobby to head off any unwanted guests. Elton's guitarist, Davey Johnstone, approached from one end of the hallway. But sensing trouble, he beat a quick retreat.

This was only my third night on tour – and I had already realized that touring was not the glamorous 24-hour party that most rock fans envisage. And I now had a clearer idea of my role in maintaining the overall health of the entourage. I was there to cushion the star's fragile ego when reality impinged. Disappointments and fears were my portfolio. Some kids suck their thumb. Not my Elton. He used me.

• • •

Although I would choose either 'Crystal' or 'Blue Eyes' as Elton's best ballad, most Elton fans would probably vote for 'Your Song'. Hey, I'm not biased because those first two songs were written about me. 'Your Song' was a touch of Taupin genius, whipped off in 15 minutes over breakfast, but the song hasn't dated one iota since launching Elton's career in the early 70s – not even the line about 'buying a big house where we both could live', once he could afford it. Elton's finances had certainly moved on since those days. So had his lifestyle. Only Elton was stuck in the groove: he was even getting bored with himself.

In his early days Elton had done his share of working for £5 a week, sleeping in smelly transit vans, playing in seedy clubs, using grubby toilets as dressing-rooms, making do with borrowed, often pedal-less pianos. Now no one could begrudge Elton John touring first class all the way. The best suites in the best hotels, the best restaurants, unlimited room service, limos everywhere – even if it were only to buy toothpaste from the shop down the street. Elton's lifestyle didn't stop at the wealth stored in Woodside or the expensive gifts to his friends and business associates. As a superstar, Elton could demand that shops open for him after hours so he wouldn't be hassled by fans. He could demand TV advertising for his albums in America at a time when this was far from the norm. He didn't have to do interviews if he didn't want to: when he did, he could specify what he wanted to talk about and for how long. He could afford the best equipment, the best crews and the most elaborate stage props and costumes money could buy. He quipped on radio that after the mid-70s even the groupies were upmarket: 'They became – how can I put it – they were less sluttish!'

At one stage Elton was touring with his own private jet, equipped with stereo, movies, kitchenette and bar. At a Hollywood Bowl show, Elton indulged himself with tongue firmly in cheek: an off-stage voice boomed, 'The biggest, the most colossal, gigantic, fantastic'. The 20th-Century Fox theme burst through the PA, and Elton minced downstairs in a feathered outfit, 400 doves released to mark his entrance. When he sat down at his piano, the lids of five other pianos flipped open, each revealing giant letters of his name. It was kitsch, of course, but the audience went crazy.

Like all major tours, Elton's extravaganza was as organized as a military operation. The equipment would arrive at the venue well in advance, usually in a customized fleet of juggernaut lorries. The road crew was large and specialized. The logistics and sheer expense of keeping the entourage on the road was awesome. Just one cancelled show would have a disastrous effect on the budget as the venues, all booked in advance, would have to be re-booked. The roadies would regale me with horrifying tales of driving through snowstorms and blizzards for 18 hours at a stretch, assembling the gear, then straight after the show dismantling it again to start yet another lengthy journey to the next country. Cuts, bruises, falls and electrocutions were an ever present threat. Touring through Europe in winter was always dangerous because of the snow, so we anxiously checked the weather forecasts every night. If it was too bad to drive, we moved the equipment by chartered plane. One roadie told me of the time when during an awful blizzard, a snowplough had to clear the runway: 'We took off knowing we were the only plane leaving that day! We flew the whole journey through the blizzard . . . and we sang Buddy Holly songs all the way.'

You could tell by his chuckling that this raconteur enjoyed every thrilling minute of it – he saw a brush with death as part of the excitement of being part of rock and roll. The same guy remembered when another band's roadies packed a 32-ton truck with gear and parked it outside the hotel so the boys could grab a few hours kip. The brakes failed, and the truck rolled forward demolishing a few limos and part of the hotel sign before coming to rest in the middle of the road. He liked that story too!

Naturally, as star of the show, Elton was seldom worried by organizational problems. But the quality of the music at concerts were top priority when he toured – and if anything upset that apple-cart, he flew into a rage. Roadies who weren't up to scratch were quickly sacked. On tour, everything was organized so that

Elton's energies were confined to performance. So when he, Bob and I left Woodside for Heathrow Airport to fly to Stockholm, everything had been prepared for him by others. Both John and Ron, the husband of Gladys, the daytime housekeeper, had gone on ahead in two vehicles with the 18 suitcases. The whole scenario reminded me of something from 'Rocket Man' – bags packed the night before, pre-flight, zero hour, 9 am.

The last thing Elton had said to me the night before this European jaunt was: 'Be ready at 9 am, Chook. We can't afford to wait.' When I had been delayed, apparently Elton had become frantic. But once we were in the Corniche heading for Heathrow, he'd relaxed. Flying was a chore, and he would while away the time by reading. But I knew that this time he was excited because I was travelling with him.

In the car to the airport, jokes were flying, and the pre-taped music blared out of the sophisticated sound system. Elton was mad about the latest Prince *Controversy* LP, which he played again and again. The sort of thing he always does when he is buzzing on a record. Annie Lennox was a perennial favourite and also popular were tapes by Men At Work and Split Enz, which he had bought on his last trip to Australia. It was a cold morning, but Elton insisted having the air conditioner on full blast. I had to condition myself to his unnatural desire for chilled blood.

As flight BA 652 taxied on to the runway, Elton, sitting next to me and by the window, nudged me and indicated an elderly couple sitting a few rows in front of us in the first-class section: 'Look at that!' he said admiringly. We watched as the aged lovers spoke with affection. The man had grey hair and a long angular face. He might have been a diplomat or someone in the civil service. The woman had bundled her hair into a red silk scarf and had the quiet reserve of old money. The man stroked his wife's hair. Elton turned to me and whispered: 'One day that will be us, Chook.'

Once we hit Stockholm, the button marked Elton John Rock Star was firmly pressed, and it would stay that way for most of the next four weeks. When we arrived, all Elton had to do was to walk through customs. His bags were never checked in all the time I knew him, and mostly the customs officers were too busy telling him which of his songs was their favourite. On arrival Elton would be met by the tour promoter for that particular country and then be ushered straight into a limo. All he would have to do was alight at the hotel, walk to the lobby, suffering the bowing and scraping that inevitably greeted him, and then retire to his room.

On arriving at the Stockholm hotel, Bob dialled room service, while Elton fell into his familiar routine. As we waited for dinner, he used the remote control to flick through the TV channels. The Falklands crisis was sweeping Britain at the time and Elton, who admired Mrs Thatcher, was very much the British patriot. There was a knock on the door, and he turned down the sound. A waiter wheeled in a trolley with an assortment of plates with silver covers. As he left, the screen flashed with footage of a man dressed in green jungle camouflage, trousers tucked into canvas boots, a water bottle and Bowie knife hanging from his belt. Elton eagerly raised the volume. The soldier was talking about a skirmish in Africa. Disappointed, Elton sat down to eat.

At about 9.30 pm, wardrobe master Bob Stacey rang to say that the latest costumes had arrived from New York. We eagerly rushed to Stacey's room, and it was chock-a-block with costumes laid all over the floor and bed. As to be expected, the outfits were big and bold. Elton immediately fell in love with a number that had battery-operated mirror balls on each shoulder. These balls would revolve, reflecting the stage spots. But I don't think I ever saw him wear that gear: the batteries and wiring gave endless trouble, and it was finally banished to one of Woodside's clothes rooms.

There were a lot of military-type things as well, such as policemen's caps with exaggerated peaks for, like a lot of gays, Elton is attracted to butch men. On tour, he was forever buying police badges and caps; he'd even had a fling with a policeman in Queensland, Australia. The copper presented Elton with his truncheon, and it adorned the end of Elton's bed at Woodside.

All that Thursday we languished in the suite, listening incessantly to the *Controversy* album. Elton was busy with telexes, for he wanted to know how the rest of the tour was selling or how *Jump Up!* was doing in the charts, especially in comparison with other superstars' efforts. Elton was disappointed with the album's sales. It had reached No. 13 in Britain and No. 17 in America. 'Blue Eyes' had reached the Top 10, but successive singles from the LP had not been as successful. The song 'Empty Garden', also on the album, had been dedicated to John Lennon: Elton had been in Australia on tour when he heard the terrible news of Lennon's murder. He still vividly remembers how he and the entourage had flown into Melbourne airport when the pilot announced over the PA system: 'Would Elton John's party please remain on board while the other passengers disembark.' Then John Reid came aboard with the devastating news. Lennon was Elton's hero. It was Lennon who had begged Elton to kick drugs and drink some years earlier, and Elton had hoped for no better farewell present and tribute to Lennon than to have a worldwide No. 1 eulogizing his friend. Alas, it barely made the Top 10 in America and didn't even reach the Top 50 in the charts. Another track from the album, 'Princess', issued as a UK-only single, was also a flop.

When tours were underway, there were always requests from magazines and radio stations for Elton to do interviews. Usually Bob would deliver a message from Reid or the promoter. If Elton was happy to proceed, he usually asked for the name of the journalist or disk jockey before giving a final decision. Usually John Reid would check to see if a magazine's circulation or a programme's ratings were high enough to warrant going to the trouble. He was very aware of Elton's image on that score.

There had been a request from a German TV sports show for Elton to appear on air when the tour moved to Germany. Elton might have been one-eyed when it came to Watford but he realized that if it was not for his music, he would be just another football club director. Watford was very much on Elton's mind during the tour. The 1981–2 season had been the once-hapless club's most successful year, and Watford had become a force; some young players like John Barnes, Kenny Jackett and Nigel Callaghan had emerged as gifted stars. The soccer audiences became more hysterical with each successive win, and crowds were gathering. At this time Elton was embroiled in a fray with Watford Council. Having already loaned the club almost £1.2 million, he offered to pour in the bulk of the £5 million needed to build a new grandstand to accommodate the larger crowds. 'I can't believe it!' Elton screamed down the phone one day. 'The club's the best it's been in ages, and some bastard is slowing down the grandstand permit.'

Elton was now in a bad mood, exacerbated by the concerts' sound problems and the football club's bureaucratic wrangle, and as usual he retreated to his bedroom. But his ill humour never lasted long if people left him alone. That evening, when a party including the tour promoters and their publicists tried out a local Thai restaurant, Elton had put the hassles with Watford Council to one side, and good spirits prevailed. At dinner he had us in stitches with his anecdotes and impersonations.

That evening Elton explained my official tour duties. He suggested I should pack and unpack his suitcases on tour and receive about £250 a week for my troubles. I was to keep an eye on his eighteen suitcases – and these would increase by another four or five by the time the tour ended. When the conversation turned to living in England, I suggested that I could get a job. I knew that it would probably be difficult for me to continue a normal type of day job, but what worried me most was losing my independence and becoming reliant on Elton. It would be short-sighted of me not to think that perhaps one day things might change, and I would be alone. That sort of thing had happened before.

Elton had his luggage specially made in New York, and I loved the aroma of new leather that erupted each time I opened a bag. There were a couple of suitcases that only contained shoes. Another case contained his array of spectacles. Others were filled with shirts and trousers. It amazed me that, although he didn't pack the suitcases, he knew exactly where everything was positioned. 'This is the way to pack these, Chook,' he would say, showing me how the trousers folded in a special way with the shirts above. The sense of order appealed to me greatly.

Next afternoon Elton went with Bob to do a soundcheck and then returned to the suite to relax. He was no longer nervous before a show, but he liked to make sure everything was perfect before he walked on stage. The only time I saw him agitated before a performance was if there had been no time for a sound-check. Elton took no special precautions with his voice, but some years earlier, one of his idols, Neil Sedaka, had given him advice on how to look after his throat: gargle with warm tea and honey; and keep away from smoky clubs.

Stockholm showtime was 7.30 pm, and about 6 pm Elton began to adopt his stage persona. Elton, Bob and I went downstairs to the waiting limo that took us to the Johanneshovs Isstadion. Bob had already called ahead to tell the road crew to have the stadium's roller-doors open so the limo could move through the waiting fans without having to come to a standstill. As soon as Elton and crew disembarked in the backstage area, the car would be immediately repositioned so that we could leap in for a quick escape after the final encore.

Inside, beyond a maze of corridors, Bob Stacey was waiting to dress Elton. Once ready, Elton would invariably go into the band's dressing room to joke and indulge in a bit of horseplay, providing he remained in control. Elton well understood the need for band camaraderie and the effect it had on the audience. His long time guitarist, Davey Johnstone, was proudly displaying his tan on this occasion. Davey's skin had become tough through years of sun worship. 'Started your mad shopping yet, Elt?' Davey teased. 'Need another suitcase?'

Elton quickly retorted, 'Don't worry.' he said, stroking his face, 'if we run short of cases, we can have your hide skinned.'

The current band with Davey Johnstone had seen Elton reunited with two original band members, drummer Nigel Olsson and base guitarist Dee Murray. Nigel and Dee had been with

Elton in the early days, and Nigel had played with a band that had bought songs from Elton and Bernie. As was his usual duty, John Reid strode down the corridor into the band's changing room and announced: 'Ten minutes, Elton!' The band seemed unmoved and continued with the usual pre-show jitters, the banter, the quick bitchy jokes. Bob grinned. He'd been through this scenario many times before. Everyone was keyed-up with anticipation and wanted to be onstage – that's the way they liked to keep them – audience hungry. Like most professional performers, Elton's band knew some things were unforgivable, for example arriving late or drunk for a show, and if it did happen, the person wasn't around for it to happen twice. But a legitimate crisis, such as sickness, could throw the tour into turmoil. Elton felt at his most vulnerable when one of the band members was ill.

Nigel, a handsome, dark-haired heart-throb was a nice guy, but Elton often complained that his drummer was forever falling sick or moaning about not feeling well. Later on this tour, at one of the German shows, Nigel said that he was too ill to perform. An agitated Elton went onstage and diplomatically sought the audience's permission to play without a drummer. The reassuring applause had Elton performing at his best, and it was one of the most dynamic shows I remember – a peak experience that the audience will never forget. Risk seemed to bring out the best in Elton, although professionally he did his best to avoid the unwanted sort – that of poor administration or lack of discipline. It seems ironic when you look at his personal life. Elton had won that German crowd over, but it didn't appease him and I overhead him talking to Reid after the show: 'He [Nigel] had better get his act together, if not, we'll get another drummer!'

Dee had also been in a band scraping for a break around the time that Elton and Bernie were looking for their opportunity. Of the three band members, I thought Dee was the most forthright: the other two tended to side with Elton. They had their jobs in mind. But if there was a problem within the band, Dee, with the prompting of the other two, had no hesitation in approaching

Reid or Halley to demand changes. The tough-nut manager would normally shrug it off, but Dee would then go directly to Elton.

Although I hadn't seen Dee in many years, I remember at the studios in Montserrat in 1984, when he showed me the scars on his arms. Cancerous tumours had been removed. But it still came as a shock to me when Dee died of cancer in 1992 at his home in Nashville in the USA; Elton would later play two benefit shows in that city to raise money for Dee's widow and children. I have many fond memories of Dee.

Nigel and Dee were relaxed around Elton, but no doubt they knew that when it came to the crunch, he would dump them as he had done in 1975, when he told them of his decision to break-up the band. In mid-1979, while making the *21 At 33* album, Elton had unceremoniously brought them back. After a short break, he just as casually started writing songs again with Bernie Taupin.

According to Dee, the bass guitarist was at his Los Angeles home when a call came from Rocket Records in London: 'Oh, Elton's recording, would you like to do some sessions?' They must have been relieved when *21 At 33* went on to become a successful album. 'Little Jeannie', reaching No. 3 in America, signified the thawing of the cold shoulder that American radio had shown toward Elton since his 'I'm a bisexual' confession. The American tour, with Elton's costumes at their most flamboyant, was greeted with frenzied scenes, capped with a massive free show at New York's Central Park with 400,000 spectators.

The familiar whoosh! opening of 'Funeral for a Friend' signalled showtime, and Elton, calm as ever, made his way on to the Stockholm stage. I had an Access All Areas stage pass, so I slipped into the crowd and made my way to the sound board to sit beside Clive Franks, Elton's engineer. Clive had been promoted to co-producer during the *21 At 33* sessions, and he was one of the most warm-hearted people in Elton's entourage, a good solid bloke unaffected by the conniving and puffery that blighted many of Elton's staff. Clive always made sure there was a seat for me during a show and that I was OK. Much later when I came to know Clive, he revealed: 'You're different to most guys that Elton brings on tour. A lot of them were gold-diggers, and it was quite obvious to me what they were up to.' It became evident that it was a habit of Elton's to bring boys on tour. Which raised the obvious question – what had been their fate?

By the first Stockholm show I had been with Elton for a week, but I still hadn't settled into the first-class routine. Someone like Bob, for instance, didn't think twice about splashing out on £100 bottles of champagne. Bob figured that he had worked hard enough and earned that privilege. If he wanted a Porsche, he knew that all he had to do was to ask, and he would receive. When it came to spending Elton's money, I was still apprehensive about phoning Australia for more than ten minutes or ordering something from room service without checking the price beforehand. In all the time I spent with Elton, all I ever wanted was a Cartier watch. I never asked for it, and Elton, who gave Cartier watches to others at the drop of a hat, never thought of it. I felt it meant something, but I was never game enough to broach the topic.

On the road, Elton and I started to become closer friends. In Sydney he referred to me as Bluey, an affectionate Aussie term. And as we got to know each other better, I became 'Chook'. He was either 'Elton' or 'EJ' to me, with most of the entourage referring to him as 'Elt'. It was many years later when someone referred to one of Elton's boyfriends as ELF – an acronym for Elton's Little Fuck – that it dawned on me that, behind my back, this was probably said of me. To my face, the entourage called me Gary or, much later, Crystal, which Elton introduced as our in-joke about country singer, Crystal Gayle.

I was a shy, retiring observer rather than the type to let everyone know where I stood in the pecking order, so often, at the end of the show, when I returned backstage to accompany Elton to the hotel, a security guard would question my Access pass. Security would assume I was a fan who had found the pass on the floor, and I would have to wait patiently for John Reid or Bob to retrieve me.

During concerts I would usually watch from the wings or chat to one of the girls that the crew or band had brought along as a visitor. Elton had one firm rule on tour: no wives. He thought wives were a distraction or that the high life would lead to arguments, and he knew that they could upset a tour.

Members of the entourage were allowed to bring their one-night stands into the dressing-room areas with the unspoken condition that the girls kept quiet and stayed out of everybody's way. If a girl became noisy or caused a scene, she would have been ejected without a moment's notice. I felt sorry for some of these girls. Most of them seemed to accept that their bodies were to be used for the night and then turfed out in the morning. The compensation was that they could brag about having been fucked by someone from Elton John's crew. The lucky ones might even be treated to a good breakfast. There were the occasional sad girls who'd mistaken lust for instant love. If they didn't take the hint in the morning and tried to become part of the entourage they would find the door slammed in their faces. It was very harsh.

Elton had learnt to be tough on fans. In the early hysteria days he had been mobbed, forced to run down streets in cities he didn't know to escape the fans; he'd left theatres in the back of vans while the kids chased a decoy in the limo; and his luggage contained dozens of spare spectacles because they were inevitably smashed when the fans attacked. Although those days of placing himself at public risk were long over, intense fan worship continued then as it does now. After all, Elton provides hope in a world devoid of direction. That means a lot to people.

On tour Elton tends to attract celebrities. In America, it wouldn't be unusual for the audience to be studded with names like Cher, Barbara Streisand, Warren Beatty, Fred Astaire, Paul and Linda McCartney and Axl Rose of Guns 'n' Roses. Elton sent Princess Diana a copy of *Jump Up!*, and she wrote back a very nice letter telling him that she enjoyed the 'Ball and Chain' track the most. Elton was thrilled with the royal seal at the top of the letter. It made him feel respectable. By 1982 he was one of the rare rock performers who'd got in with the British royal family. About ten years before, Elton had been asked to play the Royal Variety Show. Unwilling to say no to the Queen, he shuffled around dates on his American tour, blew out Phoenix, spent between £15,000 and £25,000 to return to England, flew into London where hundreds of screaming teenies waited at Heathrow for the Jackson 5 and the Osmonds, went to rehearsals from the airport and played the show after going without sleep for 49 hours. Mind you it was partly because the perfectionist wanted to listen to some newly mixed tracks in the London studio. Elton flew back to America the morning after. Such was his sense of patriotism. Or was it a measure of his need for royal approval?

Elton first became pals with Princess Margaret when he played a benefit show for one of her favourite charities, the Invalid Aid Association. She had told the Queen Mother about Elton, and Her Majesty invited Elton to perform for her at Royal Lodge, Windsor. He later played at Prince Andrew's 21st and, if the British gossip columns are to be believed, even gave Prince Charles and Princess Diana some friendly advice when their marriage hit the rocks.

Elton would often tell me about madcap things that went on at those early royal meetings: 'I don't know what they must have thought of us rock and roll creatures,' he'd guffaw. 'I was sitting at dinner with the Queen Mother, and I was so nervous that I picked up the wrong container, I thought it was salt, and it was sugar. I had to eat the entrée covered with sugar. Then I went off to another room to change into my playing clothes, and I was standing there in me undies, and Princess Margaret popped her head in. But they were so relaxed. Later on at the end of the night, the Queen Mother put on some of her favourite music, and we both danced around the room.' Elton often reminisced about the Queen Mother with great affection. Once she advised Elton that the best way to keep diamonds gleaming was to give them a good soaking in gin, reportedly one of her favourite drinks.

On the European tour Elton socialized with a few close friends in the entourage. If there was a crisis, Halley or Reid would sort it out. If Elton didn't feel like speaking to a business associate, they would make his excuses for him. Although Elton would never blow out a concert, he wouldn't think twice about cancelling a business meeting or TV or radio appearance. During the tour, he occasionally called his mother. When Watford were finally promoted into the First Division, Elton was so excited that he spent about an hour and a half on the phone congratulating each player.

When the tour hit Oslo on 4 May, we noticed that the Holsberg Gate Hotel was full of grey-suited men in shades, and we later discovered that ex-President Carter and his family were guests. As we were about to leave for the concert, we received a message from the former First Lady asking if she could meet Elton. When granted an audience, Mrs Carter came over and introduced herself, declared herself a fan and chatted about Elton's music. The star was most impressed and was delighted when Mrs Carter asked for his autograph. He beamed for the rest of the evening.

One of Elton's prized possessions was his phone book. He guarded it zealously. Obviously it would be disastrous if he mislaid it and the home numbers of showbiz celebrities fell into the hands of the wrong people. Having never dreamed as a child that he would come to know so many famous people, having their names listed in his phone book meant a lot to him. It gave him instant access to his famous friends.

Once he was quietly reading a newspaper when I heard him chuckle and hand the paper to Bob. As he read it, Bob began to laugh. I reached for the paper and read the startling news that Rod Stewart had been threatened in a car park at knifepoint and had had his car stolen. I didn't see the humour. The next thing I knew Elton was prancing around the room mimicking Rod, saying: 'Take the car, lovey, but don't touch the face . . . Ohh, I've just had my hair done!' Elton and Bob joked and then began discussing how scarey the incident must have been, and I agreed. I realized later that the joking was in fact part of how they coped with their own fear and a sign of relief that their friend had survived.

Elton flicked through his phone book and in no time his fingers were jabbing at the digits on the telephone. He was ringing Rod to find out how he was and at the same time to invite him and his wife, Alannah, to Lille to catch the final show of the European tour. Usually, with close friends, Elton would ring or, if he was busy, ask Bob to make the call. He would bark into the phone, 'It's Elton,' and go into his royal dowager routine. But I noticed that when he rang up Yoko from Oslo, the conversation was matter-of-fact. Elton was ringing to check on his godson, Sean Lennon. Elton's enthusiasm for the child was obvious, and though the conversation was brief, I remember Elton whistling cheerfully afterwards.

When we got to Berlin, we discovered that Queen was also playing in that town. Faced with the prospect of exchanging juicy gossip, Elton was keen to dine with Queen singer Freddie Mercury. But we had the devil of a time trying to catch up with him – he was going through those Berlin leather clubs like a bull at a gate. I'd been eager to see what these leather clubs were like so the jaunt was a bit of fun. Someone had told me how club patrons dress to signal their sexual desires. A red handkerchief hanging from one pocket meant the male liked to be the dominant partner, a red hankerchief in the opposite pocket signified the reverse. Another colour would send the message that the person enjoyed fist-fucking or golden showers. You could be in trouble if you were colour blind. We never did find Freddie. Another night we had dinner with Tim Robinson, who had enjoyed a brief splurge of success in the late 70s as a gay icon and had written a song called 'Elton's Song'.

It is not surprising that gay teenagers seemed to see Elton as a role model. On tour, the star would receive many letters from boys saying they had been confused about their sexuality and that Elton's songs and messages in interviews had helped them define their identities. Elton was pleased to read the letters because he felt he was making a worthwhile contribution.

Touring became yawnsville for me, but I certainly enjoyed seeing the different countries, no matter how brief the visit. For most of the day Elton and I were surrounded by people, so our sex life was confined to the night. I was starting to relax although at the back of my mind there was always the threat that I could be thrown out on a whim. Being anxious, it was difficult for me to give myself completely, and I felt true love with Elton was yet to come although sensually I was finding him very satisfying. We really enjoyed being in each other's company and when others were in the room, Elton would smile and wink at me, and occasionally we cuddled.

Despite the attention, I was irritated because Elton couldn't appreciate that he was cocooned in a bubble, where every move and conversation centred on his interests. We needed to break away from that for our emotional life to develop. But he was selfish and if I talked about flying, or fast cars, he would feign a snore to indicate he was bored, or abruptly change the subject. Elton's celebrity friends were polite to me, and Elton always tried to include me in conversations. These people shared his past, whereas to me they were complete strangers, and I often felt left out. It was difficult to make friends with the crew because there wasn't time, for tours were so highly organized. When the show hit a new town, usually in the afternoon, everyone in the 50-person juggernaut would scramble out in an erratic but efficient tumble of activity.

In the few hours to showtime, a complex ritual was completed with very little time to converse. After the show the road crew would disassemble the stage, load it into the trucks and start the overnight drive to the next town, and the band would go clubbing or be entertained by the promoter or record-company representatives. On returning to their rooms, the players would start packing for the next day's journey, and it was, in a way, just as lonely a life for them as it was for me. They would share jokes and good times with new-found friends, but it was all superficial, and although addresses and telephone numbers would be exchanged, there would seldom be further contact. The tour was a commercial enterprise, so socializing was secondary. Sometimes I felt Elton saw me as his pet, to have around at his convenience, and he never encouraged me to fraternize with his battalion of 'soldiers and officers'.

The worst aspect of touring for me was that Elton and I spent most of the time confined to our suite, for he seldom went clubbing or sightseeing. He had been touring Europe for more than ten years and for him the outside world was a case of 'been there, done that – or not interested!' At the same time, Elton didn't want me to go anywhere without him. Emotionally and physically, he was tired by his tour but satisfied. Being less involved, I had energy to spare, and it was this energy that Elton wanted to have in reserve when he needed to top up his emotional batteries.

Touring was a well-oiled process with only the occasional surprise to break the monotony. In Stockholm the promoter presented the entourage with Swiss knives as mementos, and John McEnroe had sent around two pairs of one-off camouflage style Nikes that had been specifically made for the tennis champ. To my surprise, Elton gave me a pair. And gifts from fans would rain down like an unwanted flood. Things like teddy bears, novelties and Elton John dolls. All would be packed away in the suitcases. The boredom of the endless round of room service was alleviated when waiters and waitresses, chuffed to be in the star's presence, would pause to chat. Plucky ones would summon up the courage to ask for an autograph; the bolder ones would ask for tickets. If they were sassy – and certainly if they were cute boys – they were accommodated.

I had been travelling for four days, and I still hadn't been allowed to see the sights; it was really starting to get me down. Helsinki didn't give the impression it could be a fun city, but as this was my first time in Europe, I decided to see for myself. As the backstage area of the venue, Ishallen, was so depressing, I left early one night to take in the sights on my walk back to the hotel. Dawdling along by myself for the first time since joining Elton, I felt great – free and invigorated. On returning to the hotel I went to bed, and it seemed only minutes before I was woken by Elton, sitting at the end of the bed, weeping and calling out my name: 'Gary, don't you ever leave me like that again!'

'I'm sorry, but I did tell Clive I was leaving,' I pleaded.

'Yes, I know . . . but that's not the point . . . don't leave early again!'

We had a quick cuddle; I felt upset that I'd distressed Elton like this, as I felt a genuine warmth for this man who obviously cared for me. But I certainly hadn't expected him to reach out as desperately as this. It was a side to Elton I'd not previously experienced. I'd always associated him with strength and achievement, yet here was someone who was frightened of being alone. 'Please,' he begged, 'I want you to stay with me at the shows.'

Elton seemed fine the next morning, and no mention was made of the previous evening. Over lunch, I decided to ask him if I could do some more work on the tour, something to make me feel more than just Elton's boy.

'Perhaps I could work with the crew, loading and unloading the trucks,' I eagerly suggested.

'No,' Elton said affectionately, 'because I want you to be there with me, Chooky.'

But a day or two later, Elton's sensitivity had moved a notch or two away from himself and towards me. He made a promise: 'Blue, when we get to LA, we will have a week before we start the tour, and I'll show you around the place. There's some great shopping there, and I want to take you to Disneyland . . . you'll have a ball!' I felt I was becoming a person rather than an attachment, but later on this was to prove as much of a curse as a blessing. Still, at the time, I responded enthusiastically. It was then that Elton also suggested that in case he should get tied up with work, I should ask Cameron to come to LA to keep me company. He'd hire us a car.

I immediately phoned Cameron in Australia. He said he was doing his plumbing apprenticeship, and as it was approaching exam time, he'd only be able to make it a short visit, if he could make it at all. But as we chatted I could hear the excitement in his voice, and I knew he would make the effort. I told Elton to make the arrangements, and he had Bob contact his LA office to sort out the details of the flight.

The European tour continued. On arriving in different countries, some promoters or the hotel would present Elton with a sightseeing book, which he would pass on to me. I pored over the photos, wishing we could explore these places first hand rather than mope around the suite listening to music or watching TV. Sometimes waiters would talk about great times at the clubs the night before, or the band members would return from a shopping spree with souvenirs. Listening to them had me even more depressed.

Although we normally took commercial flights, occasionally Elton would break the monotony. Once, when we had time off before the Rotterdam show, we flew from Copenhagen to London to catch a Watford match, and after the Rotterdam performance we drove to Brussels for two days, luxuriating in a splendid suite with a spiral staircase leading to the upstairs bedroom and a massive mirrored bar that covered one wall.

By the second week of the tour, we'd already visited six European cities. Some of the European shows were really brilliant, and Elton would want to celebrate. In Göteborg we went to a fabulous drag show, which compared most favourably to the tacky drags I had seen in Australia. It was high-class cabaret. In Nice Elton took ten of us to a restaurant in the hills, and the bill came to £5000. That night Elton ripped into the wine, and on the way back to the Negresco Hotel he pulled his pants down and stuck his bare bum out of the car window, a stunt he was later to repeat many times and one that delighted the tabloids.

As the tour proceeded the cities seemed to flash past. I only remembered them by the hotel we stayed in and the venues we played. By Germany, the eighth country on the tour, things came to a head. Frustrated, I confronted Elton. I wanted to go out – with or without him. Elton hit me with another delaying tactic, promising that when we got to Paris, we'd do the sights. But as soon as we'd booked into the Hotel Plaza-Athénée, a fine Versailles-style hotel with magnificent fittings, Elton declared he was too busy. So I slipped away and checked out the Eiffel Tower, strolled the cobbled streets around the Ile St-Louis and glimpsed leafy courtyards beyond yellow stone archways, visited museums, cruised the Seine and watched a young couple making out, sadly wishing that Elton was with me.

On returning to the hotel, I sat outside the suite and contemplated the possible outcome of my rebellious behaviour. I decided that I wanted Elton to realize that I had gone without him and to wonder where I was – so I stayed out even longer. Soon I could hear his voice booming: 'Where's bloody Gary!' He was furious, but by this time I'd had enough. I didn't care. I felt genuine affection for Elton, but I was sick of being treated like a prisoner. For the first time, I had lost my patience. Elton couldn't live with himself and had been bingeing on everything he could find – and now he was bingeing on me. I walked in and confronted him:

'I want to go back to Australia,' I snapped. 'I'm not having a good time. You keep making promises that we'll spend some time together sight-seeing, and we never go!'

Elton looked as if he were about to have a heart attack but managed to blurt our: 'All right, Chook, all right. When we get to America, I'll have a week before the tour starts. I promise I'll take the whole week off, and we'll go to Disneyland. We'll have the time of our lives. I don't want you to feel this way.' Elton had become very emotional, and I could feel the tears welling in my eyes. But I'd already made up my mind and told him so. That night was the first time on tour that we didn't make love. Rather than wait for Elton, I went straight to bed. My doubts about our relationship had me feeling that this whole venture was a mistake. I had visions of being back in Australia with nothing, and I fell into a deep sleep, emotionally exhausted.

On waking I was startled to find Elton standing over the bed, staring pensively down at me, and as my eyes focused I sensed something different about him. All of a sudden I saw it and shrieked: 'What on earth have you done to yourself?! You look like a drag queen!'

His eyes looked sad but funny. In fact, the sight of him was so comical that I started to laugh. So did he: 'Chook, this is my protest. I want you to stay.'

I had to give in. 'Well, if you can go without your eyebrows,' I shrugged, 'then I guess I can suffer being cooped up in a hotel.'

A short time later, guitarist Davey Johnstone came into the suite and began talking to the pair of us. 'When we get to Nice, I was thinking that . . .', he stopped in mid-sentence and did a double-take. 'Hey, man, you look different!' he said to Elton. 'It's your eyebrows. You've shaved off your fucking eyebrows, man!'

Elton was making a public display of his affection: 'I did it because Gary threatened to leave me and go back to Australia . . . but he's staying now.' The guitarist shook his head and withdrew: 'Elton, you're weird man!'

Over the next few days, Elton pushed his hat over his forehead and wore shades, and those who did think he looked strange were too polite to say anything. As for me, I was glad that John Reid had gone back to London for a short time and so wouldn't see his star touring without eyebrows.

Elton's bad moods were legendary. At these times, the slightest thing could throw him into a rage. He once admitted: 'I don't know why I get into these moods. But I do. When I snap out of them, I think, What a silly thing to do. Because, really, I have absolutely no reason to be unhappy about anything. I've been very lucky.'

Before meeting Elton for the first time I had read about him in showbiz magazines and was aware that he'd thrown some mighty wobblies in his time. I'd heard that he had been moody as a child and that this appeared to have worsened as he became more successful.

There were very few battles between Reid and Elton, as they knew each other well having lived together in the early days, and they tended to project their anger away from each other. There was the potential for conflict as this star and his manager were opposite temperaments, but they had come to understand how this could work to their mutual advantage. Reid had ambition, administrative skills and aggression – it is said that when he was 19 he had boasted to a friend that he aimed to have a Rolls-Royce by the time he was 22.

When it came to making a buck you couldn't accuse Reid of riding on Elton's coat tails either, as he had successfully managed other groups. The bond between these two men was more complex and powerful than a financial arrangement. Reid had earned his stripes with Elton as a politician, a manager and a promoter.

Elton would sometimes use his anger to advantage. With his first American performance in LA, the audience came along expecting a laid back Richard Clayderman-type performer, and Elton was soon ignored, the crowd chatting, oblivious to the music. When he finally lifted his head from the piano, Elton noticed that his act was dying. Angry, he rocked into some Jerry Lee Lewis pounding, and the crowd – shocked because they'd assumed from the cover of his first album that he was incapable of a dynamic performance – roared their approval. That night they had been witness to the unmistakable aura of a rising star. Elton was an overnight success.

Elton's response to professional criticism since that time is well documented. For example, a few years after his LA debut, he was mortified when respected *New York Times* critic, John Rockwell, described the visiting star's performance as: 'Smooth . . . wallpaper music of the most banal sort.' Elton's response was over the top, given that the review had been, in the main, quite complimentary. There were a few uncharitable phrases, but Elton was usually prepared to be open to criticism. However, one afternoon, Elton commandeered the disc jockey's chair at Radio WNEW-FM, and he was in an antagonistic mood. His courage enhanced by two bottles of Dom Perignon, Elton lashed out at Rockwell, challenging the critic to face him: 'I bet he's 4' 3" . . . I bet he's got boogies up his nose . . . I bet his feet smell.'

Rockwell, who is 6' 4", mature and not unduly concerned about body size or functions, wasn't perturbed by Elton's petulance, and he diplomatically refused to take the bait, saying: 'I don't think it's me he's talking about . . . I think he's reacting to years of critics' pans!' The astute Rockwell was probably right. Elton had never recovered from that first night when, as a lad, he performed in the Pinner pub, and the bored crowd threw chip bags at him and poured beer into his piano.

In Australia, and at Woodside, I had seen the amiable side of Elton – loving and mostly good natured. But on the 1982 European tour I had a glimpse of the devil within, and it was quite disturbing. In Germany I was a silent party to a furious debate between Elton and John Reid that rapidly escalated. The manager finally left the room in rage with Elton screaming: 'Fuck it, I'm not going to do the show tonight! I'm going to cancel the rest of the tour!' If it had been someone else Reid would have probably decked Elton. But the notorious bruiser knew his mark. Normally, when Elton was upset, I would put my arms around him to calm him down. This time I was stunned because it was the first time I'd seen the ego raging. Elton was outbullying the bully. I'm not sure what the argument was about, but where business is concerned, Elton sometimes needs to have his mind changed. He loathes being told he is wrong.

Around this time Elton's desire for multiple sex partners was emerging. Or re-emerging, I should say. In Copenhagen, as we were about to have lunch in a restaurant down the road from the Plaza Hotel, he casually told me that a friend of his would be joining us. Carl was a fair-haired, good-looking boy who carried himself with style. That day the 21-year-old wore boots, white jeans and T-shirt and a green suede jacket; as we chatted I noticed that he evaded questions about his livelihood. I never did find out if he was a rent boy or simply one of Elton's ex-boyfriends. Even though Elton had always told me: 'I'll never hide my past from you, Gary.'

That day I noticed that Carl was very comfortable with Elton and very direct: 'I read an interesting article in the paper the other week about you, Elton. They said that although you had the air of a clown, the writer thought that you didn't trust anybody, and there is something mysterious that you keep hidden.'

Elton frowned, thought for a moment and said: 'Do I come across like that to you?' There was a pregnant pause, and our lips were sealed so he continued on: 'I hope not . . . because I don't like people who're closed off . . . I respond better to people who are open with me . . . I go nuts when they try to play mind games!'

After lunch Elton invited Carl back to our room and plied him with Scotch and coke, and Elton winked at me, eyeing the two of us. I knew exactly what he had in mind. Carl hung around all afternoon and then accompanied us in the limo to the show at the Broendby Hall on Broendbyvester Boulevard. I knew Elton had been testing me to see if I would agree to a threesome with the boy. I didn't think I could have handled it. In any case Carl returned to our room after the show, had a few drinks and left.

The tour continued for another nine cities. In Frankfurt three young British soldiers came backstage to be introduced to Elton. One must have taken his fancy because he invited them all back to the hotel. The champagne and spirits flowed, and soon everybody was merry and at about 1 am two of the soldiers left, but one lingered.

Elton signalled for me to come to the bedroom and whispered in my ear: 'What do you think of Soldier Boy, Chook? Perhaps he should stay the night?' He looked at me knowingly. This time there was no guesswork. My desire was certainly there: Soldier Boy was cute, but I knew it would spoil my relationship with Elton. Before I could reply, the young man staggered into the bedroom. From the expression on his face I knew that he had sussed the plan and that he approved.

It was time for me to make a move, so I said: 'Excuse me, EJ, I have to go to the bathroom.' Instead I left the suite in despair and wandered out of the hotel. From the pavement I could see the bedroom light on in our suite and waited for an hour, then returned. Soldier Boy was gone. Elton was fast asleep in bed. Looking back I can see that Elton was beginning his spiral into the mire, and although he knew the consequences could be disastrous, he was prepared to take the risk. I was second fiddle to his excesses.

The next morning Elton acted as if nothing had happened, but I was distressed, and I sensed he knew it. In a gush of anger I blurted out my desire to return home. There were no tears in my eyes this time. Elton, apparently emotionless, nodded and grunted that he'd have Bob organize it. He left the room, and I overheard a heated conversation between him and Bob, and a little later the assistant approached me and said coldly that every-thing was arranged for me to go back to Australia.

I resigned myself to retrieving the threads of my life in Melbourne yet again. Later that afternoon, while having a bath, I heard a knock on the door, and Elton walked in wearing his usual hotel robe. We had barely exchanged words since the morning's stand-off: 'I don't want you to go, Chooky!' Elton was weeping, babbling: 'I want this to work . . . my life is so unhappy . . . please don't go!' I burst into tears. I didn't really want to go back to Australia, I just wanted Elton to be happy with me. There was no need for other lovers. We both stumbled out of the bathroom, tears streaming down our faces and when Bob came into the room, for the first time I saw his tough exterior soften:

'Oh, good, Gary, I take it you're staying.'

Elton broke the tension: 'Look at us, Chook,' he put on his dowager voice, 'aren't we like an old married couple?'

What a whirlwind European tour. Some 23 cities and 25 concerts would be covered in 32 days. Quite an experience for a young boy from Oz. For the last concert we were to fly to Paris to meet Rod and Alannah Stewart. After that, Elton and I would tour America. Then a speedy return to Woodside to built on our relationship. Or so I thought.

5. I Guess That's Why They Call It the Blues

The next morning I woke to find Elton and Rod still doing lines of coke through £50 notes.

T HE SOUTH OF France has an easy well-worn feel about it, which caught Elton's imagination. The raffish Nice is one of his favourite spots. 'Cheap and old and exotic and beautiful,' the American novelist Clifford Irving wrote of another Mediterranean resort, Ibiza, but he could have been describing Nice except Nice certainly wasn't cheap. It had the same ambience: wine from the bottle, fish freshly caught from the harbour, a timeless bourgeois playground.

I found the buzz of Nice both enticing and intriguing. It was stocked with the beautiful people; star-struck tourists and young bronzed locals would spend their days roaming from disco to high-class restaurant to exclusive beach trying to spot a famous face. Elton was in his element here. Good humour abounded, and our sex life was heaven. He was eating well and looking after his weight. Elton liked the city so much he filmed his 'I'm Still Standing' video in Nice, a clip cast with lots of good-looking boys and directed by Russell Mulcahey and his friend, Jerry. Elton was introduced to Duran Duran during the shoot and would later confess they turned him on to the joys of drinking Martinis. He soon developed a partiality for downing eight of them in half an hour.

On a whim Elton decided to base himself at Nice's splendid Negresco Hotel, and to fly in his private aircraft to his remaining gigs around France. In the hotel you could bump into Roman Polanski, Jack Nicholson or Adnan Khashoggi. Characters such as these drew much speculation and comment.

Elton had another reason to feel an affinity with France. The French were one of the last European audiences to fall to his music. In the early days Elton had had difficulties there, when audiences booed and pelted things at him; this rejection made him more determined to win their acceptance. So Elton taught himself French and threw himself into cracking the French market. It worked. 'Nobody Wins' from the *Fox* album was one of the longest-running No. 1 songs in France, and Elton released two versions of this track – one in French and the other in English.

In concert, Elton spoke and sang in a mixture of English and French, and it sent local audiences wild. However, his compet-itive nature would never allow him to forget the early days, and he would occasionally change the lyrics of a song he was singing in English. For example, in 'Blue Eyes', instead of 'Baby has blue eyes', Elton would slip in 'Baby has no legs.' The crew would chortle but the audience were blissfully unaware.

The best show during this European tour was in a circus tent in Toulouse: the sound was fantastic, and I'd never seen Elton work so hard. The crowd responded with Gallic fervour, and it topped the excitement of any of his other shows. The French part of the tour was divided: Elton did two shows in Paris at the Palais Des Sports before winging off to do five dates in Germany and then returned to Lyon, Avignon, Toulouse, Bordeaux and Nantes, with the grand finale at Lille. The Paris shows were hectic, with two gigs on the Sunday and one on Monday. It had been planned that Elton, Bob and I would stay at John Reid's apartment, but at the last moment, Elton decided that we would stay at the Hotel Plaza-Athénée, while the band stayed at the Holiday Inn. You just couldn't escape Elton's music in Paris. If you turned on the radio they were having Elton John specials. If you walked into the hotel bar, the cabaret band would be doing Elton songs.

On reflection it was during the latter part of the French tour, after the highs of Nice, that our relationship started to flounder. When I first met Elton in Melbourne he'd been clean for a while and would tell his close friends how great he felt, vowing never to return to drugs. But when we hit Paris, he went back to his old ways.

Kiki Dee, Elton's longtime friend from the 60s, visited our suite. Elton had boosted Kiki's career in the 70s with a duet 'Don't Go Breaking My Heart', and she was grateful. It was a No. 1 hit around the world and made Kiki a household name, albeit briefly: it was also Elton's first No. 1 hit in England. When Kiki arrived, I was sent to the bedroom, ostensibly to unpack suitcases, and on returning to the lounge I saw Elton bent over a mirror on the coffee table. There was white powder in neat lines on the mirror. Elton was back into the 'toot'. After Kiki left, Elton was on a high, but his cool manner towards me suggested he was apprehensive about how I was reacting. I was very confused.

What had happened since the good times in Nice when Elton was determined to take the time to show me one of his favourite playgrounds and indulge me in a visit to Le Moulin de Mougins, one of the most splendid restaurants in the world? After a drinking binge at the restaurant, as well as a fantastic meal – for which I still possess the menu signed to me personally by the brilliant chef, Roger Verge – the entourage had driven back to the hotel in a couple of vehicles. Elton and I were in separate cars and the people in my vehicle started to hoot with laughter as we passed Elton's car – he had shoved his bare bum out of the car window, pointing it straight at me. I wouldn't have laughed so much if I had known there was more to this gesture than a cheap laugh.

As I grew to know Elton, these seemingly spontaneous displays of bawdiness signified an emerging mood. He was beginning to closet himself too often in his bedroom, withdrawing. Cocaine was no help, for it keeps you going all night, so in the day you are tired and irritable. As for sightseeing, that was last on the agenda. At the time I thought it was only the drug that was creating the mood; only later did I suss out, after much heartache, that it was the mood that was dictating his need for the drug. Elton's metabolism seemed to run in cycles.

After concerts in Paris on 16 and 17 May, we skirted through the other countries to finish the European tour with a last run of French shows. In private, Elton's darker side was emerging. He no longer cared about his diet, became more aggressive in bed and wrecked our most intimate moments. He was pushing me to the limit, testing for something that perhaps was missing in himself.

He was disappointed in something, but was it in me or in him? I noticed he was swearing more often, suggesting bizarre sex; distractions and angry emotions dominated his thinking. He was now at the point where his moods were upsetting staff, and at one stage the pressure got to Bob Halley. The clashes between the personal assistant and his charge increased in ferocity, until Bob resigned, threatening to work for Rod Stewart. Rod had mentioned to Bob that if he ever left Elton, a personal assistant job was his for the taking. When tempers quietened, Elton joked about the flare-up and talked Bob into reconsidering, no doubt with a promise or two.

Before he started to go downhill, however, being in France seemed to have cheered Elton considerably. He had a lot of friends there. More importantly, he was looking forward to meeting Rod and Alannah Stewart in Paris and flying with them to the final show in Lille.

The two vintage rockers, Elton and Rod, were about the same age and had been friends for a very long time, since the early 60s, when they struggled in small-time London bands. Singer Long John Baldry had given them both their breaks. Rod had sung in

Baldry's band Steam Packet, and Elton had played in the band Baldry formed after that, during which time Long John had his enormous hit, 'Let the Heartaches Begin'. Baldry was a forthright character, and Elton remembered that even after the hit made him a pop star, Baldry would still react in a distinctly un-pop star manner, threatening to hit people with his mike stand or screaming abuse if they didn't react to his performance. Rod and Elton adored Long John and, when they hit star status in the early 70s, both produced an album for him.

Rod's and Elton's careers had other parallels. They both emerged in the 70s with critically acclaimed singer–songwriter albums; they were flamboyant; and both spent most of their spare time listening to music. They were also both superb showmen who lived football and were very English in their outlook, with strong family ties. Their audiences spanned generations and continents, and their overriding mutual interest was rock and roll. Elton and Rod had been embraced by the gay culture, and their entourage included gays. Rod's hit, 'The Killing of Georgie', was about a gay friend who had been rejected by his parents when he outed himself, travelled to New York 'as a victim of these gay days' and was killed during a violent robbery.

In a *Gay News* interview Rod proudly admitted that, in his younger days, men would try to seduce him; that one admirer had even offered him a month's wages; and that he often visited gay clubs in LA and New York. However, he also made it clear that he never danced in these places: 'No, I just sit there. I don't think I could dance with a fella. A member of my management is gay, and he won't let me (anyway). We have lots of rows about it.' Clearly Stewart was neither homophobic nor gay – nor was he judgemental.

Rod was of interest to the homosexual community and when *Gay News* asked the singer if he regretted not having sex with any of his male friends, Rod replied: 'No, it's just not my bag at all. Not in this year of 1976. I don't know what I'll be like in three years' time.' It was probably a throwaway line, but the British press preyed on it gleefully and for the next few years they hinted that he was homosexual, despite the fact he surrounded himself with young beautiful girls. Rod had angrily denied these insinuations, and when the *New Musical Express* had referred to him as 'a Nancy boy', Rod sued the paper – at which point all insinuations abruptly ceased.

An interesting difference between Rod and Elton was that while EJ was renowned for his generosity, Rod had a reputation for being a mean man with a nose for a bargain. To entice him to join in the all-star cast for the soundtrack of the film *Tommy*, the producer Lou Reizner had to hand over his £5000 pre-war Rolls-Royce. Rod also knew about the property market. He purchased an eight-bedroom Georgian place with six receptions rooms, five bathrooms and its own staff quarters for £89,000 – and two years later turned down an offer of £300,000 for the estate. Rod bought and sold his mansions within a few years – making a profit each time.

Being the best of mates, Rod and Elton would have fun hurling good-natured abuse at each other in the press, and they played countless, highly public practical jokes to make each other look foolish. Rod would buy some cheap wine, put an expensive label on it and sent it to Elton. Another time, just before Rod's concert in London, Elton had his roadies erect a huge sign banner outside the theatre: BLONDES HAVE MORE FUN BUT BRUNETTES HAVE MORE MONEY! HAPPY CHRISTMAS. However, theirs was friendly rivalry. In a camp way, Rod and Elton also had girlie nicknames for each other, which they would endearingly and frequently call each other in public. Rod was 'Phyllis', and Elton was 'Sharon'. Everyone in the inner circle had such nicknames. John Reid was 'Beryl'. Bob Halley was 'Betty'. I was to become 'Crystal'.

I was looking forward to being together with these two great stars. It had been some time since Elton's concerned phone call to Rod during the Scandinavian part of the tour. By now Rod had recovered from the mugging and had agreed to fly to France with Alannah to catch Elton's final European concert. My excitement about Rod's arrival had been building since the first phone call, and I was impressed at how no expense had been spared to accommodate the Stewarts. A ten-seater Falcon 20 was chartered to fly the couple from Paris to Lille.

The two old friends were clearly pleased to see each other at the airport, although I noticed they didn't refer to each other as Sharon or Phyllis. The flight to Lille was only about 20 minutes, and Elton was soon boasting about how his Watford team was climbing the ladder, while Rod's soccer team, Arsenal, was falling at a corresponding rate. Elton was enchanted by his team's achievement and gleefully rubbed salt into Rod's football wounds: 'First division, lovey, first division!'

When we landed at Lille there were two limos waiting on the tarmac, and we went straight to the 3500 capacity Palais de la Foire. As it was the end of the European tour, a marquee had been installed inside the backstage area, and snacks and champagne were supplied for 40 or so guests. Singer David Essex was there, along with local promoters, journalists and DJs. Everyone seemed to be in a good mood, particularly Elton, who broke his own rule by having a couple of glasses of champagne before he went on stage. I could sense it was going to be a great show, and so it proved to be.

If you believe in the cliché that insecure people are drawn to the stage to bask in adulation, then tonight's reaction would have cured the self-esteem problems of a neurotic mouse. It was the sort of response the biggest superstars would kill for – hero worship. There was a curfew at Lille airport that night, so after the show we immediately jumped into the limos and headed for our Falcon jet. Within the hour we were lounging in our suite at the Paris Plaza-Athénée. Alannah left quite early without Rod, but with a terse expression on her face and a tight flick of her shapely hips.

After that the cocaine was cut in the bathroom, and Rod and Elton wasted no time in snorting the white powder, doing a line every 15 minutes. During that evening I felt that Rod was a lot more relaxed when Alannah wasn't around, so it didn't really surprise me when they separated a short time later.

Rod quickly regressed to being 'one of the boys', cackling

loudly at jokes and recounting hilarious dirty ditties. The chief effect of cocaine is that not only does it make you start talking at 100 mph but it also gives you a feeling of grandeur. You think you're talking meaningfully, when you're spouting nonsense.

Around 12.30 am I headed for bed. Bob was in his room playing solitaire; the other guests had left, and I was bored. Elton noticed me leaving: 'Good night, Chook, I'll be there shortly.' The next morning I woke to find he had still not found the bedroom. Stumbling into the lounge, I was amazed to find the two stars still doing lines of coke through crisp £50 notes, chattering like gibbons. After about half an hour, Rod said his goodbyes and staggered off. Thank goodness that, like Elton, Rod gave up taking drugs long ago.

Elton had a simian smirk on his face, and he yelled for Bob, who appeared at a trot. Elton had gleaned some information from Rod. Apparently Rod had made some bad investments. He'd put his money into a chain of hotels and blown about $3 million. Elton now had more money than him. Outdoing a stingy bugger like that meant a lot to Elton – and he was clever in that regard. His investment advice was always sound, and he preferred sure-fire things such as paintings and jewellery. His best investment had been Woodside, which his mother had bought for a song and which is now worth several million pounds.

I spent the afternoon packing Elton's bags. He insisted that Bob charter a flight to London that evening. The way he was feeling, I didn't blame him: bombed out, he couldn't cope with the drag of talking to people and waiting in queues for a commercial flight. We spent only a night in London, where my American visa problem was solved. An official was dragged out of bed to ensure any red tape was cut to give overnight approval. This all followed a tantrum Elton had thrown in Nice, screeching that he would cancel the US tour if I didn't accompany him. He knew his tour manager would fix everything, and, of course, Reid did, despite the lateness of the hour.

The next morning we were back at the airport to catch a flight to Los Angeles. Elton was withdrawn on the flight, and at best our inflight conversation was forced. I assumed it was the lows that follow cocaine, but I was so excited about our destination, I couldn't see that his mood was continuing on its downhill swing. At the time it didn't bother me in the least. I'd always been fascinated with Los Angeles, and here we were. Disneyland! Shopping at Rodeo Drive! Venice Beach and the musclemen! Hollywood! Pink caddies and palm trees! Even better, my Australian mate, Cameron, was to meet me there. Then on tour to legendary cities like New York, Dallas, St Louis and San Francisco – places I'd always dreamt about visiting – all first class.

In every sense LA is on the edge, and it suited Elton's mood that day. It was certainly his sort of town, and one with which he had conducted a love affair since his first trip there in 1970. It was little wonder that Elton made it a point to play the city every year between 1970 and 1975. There's no doubt that he had a special relationship with southern California. His debut at the Troubadour made him a star overnight. The next day, one of the country's biggest rock producers, Bill Graham, asked him to play the Fillmore East in New York for a fee of $5000, then more than a year's salary for an average worker. This payment was the largest fee paid to an unknown act at that time, and there was a buzz about Elton that quickly spread to the rest of the country. Elton's first American album release sold 30,000 copies in a week.

When Elton toured a year later, there was such a demand that he added four extra shows. In 1974 he played five consecutive nights at the 18,000-capacity Forum. A year later, after he announced that he would play a week of shows to raise money for UCLA's Jules Stein Eye Institute, there were 100,000 applications for the $25 tickets, with high rollers like Cher, Tony Curtis, Mae West and Ringo Starr paying $250 a head for VIP seats. Elton raised $150,000 – a considerable sum in those days.

Elton eventually became the most popular male performer in America and sold five times more records than the Beatles. His *Greatest Hits* set sold five million, and radio stations would boost their ratings by dubbing themselves 'your Elton John radio station'. An American critic who did an experiment by flicking his radio from station to station for six hours discovered an Elton John track was played somewhere in America every two minutes. *Captain Fantastic* set a new milestone by crashing into the charts at No. 1 – a feat that Elton promptly repeated with *Rock of the Westies*. An $8 million deal with MCA was the biggest of its time.

From the proceeds of these successes Elton bought himself a US$1 million Spanish-style house in Benedict Canyon. This once belonged to a number of film legends, including Greta Garbo, director David Selznick and the original owner and builder, silent screen star John Gilbert. Elton filled that place with teddy bears wearing huge spectacles, hundreds of records and two pinball machines that illuminated the names of his last two albums, but the Gilbert house was gloomy and dark and rumoured to be haunted. Elton's neighbour was Alice Cooper, a rocker whose horror-show persona attracted freaks. It was an upmarket, offbeat street.

In LA Elton moved in circles of film and rock celebrities that never numbered less than a dozen. When not at home the stars were seen dining at the best restaurants. Some of these acquaintances were friends, others parasites; in any case their role was to indulge every rock-star whim and to distract the star from himself. Elton lived in style, travelling America in his hired private 707 *Starship*, which came with a bedroom with Plexiglas nightstands and foldaway bed, a bathroom, a long bar surrounded by mirrors, a lounge with groovy furniture and an artificial fireplace. To add to the feeling of power and immortality, Elton surrounded himself with a gaggle of waddling bouncers, led by posturing muscleman Jim Morris, who had once been Mr America.

Around this time though, it was becoming obvious that Elton was suffering a personal crisis. Longtime friends found him elusive. Journalists who had enjoyed open access were startled when refused interviews. Fans complained that Elton was no longer friendly when they met him in public. He had been so absorbed by his rock-star lifestyle, the endless round of parties, clubs and limos, that he had lost touch with himself. He had lost his private space. At least when in England, being involved with the Watford soccer club had him interacting with unpretentious people. But Elton's American adventures also meant he was out of touch with his family and in particular beyond his mother's steadying influence. By 1978 he was in trouble:

'I just couldn't stand the thought of constantly being surrounded by people any more. I'd get off a plane, into a car, go to a gig, back in a car, back to the hotel . . . I became totally disillusioned with the entire lifestyle.' Reggie Dwight resented what Elton John had become, and in an interview he said: 'No, I have no regrets. I enjoyed it. But towards the end I wasn't living a happy personal life. Everything was geared around my professional existence and – I know it must sound like an awful cliché – I thought, there must be more to life than this.'

Elton was drained. There was no spiritual direction. The star was learning the price of fame, what happens when you give without taking. I felt audiences sensed when Elton, or any other performer, was in an emotional crisis, whether it be a high or low. This sharpened the onstage vibrancy and generated the energy that led to emotional and sometimes great performances. However, as I'd seen, such performances take a heavy toll. It is as if the audience feed off the star, their hunger is insatiable, and there is a limit to what can be given. Like an exhausted long-distance runner consuming his own muscle when the fat is depleted, Elton's emotions were beginning to work against rather than for him.

The void between Elton's private life and professional career, the inner battle between what he wanted to be doing and what he thought he should be doing came to a head in October 1975. That was when Elton was given his own star on Hollywood Boulevard, and LA declared an Elton John Week. He was to play two shows at the giant Dodger Stadium, to 55,000 people each concert, and all the tickets were sold within half an hour. To celebrate, Elton charted a Boeing 707 at a cost of US$100,000 and flew over a party of 12 people from England. These included Sheila, Derf, Ivy, childhood neighbours, various journalists, TV presenter Russell Harty, and footballer Rodney Marsh. And as each person found their seat on the plane, a gift was waiting: a camera. Elton graciously met the party at LA airport but quickly retreated to his limo and split. The visitors were taken around Disneyland and Universal Studios and the swish boutiques of Beverly Hills without their host.

Elton often told me about an incident that occurred at this time. One afternoon his family and some close friends gathered around the pool of his Benedict Canyon home to bear witness to his success – or excess? Frustrated with what he had become, Elton's depression was compounded because a boy who had taken his fancy had rejected his advances for over a year. The star's fragile ego was shattered and wandering out to the family gathering, he announced: 'Well, that's it then. I'm going to end it all. I've just taken 85 valium!'

The guests looked askance as the famous artiste, clad in his white towelling bathrobe, ceremoniously climbed on to the diving board. No one moved as Elton waddled to the end of the board before pinching his nose and dramatically stepping into the pool. Disappearing under the surface, a sudden change of mind came over him, but he was descending into the blue at an ever faster rate, the sodden towelling pulling him to the bottom of his watery grave. Seized by panic he tore the garment loose and headed for the surface, lungs bursting. As his reddened face cracked the surface of the pool, spluttering and gasping, he could see family and friends peering at him in disbelief.

According to Elton, his grandmother Ivy, who was enjoying her first trip outside England, walked to the edge of the pool, looked at Elton and said very matter of factly: 'Oh, well, I'd better pack my things and bleedin' well go home.'

Elton later admitted that this stern attitude was the best approach: 'I was an immature little schoolboy craving attention on a totally different level to that I was getting as Elton John.'

The suicide attempt was no joke though, and Elton was in a coma for three days after the incident. He said that the display and aftermath had upset his mother so much, he vowed never to contemplate suicide again. Well, he never attempted dramatic suicide again, but, like Elvis, he was slowly destroying himself. Elton would retell the story of Ivy's remark with great affection. I figure Grandma Ivy, the wise one who'd been around for a long time, had seen this type of behaviour from adults in the family long before Elton hit the scene. She'd intuitively known what to say.

In any case, fans never knew that the pool drama energized Elton's performances at the Dodger Stadium concerts, and these were among the most magical he ever played. It confirmed my later observations that his fans loved him as much when he was down as they did when he was up – as long as he was prepared to stay on the razor's edge. Elton must have known it too. To a crowd of sun-kissed Californian beach kids, he played a stunning three-and-a-half hour concert, leaving the stage after the first set to return in a sequinned baseball outfit in local team colours. That, of course, sent the audience wild, and even more so when Billie Jean King joined the chorus for 'The Bitch is Back'.

The Dodger shows were the last of the West Coast tour of the mid-70s. Elton's memories were of being continually ill and suffering severe weight loss, and it would be a few years before he played California again. That tour was like a scene from a Stephen King movie: the audience devouring their idol. This star realized the horror and was scrambling for survival. He nearly didn't make it.

During that period, Elton's personal problems flowed over to his staff who were becoming abrupt with TV reporters and newspaper journalists. The media complained that his people were evasive and severely restricting access. Suddenly the intelligent and funny man to whom journalists loved to talk would only do phone interviews that lasted no more than five or ten minutes. A film crew that toured two cities with him had to dump the project because he gave them no more than a minute's interview.

• • •

From the air Los Angeles looked like any other city, in fact, it looked quite ordinary. However, like Elton a decade or so earlier, once on the ground I fell in love with its infectious vibrancy. We were to stay at Bernie Taupin's house, and on the drive there Elton sat quietly huddled to one side of the limo, apparently oblivious to the scenery. To me, however, it was exhilarating to watch the palm trees and broad concrete motorways, recognizing familiar street scenes and road signs from TV shows and movies. We soon arrived at Bernie's home in North Doheny Drive, bought by the songwriter years earlier when he needed a permanent place to stay during his frequent US visits. His feeling for the American Wild West was so acute that few believed he had written the lyrics on *Tumbleweed Connection* without ever stepping foot in the States. When Elton eventually arrived, he also knew he was on home ground.

Bernie started visiting California on a regular basis, and he was to marry an American dancer called Maxine, for whom he wrote 'Tiny Dancer'. He based himself in LA. The marriage dissolved four years later. To distract himself from his personal troubles, he embraced the style of the LA showbiz set, surrounding himself with famous friends and the never-ending good-time party. What Bernie could not disguise was that, despite his genius, he lived in Elton's shadow. It's not surprising that the gifted lyricist developed a drink and cocaine problem, which culminated in a trip to Acapulco to dry out. Bernie wrote about this in songs, 'Two Rooms at the End Of the World' and 'White Lady White Powder' on the *21 At 33* album released in May 1980.

In 1976, Elton and he stopped writing together. They'd fulfilled their ambitions, playing to sell-out stadiums and reaching a point in their popularity where each new single came crashing into the charts at No. 1. The *Blue Moves* album reflected Bernie's lack of confidence after his marital break-up, with lyrics that skirted suicide and feelings of worthlessness. There was never any formal split between Elton and Bernie. A year later, when Elton started to write his next album, Bernie was 5000 miles away in Los Angeles stuck firmly in a party mode and still not sure if his writing offered him any new challenges. Elton drifted into writing with one of his new friends, Gary Osborne, who'd frequently call over to Woodside with his wife to play pinball and backgammon. After the games, they'd fool around on the piano together and discovered songs were coming together quickly.

In 1979 Bernie met a model called Toni Russo, whom he later married. I had briefly met Bernie and Toni a few weeks earlier in England, when Elton and I flew back from the European tour to catch a Watford match. On arriving at their LA home I found the Taupins very loving and caring towards each other and their guests, and they had even moved from their bedroom to a smaller room for our sake. The corner-block house was full of books and framed records; its modernist style in stark contrast to Woodside, whose interior reminded me of a museum. Toni had an American brashness that I loved: and when she and Bernie became an item, she oversaw his finances and encouraged him with his career. She had become Bernie's soul mate, and I was shocked later to learn that they had separated.

Toni's arrival into Bernie's life coincided with Elton and Bernie working together again after their break. Elton had casually asked the two to join him in France for a holiday, and before long they were churning out songs. The composer and his librettist adored each other and had a brotherly relationship. In the early days Elton did have a crush on Bernie but when he admitted it, Bernie had replied with typical Lancashire forth-rightness: 'You're sick!' That honest comment didn't affect their relationship. They had, after all, spent a lot of frustrating times together in the early days, knocking on doors and coping with rejection.

The morning after we had arrived in LA I eagerly awaited Cameron's arrival from Melbourne. Elton sent a limo to collect him from the airport, and it was such a buzz to see my old friend standing at the front door, grinning broadly and wearing the ski jacket I had helped him select before leaving Australia. Cameron was to stay a mere six days. He was departing on the Monday and Elton, Bob and I were to fly to Texas the day after, from where the tour was to begin.

Bernie and Toni settled Cameron into one of the downstairs bedrooms, complete with ensuite bathroom; later that day Elton took us shopping at Century City on Santa Monica Boulevard, an open air mall with sidewalk cafes and about 80 shops. After recovering from the shock of the prices of clothes, I settled on buying some trousers, while Elton loaded up with the latest records and videos. When we returned to Bernie's place, Elton interrupted our pinball game to surprise us with a gleaming new white Mercedes Sports convertible, displaying *So-West* number plates. It had just been delivered to the side driveway, and it was ours. Cameron and I immediately leapt in. I turned the key and the two of us grinned as we played with the electric windows, gave the sound system a blast and lowered the roof. Before long we were cruising the rent-car down Loma Vista Drive before turning right at Sunset Boulevard to check out the scenery. Then it was off to West Hollywood, with Cameron's eyes popping out of his head at well-tanned girls in brief and very expensive dresses sauntering along Melrose Avenue. Then past Chanel, Armani, Cartier and Lauren boutiques. In my home town, two young guys on the prowl in a Merc would have turned heads and invariably have got us laid. Alas, this was Beverly Hills, and Mercs were a dime a dozen. That night, along with some music industry folk, we all went to Spago on Horn Avenue, a restaurant where you had little chance of being offered a table unless you were a regular or a celebrity.

Next morning the limo came to take us to Disneyland. Bernie and Toni had other commitments, so Michael Hewitson, Elton's ex-PA, accompanied the three of us. Elton had arranged for the VIP $1000 a head ticket, which provided a guided tour, countless rides and priority service. He seemed excited to be with us, although he'd visited the famous fun park dozens of times. A few autograph seekers stopped him here and there, but it was fairly quiet and the three of us went on most of the rides. The following day we visited Magic Mountain, but this time a personal bodyguard accompanied Elton. The guard certainly earned his money: Elton was mobbed. An 18-year-old girl became emotional at the sight of a real, live, pop star. She started screaming hysterically and was quickly ushered away in case others took her cue. Again we had an absolute ball, and Elton was the perfect host. That night, although we were all tired, Elton insisted that Cameron join us for dinner. The patrons waiting outside the Mumtaz Indian restaurant must have rubbed their eyes in disbelief when we arrived in the Merc, with the star crammed in the back of a two-seater.

Looking back I realize that Elton, by insisting that he kneel in the back of the car, was just playing martyr. Cameron had offered the front seat, but Elton declined. Something had clicked in his mind. That night in bed, Elton shook me awake and whispered in my ear: 'Why don't you go and sleep with Cameron, Chook?' I didn't want to, but Elton became insistent, eventually saying, 'I meant it Chook. I really need my rest.'

I knew Elton had started taking cocaine and was becoming edgy, but as I wandered sleepily down to Cameron's room, I still wondered what was going on. Was he jealous of the camaraderie I had with my old friend? I had told him about my love for Cameron, but that it had not been reciprocated because this plumber's apprentice was straight. When Cameron and I were goofing around Disneyland and Magic Mountain I hadn't intentionally paid a lot of attention to him but maybe, without realizing it, I had. Or was Elton subtly suggesting a threesome?

I crawled into bed with my friend. It was to be for the last time. The next morning I slipped upstairs because I didn't want Bernie and Toni to find out. Over breakfast Elton seemed relaxed and good natured, and he never once asked me about the previous night's events. Over the next few days Cameron and I went for long drives together, and it was fun to be out and about without pomp or ceremony.

The day after Cameron's departure I woke early and lounged around the pool for an hour before packing Elton's bags. He had slept late and was still in his bathrobe when he delivered his unanticipated bombshell: I was not going with him to Texas. He was sending me back to Australia. I was stunned, but he was adamant and quite cool about it. I couldn't accept what I was hearing, and stated my feelings clearly, though Elton wouldn't be moved. He'd decided it would be best if I left.

By now I was shaking, and the significance of what he was saying was beginning to seep in. I pleaded, hysterical, and tears were welling in Elton's eyes. We embraced, but he had no intention of debating the issue or changing his mind.

Elton was running late for his flight to Dallas, so on that pretext he abruptly excused himself and began dressing. I slunk downstairs. As I walked to the kitchen, Toni and Bernie were preparing breakfast, and I sensed Elton had already told them of his decision; they consoled me and made it clear that I was welcome to visit them anytime. I was grateful for their concern but felt humiliated and embarrassed by Elton's abrupt and inexplicable pronouncement.

Half an hour later, when Elton walked into the kitchen, you could have heard a pin drop. He ate his breakfast in silence, and a short time later, when Bob arrived, left the kitchen to direct his assistant to arrange my immediate departure. All in a day's work for Bob, and he wasted no time in organizing my evening flight back to Australia.

I approached Elton again, attempting to regain my self-esteem. I was grovelling – no dignity, no pride. Ignoring my pleas, he quietly replied: 'John Reid will be around soon and will take you to the airport. You can have the car for the rest of the day.' Bernie put his arm around me, and I watched in despair as Elton strode towards the limo. 'I'll call you soon, Chook,' Elton muttered, feigning a half-wave and then he was gone. It would be months before he made that call.

6. Madman Across the Water

'If you want a relationship, you'll have to agree to three-way sex,' Elton said, staring at me.

I WOKE IN A sweat during a nightmare: my recurring reminder of unresolved conflict. Am I going mad? The clock radio showed 3.15 am. I'd drifted into sleep with my small TV set flickering silently in the corner, its glow a stimulus for my frightening dream. That and the sleet rattling the window panes heralded a night of self-doubt and broken sleep. I drew the covers around me, trying to forget my thoughts, hoping to sink into the black abyss of unconsciousness, distant from thoughts of Elton and other horrors.

My self-esteem was so low at the time I could not face anything. The bottom line was that I regretted falling out with Elton; I was infatuated with him, and that was that. My mother was worried about the severity of my depression and in her well-meaning way trotted out the usual platitudes, encouraging me to put the experience behind me. But I had to deal with it. There were continuous reminders of what we meant to each other, and I only had to turn on the radio or see a poster on a newspaper stand to have his presence return.

This was to be a testing period for me as my parents, with whom I was living again, were flying to England for my aunt's funeral. I would be alone. As they hastily packed for their flight to London, I decided to contact Sheila and Derf. It was an excuse to make some sort of contact with Elton and a genuine use of an opportunity to recover my belongings. My parents would be in London so why shouldn't they retrieve possessions that I had left at Woodside?

It wasn't the first time I had rung Sheila since her son had dumped me. In fact I'd phoned a couple of times since returning to Melbourne, just to say 'G'day'. Sheila had been as warm as ever, if a little puzzled about what had happened, but she was genuinely sympathetic and quite happy for my parents to drop by and pick up my things.

A week or two later I received a postcard from Dad to say they'd made contact with Sheila, who would take them to Woodside. About five days later, I received an international phone call. It was Dad. He told me that when they'd met up with Sheila and Derf, they'd really hit it off and were now staying with the Farebrothers. How bizarre! Elton and I had in-laws cohabiting, and we weren't even talking. But, as you can imagine, it was an exciting development for me, for I could feel Elton observing from somewhere in the wings. Then to cap it all, Dad rang one night to say that he and Mum were staying at Woodside. While my relatives were having fun in London, here was I stuck in a tiny unit in Melbourne, staring out at grey drizzle. Oh to be back in a summery Britain, at Woodside, back in Elton's fold.

On a wintry evening, while dolefully washing the dinner dishes, the phone rang. International pips. Had to be Dad. 'Hello, Chook.' It was Elton – at last. He was casual and relaxed, as if nothing had happened. I felt the adrenaline pumping. I knew I missed him but didn't know just how much until that second. I could hardly speak. My heart was thumping, my breath was short. Elton broke the silence, 'Chook, I'm going to be in Sydney next month. I'm doing a Parkinson talk show.' I couldn't manage an answer, and Elton, after hesitating for a moment said casually, 'Why don't we get together then?'

And so Elton was back in town, and I was back in favour. It

was mid-1982, and Michael Parkinson was in Sydney for a series of celebrity chats for an Australian TV network, on which Elton was to appear. The year wasn't panning out all that well for Elton. After the big worldwide hit with 'Blue Eyes', his chart success through 1982 was limited. Particularly in Britain where names like Duran Duran, Spandau Ballet, the Eurythmics and Wham! were all that seemed exciting in pop. Elton's 'Empty Garden', the tribute to John Lennon, had failed in England, not even reaching the Top 50, but it went into the Top 15 Stateside. The follow-up, 'Princess', didn't even rate.

Elton was also involved in a lawsuit against his publisher, Dick James Music (DJM), to whom he had been contracted as a songwriter for £15 a week. This was when he was unknown, at the tail end of the 60s. It was claimed that DJM had taken unfair advantage of Elton's inexperience with music-industry practices and had underpaid their protégé. In particular it was considered not appropriate for a contract still to be in force that had been signed in 1967 and 1970. Particularly when the contract stated that copyright for all of Elton's songs were DJM property. In effect, Elton and Bernie were receiving what might be viewed as an unfair share of the £200 million worth of Elton's records that DJM had sold over the years.

Such contracts had been common in the music industry in the 60s, but since then pop-music entertainers had forced change on the exploitative Tin Pan Alley mentality of by-gone years. For example, rock and roll writers of the 50s and 60s had signed deals in their teens that saw them lose ownership of their classics. Chuck Berry, John Lennon and Paul McCartney, Mick Jagger and Keith Richards of the Rolling Stones, Brian Wilson of the Beach Boys, John Fogerty of Creedence Clearwater Revival – the list was endless. By the mid-70s, as artists took more control of their careers, writers and performers became indignant about the way they were being treated, for it not only hurt their wallets but it also bruised their egos. Change was on its way, and the days when talent was to be viewed as a commodity, to be bought cheap and eternally owned by corporations, were coming to an end. By the 80s the creatives were taking to the courts, and it was becoming a profitable experience, for judges were upholding the notion that talent had a right to a fair slice of its own action.

With the Elton–DJM case, DJM's defence was typical of the corporate stance: they had invested in the youthful Elton, providing him with his first real recording break. If it hadn't been for them recognizing his talent in the first place, DJM suggested that there would have been no millions to argue about. The facts were undeniable, Elton needed DJM. But at what price?

When Elton recorded his first album, the pretentious and thematically weak *Empty Sky*, very few wanted to know about him. Not only that, but marketing Elton was no easy task. This lad was not the James Dean type whose poster would decorate an adolescent's bedroom wall; nor did he conjure images of rebellious youth at the height of its primal rage. Elton didn't present as a believable spokesperson for a generation, like Dylan or so many of his impersonators at the time; and when moving on stage he had the elegance of an overweight penguin. To all but his family and friends, his charisma was zilch. But he knew his music, and he could play piano and sing.

In terms of effort, DJM had a good story to tell the court. They had gone out on a limb for Elton, forking out £2000 to make his first record and, under duress, cancelled their distribution deal with the large Phillips company. In essence, Phillips would not distribute what they thought was a worthless record. So it could be argued that the company, DJM Records, came into being essentially to release *Empty Sky* and that the James family marketed to the extent of their resources. They took out ads on the back of double-decker buses and persisted with Elton for two years, unstintingly agreeing to extra dollars when Elton exceeded the budget set for his second album. This extra money, spent on arrangements that included chorals and strings, released the full potential of Elton's music. It was these decisions that gave 'Your Song' its spark and launched Elton's career in a big way.

Much later, as Dick James and his son Stephen pointed out, Elton was still signed to their record label when he formed his own Rocket label and launched the *Blue Moves* album. DJM stated that they had not sued Elton or claimed damages against him because they wanted to encourage his initiative, not block his progress. Dick had published the Beatles in the past, so he had plenty of experience in developing talent.

This DJM history of close and supportive involvement had no effect on the world-weary Reid. He knew the precedent had been set, for in mid-1982 the decision of a very important court case was to change the fortunes of many English songwriters. The case involved singer/songwriter Gilbert O'Sullivan, who, like Elton, had been signed to his manager and publisher, Gordon Mills, for a small retainer. O'Sullivan records, like 'Clair' and 'Alone Again (Naturally)' grossed nearly £15 million – and the writer had received a mere half a million. The judge found that the contract O'Sullivan had signed with Mills had been unfair and that the company had taken advantage of O'Sullivan's inexperience. The judge then ordered that Mills return all the master recordings and ownership of O'Sullivan songs, and make retrospective payments with interest.

Reid believed that with DJM, if he played it hard, he was on a winner. All he had to do was block any sentiment that Elton might carry for those who placed their faith in an immature, chubby little piano player with more talent than hope. Otherwise the similarity between O'Sullivan's and John's court cases was undeniable. Early in the negotiations DJM knew they had their backs to the wall, and they were keen to reach an amicable settlement. Why waste money on lawyers? But when they asked Elton to meet with them over lunch to discuss the possibility of DJM relinquishing ownership of Elton songs, proceedings were instituted. Once the action commenced, the case dragged on for four years. In that time Dick and Stephen James attempted to make personal contact with Elton for they wanted to dissuade him from continuing on the expensive legal route, which would eventually amount to around £1.5 million. The star made himself unavailable.

When the DJM–Elton judgement was made in 1986, it seemed the troubles between the two parties were a storm in a teacup, something that could have been resolved without four years of litigation. The judge ruled that DJM retain copyright of the songs: it was Dick's reward for helping Elton and Bernie become more wealthy than they could ever have imagined. The judge also noted that for many years prior to the case Elton appeared to have had a good personal relationship with James, and he said that this indicated Elton must have been reasonably happy with the contract otherwise he would not have waited until 1982 to commence proceedings. In fact, in 1969 when Island Records tried to poach Elton, they had studied his DJM contract and said it was full of holes and that Elton could break it any time. The judge had made a good point.

But DJM did not have things all their own way. They were told that Elton's share of the recording royalties, at 5.4 per cent, was unfair. The judge found it should have been 12 per cent, and DJM had to make good the difference. The judge also decided DJM's foreign subsidiaries were to reduce their service charge. Although newspapers screamed that Elton would make £5 million out of this judgement, in the end, the sum turned out to be less than £1 million.

Elton was devastated by the outcome of the case. Not only did he not win the money and song ownership that he and Reid wanted, but he also knew that the experience had been a weight that added to Dick James's poor health. It wasn't only because Elton had turned against Dick, but during cross-examination Elton's lawyers had attacked Dick's business ethics and, at one stage, suggested that profits went directly into a private bank account in Switzerland and that this was done without Elton's knowledge.

This was sheer dramatics to influence the judge, but Dick James took the slur to heart, and it shattered him. Worse was to come. Three months after the case, Dick, a heart patient who had had a quadruple by-pass, died at his London home. His family felt bitter towards Elton and Reid, although Elton paid DJM's legal expenses.

The pop-music industry is littered with the corpses of talented people who failed to find someone to believe in them, and if Dick James had decided not to take the punt Elton could well have languished in obscurity. The boy from Pinner, Middlesex, a dormitory suburb of London, who wrote songs with his mate Bernie, the pair jammed into one room in Sheila's maisonette, may well have always played backing sessions for groups like the Hollies, or mimicked stars like the Bee Gees, Stevie Wonder, Mungo Jerry or Brotherhood of Man. Instead, Elton made a great deal of money and had a lot of fun, but he didn't have the strength of character to meet with his former benefactor when conflict arose.

I often wondered how that experience might have affected Elton, because he was quite sentimental. In relationships he would avoid intimacy by pulling down the shutters, retreating into his inner world. But he could not ignore Dick's death, and it must surface in memory and remind him of his foolishness – and his own mortality. When you live with Elton you realize his very human need to maintain connections with those who have shared his life. No doubt, for these reasons, he found the blossoming relationship between our parents fascinating. So did I.

I was keen to hear of my parents' adventures when they returned from Woodside, a few weeks before Elton flew into Sydney to tape his interview for *Parkinson in Australia*. Mum and Dad were full of anecdotes about Sheila's and Derf's friendship and impressed by the luxury of Woodside. They had become big Elton John fans overnight, listening to his records, identifying with him intensely and becoming excited if they saw his name in the newspapers. And now it was time for the star's arrival.

Elton rang me just before he left America for Sydney. Needless to say neither Cameron nor my Los Angeles deportation were raised as topics of conversation. It was almost time for me to fly to Sydney. I was ready for an emotional experience but had no inkling of what was in store. When I left I told my parents that for all I knew, it might be a short stay. In reality I was expecting a week at the most, but I would have not been surprised to have been back within 48 hours. And, if my hopes were fulfilled, I would be with him for the rest of my life.

By the time the taxi dropped me at the Sebel Town House, it was about 3.30 pm. Elton was still in bed, so I slipped in gently and awoke him. 'Chook!' he yelped. 'Chook!' He kissed me. Elton was unshaven and jetlagged, but he looked a treat. There were broad grins all around, and we couldn't take our eyes from each other. 'You are looking well,' I said. It's funny how I react at times like that for I think of everything and come out with the most inane clichés.

'You've had a haircut,' he said, before adding dryly, 'show us your dick.'

We chatted for almost an hour before Elton started rifling through his overnight bag, retrieving razor and toothbrush. He left the door open while he showered, and we continued to chat. This was to be a quick trip to Sydney. As far as the public was concerned, he was there for a TV appearance and then jetting off. There was no tour or record to promote, no hype, no hysteria. Yet, despite the lack of stimulation, Elton exuded an energy that was compelling. Standing near him you sensed an unfathomable source of power, a great energy that, if given free rein, could trip every circuit in your system. Elton didn't actually do anything special, but every minute with him was fun. He was in fine spirits, and I felt the two of us were communicating, especially when we were alone. But as usual there were some official duties to spoil our solitude.

The night after I arrived, our party – Elton, Bob, myself and Patti Mostyn – joined Michael Parkinson, his wife Mary and the head of Parkinson's network for dinner. Parkinson had selected a very expensive restaurant around the corner from the Sebel. At dinner I heard how Elton and Parkinson had known each other since 1973, when they both played in a celebrity cricket team, along with David Frost, Peter Cook and West Indian pace bowler Wes Hall. Bryan Forbes's documentary of Elton that year caught that game, and Bryan commented that Elton's cricket was as flamboyant as his performances.

The reason for the dinner was that the two men were to be

reacquainted prior to the interview, to be taped in two days time. The drinks flowed, and the conversation become more animated for Parkinson and Elton were both first-class raconteurs.

On the Saturday of the interview, Elton reluctantly tore himself away from the afternoon football telecast and headed to the studios. The Parkinson appearance captured him at his best. He was relaxed and very very funny. Most rock stars dislike TV because it is a revealing medium, one that shows what you look and sound like, and it's difficult to disguise a weakness. You can't censor yourself, and, unlike magazine interviews, TV penetrates the façade. On TV, stage mystique disappears and if there is no substance to the performer, it soon becomes apparent. But the articulate Elton does have substance and can use the medium to his advantage. Years later, when Elton had a run-in with the *Sun* about its reports of rent-boys and cocaine orgies, Parkinson's TV show in Yorkshire was used as the vehicle for the publicly acceptable face of Elton John.

Elton certainly used the medium to his advantage that day. The audience, like the host, were genuinely fond of him and impressed with his achievements and his humility. The interview commenced with his recent meeting with Ronald Reagan, and Elton went on to talk about his association with the British royal family and how he performed for Prince Andrew's 21st birthday bash at Windsor Castle. He recalled the evening with great humour and laughed about how he danced with the Queen to Bill Haley's 'Rock Around the Clock', while her handbag never left her wrist.

Everybody in the studio laughed when Elton recounted how Rod Stewart, who was originally offered the role of the Pinball Wizard in the film *Tommy*, came to him for advice. 'Don't touch it with a bargepole,' Elton had replied. 'They don't know what the bloody hell they're doing. Forget it.' However, the Who's guitarist Pete Townshend had contacted Elton and begged him to do it instead, as a favour. Said Elton to Parkinson: 'It was one of the most successful sequences in the film. I got paid a lot of money and Rod was subsequently furious!'

No one in the audience could have dreamt of how Elton's private life was unfolding. That morning, he'd awoken and said to me, unprompted, 'If you want a relationship, you have to agree to having other people included. I'm talking about three way sex.' Usually, if he had to say something unpleasant, he'd never look at you. This time he was staring right into my eyes. 'If you don't agree, then you'd better go back to Melbourne now!' This was ultimatum time.

Everything he was saying was the antithesis of what I expected from a relationship, but I felt emotionally trapped, a butterfly whose wings were being pinned by the collector, the type who enjoyed watching his prey wriggle. I was a captive, a hostage in the grip of the ugly side of his personality. I had to make up my mind and quickly. He was serious. Having been away from him for three miserable months, I vowed not to lose him again. On the other hand by prostituting myself, I would lose all dignity. But then again I could come to enjoy cocaine and learn the kind of sex that Elton liked. All right, Elton, I'll try.

It never occurred to me that any relationship where one person insists that everything is based solely around his or her whims is doomed to failure, no matter how desperate or pathetically willing the other partner. My bowing to Elton's demands imbued him with a sense of power, but instead of satisfying his passion it led to further testing and teasing. For example, over lunch, and for no reason at all, Elton casually mentioned the black Porsche that I had drooled over when at Woodside: 'Oh, Chooky,' he said as if he had just thought of it, 'I'm sorry but I gave the Porsche to Bob.' He couldn't have failed to notice my disappointment, but the matter rested there. No reassurances, no plans to make amends. Just dropped the bombshell and continued eating. He quickly changed the subject: 'I'm looking forward to meeting your parents.'

Aside from the Parkinson taping, Elton's visit to Sydney was a holiday. He was in shopping mode, and one night we had dinner with an American actor, Christopher Atkins, who was visiting Australia. Christopher was well known for his major role in the movie *Blue Lagoon*, co-starring Brooke Shields. I recalled the lunch with Bette Midler at Sardis restaurant when Molly Meldrum introduced me to a journalist who is now a Hollywood star reporter. He was there with a friend called Gary, and they raved on about how cute the heterosexual Christopher looked naked. It was no surprise to me when Elton sat down next to Christopher and during a lull in the conversation, turned around to me and stage-whispered, 'What do you think of him, Chook, he's cute, isn't he?'

On the Sunday afternoon Patti Mostyn joined us at the Sebel. Patti was Elton's eyes and ears whenever he was in Sydney, and he trusted her ability to manage his affairs. She chatted for a few minutes and then accompanied us in a Mercedes to her house, which she shared with her husband Eric and daughter Tara, in one of Sydney's most fashionable suburbs on the harbour's north shore. The publicist was hosting a barbecue lunch for Elton, and although most would consider it unusual for the hostess to collect their guests from the hotel, this was Patti's style.

At this stage, despite his sexual indulgences and demands, Elton seemed committed to building our relationship and to a 'normal' life and wanted me to return to Woodside. Bob Halley, at Elton's request, was to vanish for a couple of weeks when we returned. No doubt he would be grateful for the break. Elton and I would be able to spend some quality time together before flying to Montserrat to record his next album, *Too Low For Zero*.

Before that I flew, at Elton's suggestion, ahead of him to Melbourne. Later in 1984, when in Sydney, I surmised that the real reason Elton was keen for me to return to Melbourne was because he wanted to enjoy a romp with another boy. Before my trip home Elton had casually mentioned that we had to replace 'my' Porsche, the one that he'd given to Bob. 'You can't have a BMW, Gaz,' he warned. 'Paul [a friend of John Reid] has one. We'll have to do one better.'

'Well, I don't really want anything too flashy.' I suggested, 'How about a simple Ford Capri? They're nifty little things.'

Elton feigned horror. 'I won't have a Ford parked in my driveway.'

Soon after he arrived in Melbourne we were to have dinner at my parents' home. Elton was every bit the diplomat who loved nothing more than family, home and hearth. Most people I know in show business yearn for it, but they can only cope with it for a couple of days. Then they rush back to the glamour, the clubbing and the power tripping. But Elton made a genuine effort to become part of my family for the evening. On the way there he'd visited the Melbourne Hilton's jewellery store and chosen a gift for my mother, and he bought a $90 bottle of wine for my father. As it turned out, everything went well.

'It's not quite Woodside,' Dad said, waving his arm around the small living-room. The aroma of roast lamb pervaded the unit. My Mum cooked a great roast. Elton and Dad revelled in the vino, although to Elton's consternation, Dad didn't pull the cork on the expensive wine Elton had purchased, pouring only from his own stock. Nonetheless, the two regaled each other with stories. Like Dad, Elton's wit sharpened with the grog. Mum, bless her heart, wasn't vague and served one of her prize dinners.

After dinner, Mum and my sister Sue cleared the dishes. 'What would you like, boys, for dessert?' Mum said muddling her words. Elton smacked his lips and laughed, giving me a knowing wink before replying he'd kill for a custard. It was my turn at chef's duties. As I was whipping the mixture in the kitchen, Mum called out, 'Don't forget the eggs, Gal.'

Elton stopped mid-sentence. 'What did you call him?' Mum and Dad called me Gal as an abbreviation, but it had no female connotations. My friends used Gaz as an abbreviation, but Gal stuck at home. 'Gal! I love it!' Elt started to splutter. 'Crystal Gayle. That's what his nickname's going to be.'

Around midnight, after Sue and her husband Ian had gone, to my horror, Dad decided on home movies. Elton seemed keen at first, stroking my hair as I sat between his legs. I glanced furtively at Mum and Dad to gauge their response to this open display of affection. No heart attacks, so I figured they were trying their best

Right: The young Reginald Dwight, alias Elton, at primary school, where as a result of his strict upbringing he never misbehaved and was anxiously polite.

Left: In line for a school photo, Elton is third from the right. When later he became identified as a musical prodigy, Elton acquired a special status at school.

Above: Elton and his mother, Sheila, pose for me on my arrival at Woodside, Elton's 37-acre estate near Windsor. Mother and son have a close and supportive, though sometimes stormy, relationship.

Above: Elton and Hazel, my mum, at Melbourne Airport, Tullamarine. She once cooked Elton a prize roast dinner during one of his visits to Australia.

Right: Elton celebrating during the early years. From left to right, Elton, Sheila, John Reid's mother, Betty, Derf, aka Fred, Farebrother, Elton's stepfather. John Reid relaxes on the grass next to Elton's German Shepherd. Later Elton was to discover success to be a double-edged sword.

Above: With Bernie Taupin, his brilliant lyricist and long-time friend from the mid-sixties, at the breakfast table in LA.

Below: Bernie Taupin at Nevis, relaxing on the Caribbean beach

between recording sessions.

Right: Me, Nigel Olsson, Elton's drummer, and Bernie's wife, Toni, in Montserrat, where the band recorded at AIR studios.

Above (from left to right): My friend Andrew, Elton, me and Lee Smith, another acquaintance, at a party in Ian 'Molly' Meldrum's home, given in Elton's honour for the 1990 tour. Through Meldrum, the self-styled guru of the Australian pop scene, I first met Elton.

Left (from left to right): Molly, Lee, Elton's PA, Bob Halley, an early school buddy of Elton's who lives in Melbourne, and Elton, enjoying a drink in Elton's Melbourne hotel suite.

Above: Elton sampling the joys of domesticity, as he does the dishes with Bob Halley in Montserrat. Days would start early there, when Elton, Bob and I took it in turns to make bacon and eggs, before they headed off to the studio.

Right: Lunch and dinner were eaten in the studio during recording, where I would join Elton and the crew at mealtimes.

Right: Together with Chris Thomas, who produced the *Too Low for Zero* and *Breaking Hearts* albums, Elton relaxes in his usual attire.

Below: Enjoying an early working relationship, Elton with his future wife, Renate Blauel, in the recording studio at Montserrat. Initially I noticed that Renate, a soft-spoken girl with a private nature, kept herself very much to herself.

Above: Elton relaxing at Nevis in the Caribbean in 1984 while recording the album that started life as *Restless* but changed its name successfully to *Breaking Hearts*.

Left: Nevis again. This time with the band and crew. For *Breaking Hearts* Renate had been promoted from tape operator to sound engineer.

to understand. After the fifth reel of five-year-old Gary stumbling about with a football, it was clear Elton was tiring of such normality. When Dad threatened the baby photos Elton 'remembered' an appointment next morning and we made our apologies. But Dad was not to be deterred, and as we left, he presented Elton with a photograph of me, aged nine. On the drive back the limo hadn't even reached the end of the street before Elton was fast asleep.

The next trip to Woodside was to be very different from the last. The first time I was wide-eyed, star struck and naive. The world had seemed to be at my feet. Only months later, memories of the pain that had resulted from that adventure filled me with apprehension. But, this time, I was determined to make a go of it, for Elton seemed so keen to maintain our relationship. I was deliriously happy and so missed a vital clue to my future.

Before leaving Australia we dined with Molly, Leigh and an old school chum of Elton's. We returned to the Hilton suite for drinks, and when it was time for Elton to retire, he shook hands with everyone and went to his bedroom. Bob and I saw the guests to the door. Molly hugged me and said to Bob, 'Look after Gary.'

Bob grinned. 'Oh, he'll be back sooner than you think,' he said.

Back in England, we had Woodside to ourselves. Elton was full of plans. We were to spend time together – quality time – and work at our relationship. But Elton soon reverted to his bad old ways. When he was on holiday, he really relaxed. He would mooch around home unshaven, was never out of his dressing gown and spent most of his time reading or watching TV. Visitors weren't encouraged. He was slipping into the trough of depression that seemed to follow any period of excitement, a self-hatred phase when he would look at himself in the mirror and hate the pudgy, hapless figure that stared back. Years later he admitted to journalists that he would binge on food and when he could eat no more, go to the privacy of his bathroom, push his finger down his throat and make space for the next bellyful. Rewarding and then punishing his body, and himself, for not being perfect at all times. For my part, I knew what was going on for I could smell the vomit on his fingers and in the toilet, and although he attempted to conceal his problems from me, the smell was a big turn-off. I respected his privacy and never spoke to him about it.

Elton's own remedy for his eating disorder was to take cocaine, which would numb his desire to eat and replace it with the illusion of refined faculties. In fact, it further distorted his perception of his predicament. It wasn't until the early 90s that he confronted his problem, at the Parkside Lutheran Hospital near Chicago, where he penned a farewell to the drug and really meant it.

When he took cocaine, Elton would become moody and listless, staying in his room and not wanting to do anything. He looked dreadful, and when I did wander into his quarters during the day he would summarily dismiss me. On the drug, Elton was self-obsessed, not interested in anything else in the universe. We'd only interact during night-time sex. The more powder Elton snorted, the greater his fascination with kinky sex. He himself would admit later: 'I used cocaine basically for sex. My sexual fantasies were played out while I was on cocaine . . . It made me insatiable for sex.' After one of his drug binges, he turned nasty: 'You're trying to shut out my friends, aren't you!' he raved. 'You want us to be a boring Mr and Mrs type couple. I won't stand for it.' I gaped in astonishment as he banged and bashed his way around his room, his face reddening. Elton was taking it out on me, projecting his disappointment in himself on to me. And he was becoming violent. It was frightening, and I was as scared for him as I was for myself.

During the day I amused myself playing music in the disco, which was well away from his bedroom. Or I'd talk to the staff and play with the dogs. Bored to tears I impulsively went for a walk one day, out through Woodside's electronic gates and past its Authorized Callers Only sign. Marching the three miles to the closest town, Old Windsor, I caught a train to London and wandered about, gazing in shop windows. I spotted a computer for about £60 in a shop window and bought it. Although I didn't have a clue as to how to operate computers, they represented an exciting world ripe for exploration. I took the machine back to Woodside and played with it for hours on end, totally absorbed, while Elton stayed in his room incommunicado.

John Reid, who had lived with Elton in the early days, obviously knew what his client was like. Realizing Elton was spending a lot of time in his room, one week during this time he invited the pair of us to his two-storey home. In public, Reid had an image of a ruthless pirate, someone his competitors feared to cross, and one who ruled his office with a mixture of fear and gruff affection. At home, a relaxed Reid valued style and sophistication, and he appeared to know his art and literature.

By the end of the 80s, Reid's assets were estimated at £24 million, and he was ranked the 176th wealthiest person in Britain. He had accumulated his wealth not only from Elton's affairs and whatever he made from his Friends restaurant in Covent Garden but also from his prior management activities. When he parted ways with his other superstar client, Queen, because he didn't have time to manage both acts, Queen had to pay him a lot of money on severance of the relationship – Reid received 15 per cent of royalties generated from all Queen records from 1976 onward.

No doubt Reid decided to stay with Elton because they held a special, if distant, affection for each other. This made the great team that has withstood the onslaught of press, public, family, fans and critics. Reid was a ruthless entrepreneur, the perfect foil to Elton's creativity and excesses – the best person to exploit the good and bad aspects of Elton's personality and talents. These two added to each other's public image, and, as with all the great acts in rock, Elton's public persona, to a degree, reflected Reid's attitude. Reid, for his part, thrived on the role of rock manager, enjoyed and used the power; the military-style tactics used to deliver product appealed to his sense of competition.

Fear of failure in such circles never focused on losing money. Failure meant becoming anonymous: people didn't return your calls, recognize you at functions or vie to shake your hand at restaurants. Because, in the music industry, power is vested in social approval, relationships were reduced to manipulative manoeuvring and cynical insensitivity, and Reid played the game well.

Reid, who once coveted a posh house in London's Montpelier Square when he was only a clothing store assistant, made a promise to buy it; he did just that within a few years. Even in the early days, Reid carried himself with the comfortable arrogance of a self-made man, and there were only occasional flashes of insecurity. Perhaps he thought his success was based on luck rather than skill, a matter of being at the right place at the right time. He need not have worried for he is a born field-marshal, a talented administrator who would always certainly have made it in one field or another.

An accomplished cook himself, Reid selected his chefs well. The handsome young man who cooked for us that night, when Elton was on a binge, prepared a great meal. Steak, dripping with a heavenly Béarnaise sauce, and steamed vegetables couldn't be faulted. Elton started to relax, and even began to play at his impersonations. As we sat at the table for dessert, someone said, 'Time for a line.' It was more a statement than a question. Elton nodded, then turned to me and said: 'Try it if you want it, Gaz.'

What the hell. I bent down and snorted the powder through a straw. It felt so exciting. I was rewarded with a wave of euphoria sweeping my body, and I felt so energetic that I wanted to leap to the ceiling. The powder's immediate effect is that it makes you talk and talk. The others started giggling as I yapped non-stop. What's more, I didn't stop at one snort. I spent the rest of the night running upstairs to play pool and cards with the others and then running back to the kitchen for another line. By four in the morning, I started to feel nauseous and wanted to go home. On arriving back at Woodside, we went straight to Elton's room, where I discovered that although cocaine makes you feel erotic, it also lessens sexual prowess. We both found an erection a frustrating impossibility.

Over the next few days I realized why cocaine turned Elton into a sour-faced, anti-social grunter. As I came off my binge, I too found it easier to remain in my room, tired and irritable. Midway through the second week of this stay, over dinner, Elton leant across and said, 'The chef's coming over soon for a bit of fun. He and I'll watch some videos for an hour and then you come in.'

I wasn't attracted to the chef, and in any case, Elton wasn't really interested in what I thought. Within half an hour, the sound of a car door slamming signalled the visitor's arrival. After a few minutes of polite chit-chat, the pair disappeared upstairs to the video room directly above the kitchen. This is where Elton got his rocks off. The boys snorted their cocaine and then flicked on the video machine.

I ventured upstairs 30 minutes later, apprehensive about being coerced into an unwanted sexual adventure. As I approached the closed door, I could hear the video soundtrack, a giggle from the chef, then more loud laughter from Elton. Yes, they certainly were very relaxed. A chill came over me. I don't want to do this. My hand reached out for the door knob. You'd better go in, I muttered to myself, Elton expects you to – there'll be hell to pay. I stood outside, breathing hard, anchored to the spot for another half a minute of hesitation. Then I ran down the stairs, through the corridor and into the darkened squash court. I hid, curled into the back corner of the court. About 10 minutes later I heard Elton call for me and instinctively recoiled in horror. I heard him intermittently calling for another 20 minutes. Then silence.

Sleeping restlessly on the cold timber floor, come the morning I crept back to my room. At midday, while I was ironing my jeans, Elton entered the room without knocking. I wasn't sure what he was thinking and didn't dare look into his eyes.

'What happened to you, Chook?'

I shook my head, tensing myself for an explosion. 'I don't

know. I just didn't want to go through with it.'

To my relief, Elton nodded his understanding and wandered out. The chef was never mentioned again, and Elton somehow stopped his cocaine bingeing. He knew the recording sessions for *Too Low For Zero* at George Martin's AIR Studios in Montserrat were approaching, and the professional side of his personality was taking control. The star instinctively knew that his reputation depended on being clean by the time he left Woodside. He was in need of a hit record, and there was to be a big one in the offing.

7. I'm Still Standing

Elton began to say something then swayed and fell into a dead faint. I grabbed him just before he crashed on to the floor.

*A*S WE FLEW into Montserrat, the setting sun had splashed a blaze of red across the horizon. The island's airport was no more than a large shack with hot wind swooping through its open space, and lazily churning overhead fans provided the only relief for perspiring customs officials. A portrait of the Queen stared down from one of the walls. I was amazed that we had to clear customs on a tiny island that was probably no more than ten miles across at its widest point. Perhaps they were only there to check the recording studio's clients. It was dark by the time we piled into a Nissan station wagon and roared off towards the hills.

The next morning, when the strong morning sunlight woke us at about 7.30 am, Montserrat showed her unreserved beauty. From the balcony I had a magnificent view across the ocean with the edges of the green tropical verge framing a clear blue sky. Our villa was a white-washed Spanish-style building, one of many owned and rented by American or British business people. We stayed here for about a week before Elton complained to the studio's manager, Yvonne, that it was not grand enough, and we were moved to a larger one with an even more splendid view.

The day started early in these tropical climes. Elton, Bob Halley and I took turns making bacon and eggs from the supplies we had brought with us, or one of the locals, Mary, would arrive and help prepare breakfast – a fruit platter, mostly bananas and oranges, and a sugar-cane drink. By 8 am Elton and Bob were heading for the studio, about ten minutes away, where I would later join them when they stopped for lunch around midday.

The studio was high on a hill; George Martin had established his production company, AIR, in 1965 in London. Later he discovered Montserrat and decided to establish studios there, as it was the perfect place to record – a tropical paradise to inspire creativity, well away from all distractions. In time acts like the Police and Phil Collins were attracted there, as well as Paul McCartney, Ringo Starr and Stevie Wonder.

An added bonus was that there were no security problems for Elton. The band lounged around in shorts and T-shirts, occasionally bare chested, and the temperature never dipped below 80 °F. Everyone was relaxed, and camaraderie blossomed. Although Elton had a rule about wives and girlfriends touring, he didn't object to partners being around when the group was recording in a place like Montserrat. There simply was nothing to do after sessions except drink the local rum and beer, and having intimate company was good for morale and reduced the hangover rate. The only unofficial rule was that partners kept clear when recording was in progress.

The women attached to the musos and production team soon knitted into a tight group. They included Bernie's wife, Toni Taupin; Nigel's wife Lisa, whose twin sister was dating Dee; engineer Bill Price's wife; and producer Chris Thomas's Japanese girlfriend Mika. If there were any squabbles between the women, or between the women and their lovers, it would be kept quiet for we all knew that one loud argument could mean Elton banning partners from the studio complex.

This was the second time that Elton had recorded at Montserrat, the first time being for *Jump Up!*. On this occasion, though, he was taking more care with his approach to his music.

Bernie had insisted that he should write all the lyrics or there was a risk it would be a patchy album like *Jump Up!* Elton agreed and disposed of his previous lyricist, Gary Osborne, working only with Bernie, 'The Brown Dirt Cowboy'.

As soon as sessions began it was obvious that the magic between Bernie and Elton was about to weave its spell. When they were on different continents, Bernie would telex his lyrics and reams of paper would arrive in the studio. Elton would study them, sometimes changing a line or asking for a rewrite. The technique was the same at Montserrat.

When the lyrics were right, they would talk them through. Bernie might already have an idea, suggesting an up-tempo beat or a ballad. Elton would then hum a few bars. He would give himself 20 minutes. If the song didn't click, it was shelved, but occasionally they would come back to a troublesome song a day or two later. In fact they were operating in a similar fashion to the early days, when Sheila provided refuge from distraction in Pinner. In those days they would share a bedroom, sleeping in children's bunks, and Bernie would write sitting cramped on the bottom bunk, delivering text to Elton, waiting at the piano in the living-room. It was astounding to watch the two of them work. They would throw lines at each other, out of which a song would be created, a piece of perfect pop art.

Being with Elton at Montserrat put me in mind of Sam Phillips, who in the 50s established Sun Records, the company that did most to encourage rock 'n' roll in the early days. Phillips, an altruistic entrepreneur, explained what drove him: 'I got pure gratification, far more to me than monetary gain, and it came from helping these people unlock their lives.'

When recording with Elton that's just how it feels. You can sense the talent being unlocked, and the artists' marginal conscious control of the creative process. It's as if a song has a life of its own, that it was always there waiting to be discovered. Gems like 'I'm Still Standing' and 'That's Why They Call It the Blues' were born over a few days. When they were replayed, everyone in the studio knew they had a classic on their hands, music that would inspire, music that would last. There would be agitated discussion about which track should be issued as a single. For example, as soon as 'I'm Still Standing' was recorded, everyone immediately knew it would be the first single. It was up-tempo, perfect for radio, and its success on the charts would guarantee the album's exposure.

In Montserrat, Bernie was going through a particularly creative period. He had overcome his drinking problem and his recent marriage to Toni had given his life a purpose and joy that had been lacking for some time. 'That's Why They Call It the Blues' was a summation of his life to that point, a wry, backward glance at the dark clouds and an affectionate thank you to Toni, for having rescued him from the abyss. With this team, Elton's music always carries the lyrics, and he is never a slave to poetry or prose. That was the beauty of his partnership with Bernie: it is a symbiosis, in which the lyricist appreciated that the music could travel well without the words, but the reverse was not necessarily true. It is a fact that Elton has never exploited.

But there is more to Elton's music than Bernie and the players, there is also the creative skill of the producer. In this case it was Chris Thomas who added greatly to the depth of the music, always looking for ways to embellish without distracting from the directness of the arrangement, or adding to the excitement of a composition by introducing other musicians or technical enhancements.

For an outsider, recording could be perceived as a tedious process. For someone inside the bubble, of course, it was exhilarating. One of the first tracks they worked on at this Montserrat session was 'Too Low For Zero'. Elton went in first and performed on the piano. The track had a subtle, West Indies feel, and Nigel Olsson improvised with drum patterns until the track came to life. They would all listen to a replay, snapping their fingers or beating out the rhythm on their thighs. Chris, the producer, was a droll perfectionist when at work and silent outside the studio. During recording he would close his eyes, nodding to himself, then suggest a change. Maybe one of the musicians would be asked to do a solo, and if it worked the piece would be laid into the master.

The musos and producer would discuss the completed track and painstakingly work on every single detail. To some, such slickness robbed the music of spontaneity, but it is probably what has made Elton's music endure over two decades. Turn on the radio and Elton's voice will inevitably be heard, and even if the music was performed back in the early 70s, you will find it, if nothing else, exceptionally competent.

In the studio Chris Thomas was in control. But he was essentially an outsider. Within Elton's entourage, Elton was the king. The band knew their place, and although they cracked jokes and enjoyed Elton's and each others' company, the boss remained distant. Elton only saw the band on business – they were never his playmates. The idea of popping over to Woodside for a cup of tea would never cross the mind of any of the band's members. Essentially they kept to themselves, did as they were told and never threw tantrums.

Recording would continue without a break until about 6 pm, when the wives and girlfriends would arrive at the studio for dinner. The food was scrumptious, a buffet spread that could be either British fare of chops, spuds and peas followed with custard, or local dishes like fried chicken and cinnamon bread or lobster with coconut milk. We would mix freely at dinner, cracking jokes, arguing about politics and occasionally watching a video. Once in a while someone would open a can of beer at the studio, but there was very little partying. Elton and the band were highly disciplined when it came to recording, for their careers were on the line.

Immediately after studio work was completed for the day, Elton, Bob and I would return to the villa, have a shower and be in bed by 10.30 pm. Throughout the day, I made a point of popping into the studio for half an hour just to see what was on the boil. Then I'd either return to our villa or relax near the pool with Bob, reading and sunbaking. I sometimes met up with the wives and girlfriends, and we might go into Plymouth, the capital.

My birthday fell during these Montserrat sessions, and at dinner the staff served a cake to celebrate the event, and everyone sang 'Happy Birthday'. Elton and Bob presented me with cards, and Elton's had a drawing of a huge dill with the message, 'You mean a great dill to me.' Life with him had returned to normal. While off the white powder, he'd reverted to being the sweet, lovable man I'd fallen for. We laughed and joked a lot, and he would reach out and cuddle me for the slightest reason.

One morning he looked over the breakfast table and said, 'Chook, I want you to follow me to the studio. I have something for you.' When we got there Elton sat down at his piano. 'I've asked Bernie to write this song for you,' he confessed. I stood transfixed as he played 'Crystal', his eyes never leaving my face. Elton finished with a dramatic flourish and leapt to his feet.

'What do you think, Chook?'

'What . . . what can I say?' I blubbered, somewhat embarrassed, 'it's fantastic . . . beautiful!'

He put his arm around me, and I kissed him. My mind flashed briefly back to that happy dinner at my parents' place in Melbourne, just weeks earlier, when he had discovered my nickname. The words to this song had exactly captured what had gone on in our lives. He leant over and whispered, 'Some of the band don't think it's a good song. They think there are better tunes around.' He was determined that 'Crystal' would be a success. This one was going on the album. After lunch, Elton returned to the studio by himself and continued working on the track.

Hanging around the studio I became acquainted with tape operators and studio hands such as Peggy McCreary, Jeremy Allan and Renate Blauel. Although they tended to their duties quietly in the background, they were knowledgeable and worked with all the stars who came to Montserrat. It was a transitory relationship, though, and once you moved on, you never expected to keep in touch. The operator I became closest to was Renate, a curly-haired German girl who lived in London. Renate kept very much to herself, and no one really communicated with her except on tape-operating business. But there was something about her that attracted me.

I left Montserrat before recording finished, because one night just before I went to bed, Elton casually mentioned that he was going to replace the black Porsche that he'd given to Bob. We chose a black Turbo Lotus Esprit, which cost about £23,000, and Elton rang Derf and asked him to angle some deals around London. 'It might be a good idea if you go back and sort the car out while I'm still in Montserrat,' Elton explained, 'we're going to be too busy once I get back.' I found the prospect of a new car exciting, and after four weeks on the island, I was ready for a change. Elton was usually too exhausted from the recording sessions for much night-time activity, and I didn't want to threaten the status quo. 'I'll get Yvonne to arrange a flight for you,' Elton said.

On the flight to London I stopped over at Antigua, where John Reid had arranged for me to be met by one of his acquaintances. Reid's friend took me for a drive around the island, and we dropped in to see a DJ he knew at a radio station. When they heard I'd come from the Montserrat sessions, the DJ was eager for me to go on air. I felt pressured and did so reluctantly. On air the DJ asked if Elton was enjoying himself, how the songs were shaping up and how I liked Montserrat. It was a five-minute chat, nothing very deep, but when John Reid found out what happened, he was upset: 'You've got to be careful with the media,' he told me over the phone, 'they can be nice to you but will twist things around.' Admonished, I returned to Woodside, where things were quieter than usual. Everyone knew Elton was away in the Caribbean so even the telex machine was temporarily silenced.

A few days later I drove the Panther Lima down to Derf and Sheila's place in Sussex. Derf had some disappointing news – the Lotus dealers couldn't obtain a Turbo in black for a few more months. I stayed on at the 'in-laws' for a couple more days and had a great time with them. Sheila cuddled me a lot, and I felt it was developing into a mother-son type relationship. We went for walks, shopped, played cards, and I did a few chores around the house. Even Derf started to warm towards me. Until one night, over dinner, Elton's stepfather made the statement that National Service was a good thing for young people because it gave them discipline. I told him that I strongly felt that war was a futile exercise and so was glorification of the military. I don't know if it's because I didn't share his enthusiasm for the armed forces, or that I'd argued back, but he became distant again.

I returned to Woodside a day or two before Elton arrived, and, when the time came, it was with great anticipation that I drove to the airport. Ron drove the Range Rover, to be loaded with the luggage, and John was behind the wheel of the Bentley. When I embraced Elton I noticed that he was a bit cool with me. I put it down to lethargy from the 11-hour flight and thought no more about it.

A few days later, when walking down the corridor, I heard the phone ring in Bob's room. Its shrill tone continued for some time, so I slipped in to answer it. It was a friend of Bob's, and I took a message. As I replaced the receiver on the cradle I noticed an assortment of photos that Bob had recently had processed. Obviously from Montserrat, I started to flick through them: Elton in the studio, two of the girlfriends by the pool, Chris Thomas looking bemused as Nigel pulls his nose. I couldn't help smiling. Montserrat represented happy times. But at the bottom of the pile there were shots of white boys in the studio. Who were these handsome men? One of them looked familiar. Was it my imagination, or was he one of the medical students who'd visited a few days before I'd left Montserrat, while Elton was working in the studio. A call had come through to the office, and a young male voice, displaying no trace of nervousness, announced himself as a medical student from America. He was in Montserrat working with some colleagues. They were big fans. Could they come up and say hello? Bob took the call and relayed the message to Elton, who said yes, cheerfully.

A group of lads arrived at the front-door and they were heaven sent – beach movie types, tall, muscular, blond and fashionably tanned. They chatted about Elton's music and their medical work, and Elton was utterly charming.

'We'll be here for a week or so,' Elton had said, as they filed out of the studio, 'so feel free to drop in again . . . you might like to hear some of the new things we've done.'

When he suggested I return to London to take delivery of the new car, it never dawned on me that he might be clearing the playing field.

Dark clouds were looming on the horizon of my future happiness. There was a photo of Elton with his arms around a couple of young American boys. They were in shorts and bare chested. They were good looking. And they looked like they were having a lot of fun. He'd obviously invited them to the villa. There were more shots that verged on the sleazy. Wide grins, tight shorts, tough young bodies. A couple of them lying back looking very relaxed and comfortable on our bed. My bed. Elton's bed. The one we shared. Damn you, Elton. You bastard. You cannot be trusted!

I stormed back to my room in a rage. Elton and Bob were out until evening so I stayed in my room for the rest of the day, staring into space. My spirit was broken, and I felt totally drained. I needed to place my feelings into context. What the hell was going on in this man's mind? He writes a song for me and tells me, in our bedroom intimacy, that he wants us to be together for ever. A few days later he dumps me for some young boys on the make. Was I over-reacting? I tried to calm down. Was it my fault? Our sex life had been a bit tame at Montserrat. Perhaps I should have spent more time seducing him. Was it the lack of three-way sex? What was it that those boys in the photos could give Elton that was beyond me? I needed to talk to someone and instinctively rang Sheila, to whom I'd become very close. I told her what had happened, and she was shocked, responding to the news with clucking sounds. 'It'll work itself out, Gaz,' was her only advice.

Dinner was a chilly affair. Elton was feeling guilty and dealing with it by being cold and distant. I could hardly eat, my stomach churning with fury at being cuckolded – and in such a public way. When we returned to his room I confronted him, but he feigned indifference, saying they were merely fans who had come to see him at the studio. He avoided my glare, but his blood pressure went through the roof and his breathing became shallow. Elton had lost control, and it frightened him. Throwing his arms in the air he pleaded: 'Oh, Chook, don't carry on!' He wasn't going to worm out of it as easily as that. I stormed back to my room, turned the radio on loud and flung myself on to the bed.

There was a knock, and the door swung open. It was Bob, looking emotional. He went straight to the point: Elton was sending me back to Australia. I pushed past Bob and ran back to Elton's room, kicking the door open. He was standing at the window, hands behind his back, and turned as I entered. I begged him not to send me away. He stared at me without moving a muscle. I started to plead again. All he said was 'Chook, it's for the best.' And that was that.

I kept on pleading. I'd continue to work for him but I'd move to a flat in London. I wanted to stay in England. I didn't want to return to Melbourne. He remained adamant. I was to return. There was to be no sleep that night. I was an emotional wreck. I'd arrived at the point where I truly believed that I would do or be anything to stay with him. He could be my master, ask for anything, and I'd be his slave. When you're young and insecure, you're vulnerable to being dominated. More so when your life seems to be crashing about you. It's about now that the prisoner begins to mimic his keeper.

The next day Elton remained silent, but after dinner he grunted at me to come to his room in about ten minutes. When I walked in, he was doing a line of cocaine. Without a word, he handed me a straw, and I obediently took a snort. He led the way to his video room. The powder started to kick in. My inhibitions disappeared as pornographic images of cavorting, naked boys filled the screen. Elton turned to me and barked at me to undo my fly and I did. He reached for his Polaroid camera and started to click away.

It is said that we all have a need to be ravished, to give ourselves entirely to another, and when that feeling is perverted it turns into this sort of humiliation. In the grip of the perversion you turn to the person in power to degrade you. The threat of banishment and the devaluing of our relationship had stripped me of dignity, and the cocaine had removed any natural inhibitions. The cocaine was also exaggerating Elton's excitement about being in control. I was his to do with as he wished.

When I left Woodside for what I thought was the last time I took my polaroids with me, for I did not want my photos mixed in with all the others – to be used to seduce other Woodside victims.

I spent most of the next day recovering from my cocaine hangover. When I saw Elton at tea time he'd thawed slightly. 'You can stay in London. You don't have to go back to Australia.' I breathed a sigh of relief. At least I would be in the same country. This stage of euphoria, however, was not to last. Sheila had been fuming since I'd told her what had happened, and she called her son and offered him some heart-felt advice. I heard a lot of yelling.

Sheila said to him, among other things: 'You're not going to send Gary back without any money.' That call really annoyed Elton. He couldn't have his boyfriend too close to his mother. Back to square one: Bob came to my room and told me I was to return to Australia – that night.

He handed me £3000 and said: 'That should be enough to set you up, Gary.' For the first time, I felt sorry for Bob. As he carried my luggage to the car I was struck by the compassion on his face. I knew he felt sorry for me, but this was his job – to do Elton's dirty work. Bob had steeled himself to avoid becoming close to anyone, and in this way he could carry out his orders without becoming emotionally involved. Hanging around the pool at the Montserrat villa, Bob had relaxed and displayed flashes of sensitivity and humour; however, most of the time he hid behind his tough guy mask.

That evening Elton had muttered a guilty farewell, with which he retreated to his room. I was hoping he would give me a good-luck hug as I left. But, as the car rolled down the driveway, the only one standing at the doorway, looking distressed, was Jenny, the housekeeper. I waved madly and she blew me a kiss. I glanced back at Woodside and at Elton's window. It was dark. There seemed to be nobody home.

By now the Melbourne media had latched on to my relationship with Elton, and within a month they were making a big deal of it. As a result my love affair began to complicate my family's lives. *TV Scene* ran a cover story by Veronica Ridge, who had somehow tracked Dad to his office. He spoke to her but wisely refused to comment on his homosexual son's affair with a superstar. Veronica, though, once on the scent of a story, would not let go. She somehow obtained my unlisted phone number, and the interrogation began.

Her approach was very tabloid: intimate and highly persuasive. She knew the areas she wanted to cover and steered me towards them. Because of this style her conversation had a flow that was difficult to follow, a jumble of supposition, fact and opinion. I found myself increasingly confused as the interview ran its convoluted course.

'We hear you're good friends with Elton John. Could you confirm this?' she said.

'Yes, I've known Elton for a couple of years now.'

'How did you meet?'

She was off and running, and I had no idea of what I should be saying. My natural instinct is to stick with the detail because I rarely make a mistake when it comes to facts. So I stated the obvious, 'Through Molly Meldrum.'

'Oh yes,' Veronica responded in an enthusiastic tone, 'he and Elton are good friends, aren't they?'

She was fishing, and in my usual careful, helpful way I volunteered another fact that I thought harmless but interesting. 'They've known each other since the early 70s.'

Then she hit me with the unrelated question, and I was thrown. 'You've stayed with Elton, at his house in England?' Oh, God, how do I handle this one?

'Yes, I went on tour with him to Europe. We spent time at his place near London, called Woodside, and then I went to America with him. I wanted to see my family, so I'm back in Australia for a while.'

'How would you describe Elton as a person?'

Veronica was going for the kill, and I was out of my depth. I had a stab at polite avoidance: 'Yes, Elton's a gentleman. I know him very well but I can't . . . I mean, it's hard to describe him.' I didn't want anything I said to be taken out of context or to hurt Elton in any way, but with these interviews you are damned if you do and damned if you don't. The interrogation continued with Veronica really pushing the pace.

'Is it true Elton and you went through a ceremony similar to a marriage and that you have the documents to prove it?'

'That's not true!' I protested, trying to deny the rumour before it started, 'it's not a Liberace deal. I don't know where you get your information from. Who told you?'

'I'm sorry, Gary, I can't reveal my sources,' she said in her most professional tone. I'd had enough by this stage and tried to bail out.

'What's happening with this story?' I asked nervously.

'Oh, we might run it, we might not,' was her breezy response. I was stunned.

Later in the week I was walking past a news agency in the city and saw a huge poster with a headline blaring: ELTON'S MELBOURNE MAN. I dashed in and bought a copy of *TV Scene*. The story was based on assumptions only, but was broadcast over the radio as well, and the press started ringing Dad at work. He handled it well, telling them to shove off. Sitting at home, with my head in my hands, I reflected on my plight. This was what my involvement with Elton had brought. I'd lost my independence, I'd lost my financial security, I'd lost my job. I was too embarrassed to face my former circle of friends. And now all was laid open to public view and criticism.

Months after all of this I'd managed to overcome the deep depression I'd sunk into after my cruel dismissal. On returning to Melbourne I'd stayed with my parents for a few weeks, but personality clashes surfaced between Dad and me. It wasn't his fault – I wasn't a lot of fun to be around. Over time my hurt and bitterness dissipated, and my life fell back into place.

I started to work in a computer company, and there I met other computer buffs, and my circle of friends grew. These were people whose relationships with me were purely intellectual. This wasn't Gary, the young piece of flesh to be used and discarded by old queens and self-destructive celebs. Montserrat, rock and roll and Woodside seemed to be another time, a distant memory.

In April 1983 Molly Meldrum tracked me down. He'd heard from Elton that I'd returned to Melbourne and said he wondered why he hadn't seen me around the clubs. He made enquiries and arrived, unannounced, at my bedsit. He took one look at the cramped quarters and urged me to move back in with him, but I declined, valuing my peace and quiet.

Molly had met Elton earlier that year when the star slipped into Australia to catch the cricket in January. Elton had arrived with Tommy Williams, an American he'd taken a shine to during the US tour. That was after I'd been sent packing from Bernie Taupin's place in June 1982. In fact, when Elton and I had reunited in Sydney around the time of the Parkinson interview in August, and he'd given me the ultimatum about three-way sex, he'd mentioned Tommy. 'When we get back to Woodside,' Elton had said, 'I want to bring him over so we can have orgies together.'

Tommy was literally the fall-back position and had been flown to Woodside after my untimely departure. But on returning to England after the Australian cricket holiday, Elton and Tommy had fallen out. Maybe Tommy had also become upset about being treated like a wind-up toy that Elton switched on and off at will. The truculent star had yet to realize that you need to work at relationships, that you couldn't expect someone to prance into your life and bring you never-ending happiness. That was your own responsibility.

It didn't occur to Elton that people attracted to his glamorous lifestyle wanted the fantasy to continue when they were with him. They didn't want to be told that he'd been there, done that. They wanted to sightsee, check out restaurants and meet celebrities. Elton appeared to be having fun with a capital F, and his companions wanted a slice of the action.

Early in 1983, the English papers had reported a mysterious burglary at Woodside. A thief had entered Elton's bedroom and stolen a £50,000 sapphire and diamond ring, a £6000 Cartier watch and £100 in cash. The police were suspicious. How is it possible, the police said, for a thief to gain entry without disturbing the dogs, triggering the elaborate alarm system, or breaking into the house? They suspected an inside job. Elton's people protested vehemently: those in the house were friends and business colleagues and above reproach.

Two years later Tommy's name was mentioned in the ensuing court case. Police crashed through the door of 21-year-old Cornelius Culwick's home and accused the unfortunate lad of concealing a stolen watch in his pyjamas. When he was asked where he'd obtained the watch, Cornelius smirked and replied, 'I'll give you a clue – the Pinball Wizard. You work it out.' Elton had played the Pinball Wizard in *Tommy* a decade earlier, and later Culwick's defence was that Elton had given the watch to Tommy, who'd handed it on to him.

At the trial it transpired that on the night the watch disappeared, Elton had returned to Woodside with Tommy and 'two other men'. The star was reported to have changed into his bathrobe and removed his watch and ring. At about 1 am, as the story goes, the four gentlemen watched videos in the privacy of

Elton's room. Elton, when testifying, didn't mention if the programme was *Gone With the Wind* or *The Sound Of Music* or any other family-type viewing. However, he did remember dozing off at about 9 am.

Once they had the facts, the police changed Cornelius's charge to 'dishonest handling'. The witch-hunt began to backfire when Culwick announced in court that he'd had a fling with Elton. Eventually Cornelius was acquitted and was allowed to keep the watch.

Midway through 1983, *Too Low For Zero* was released and greeted with some of the best reviews Elton had garnered. 'I'm Still Standing' was a worldwide hit, and Elton was in the international spotlight again. I bought the album the day it was released and took it home to play. Memories flooded back. Playing 'Crystal' endlessly, I could envisage an excited, emotional Elton composing lovingly for me on the piano. That night I had to work late. I was alone in the office, and Elton kept popping into my mind. I sidled over to the telex machine. Why not? I took the punt: 'G'day, Blue. Album sounds great. How is the football team? How are you? I hope all is well.' Hands shaking, I sent it off. What happened if I got the cold shoulder? Anyway, I included my address and telephone number and hoped for the best. A few days later he rang.

Over the next few months Elton was madly rushing about the world. A postcard came from China. He was there with Watford when it played three games against Chinese teams, one in a packed 70,000-capacity stadium, which was broadcast to a TV audience of 400 million. The tabloid newspapers were as usual interested in the important things in life. When Elton respectfully lifted his boater at the tomb of Chairman Mao, British photographers were delighted. They had proof that the six hair transplants he'd paid nearly £2000 for had not worked. Two months later Elton sent me a postcard from South Africa. He'd made a guest appearance with Rod Stewart at Sun City, which had put both

Rod and him on the hit-list of anti-apartheid groups around the world.

In September, my birthday came and went. There was no call or card. I was disappointed. A week later I received a postcard featuring a monkey lifting the tail of another and peering up its arse. 'Dear Chook, sorry I missed your birthday. I was in West Germany. Watford played their first game there for the UEFA. We got whipped but we had a lot of fun. How are your Mum and Dad?' His phone calls were becoming more frequent. On one occasion he was upset because one of his dogs had been found dead in a stream. Another time he was excited because he'd purchased a black Bentley Mulsanne.

As time went by I found myself returning to gay circles. I'd run into Bill, a queen from the old days. One of his friends, David, had separated from his boyfriend, and Bill suggested I became David's flatmate. I could help him with the rent while seeking classier digs than my abode at the time. David lived in a fabulous apartment on the twelfth floor of a condominium overlooking Melbourne's Port Philip bay, and in the morning I could sit in bed and watch tankers and yachts bobbing in the blue. Life had levelled out to a state of relative happiness, and an intimate relationship would be the icing on the cake.

It was time to start counting my blessings. I was working in computers. I was living in a nice place. My social life, through contact with Bill and David, had started to improve. I was spending more time with my parents and relating better to them than ever before. My boss had provided a company car, and I'd bought myself a 650cc Yamaha Turbo motorbike. And, most important of all, Elton and I were on talking terms.

During one of his phone calls, Elton mentioned Christmas, which was only a few months away. 'I'd love to be at Woodside for Christmas,' I blurted out. It was more of a statement than a request but Elton thought otherwise and acquiesced. I insisted on buying my own ticket. This was one way that I could make my independence obvious, for if I was going to enter the lion's den again it would be on my own terms. This time I would arrive not owing Elton anything, on equal terms. Unfortunately I'd acquired a taste for flying first class, but my bank passbook indicated I'd be booking economy.

The night before my flight David organized a farewell party. During the night someone spiked my drinks, and things went very hazy indeed, but I do remember being set up with a cute 18-year-old. When we went into my bedroom and stripped off, I discovered he was wearing undies with the back cut out leaving his bottom bare. That kinky little touch certainly helped our hot sex. As the night proceeded, my memory of it faded. I was later told I'd also bedded someone else I'd met that night, a Sean Roney, who'd been voted Mr Gay Sydney.

It was one extremely hung over person who arrived in London at dawn in late December 1983, after a 30-hour economy-class flight. Seeing Woodside and Elton again was a joy, although right after breakfast Elton disappeared behind the morning newspaper as if I'd never been away. Given that I'd travelled halfway around the world to be with him, some might have thought the welcome an anti-climax – but it felt good to me.

That night we went to a party at the home of Billy Gaff, Rod Stewart's manager. The place was full of trendies, rock celebs and soapie stars, all watching the door to spot the latest arrival while pretending to hold an intelligent conversation. We left the party as dawn was about to break and on the drive back lolled in the back seat. I felt Elton's hand on my shoulder.

'Chook, let's get back together again. Let's give it another chance.' As the Bentley raced through the night I could feel Elton's fingers fumbling around my zip. Next minute, he was giving me head. Through the car window I saw soft moonlight draped over a row of white houses on a ridge above the trees. It was quite romantic. Leaning back into the expensive leather seats, my thighs tensing, all I could think was: God, Bob, just don't look in the rear view mirror.

Although Christmas was only a week away, there was no seasonal spirit at Woodside, no decorations, not even a Christmas tree. Elton hated Christmas. It was a low point of the year for him.

He was glad to be getting out of England on Boxing Day to work in Montserrat instead of hanging around being jolly.

I decided that I'd try and make this Christmas special for him. I'd buy him something. But he refused to come shopping with me. As I mooched around the Old Windsor shops alone, I realized that I only had £300 in cash, but when I saw a swan-shaped Lalique crystal piece, I had to have it. Elton had told me he liked French crystal so I paid £200 for it and bought Bob a smaller version. I found myself whistling on the way home, despite the fact I only had £50 to my name.

A day or two before Christmas I decided to walk in the nearby fields, and as I left the house I heard the cleaner, Gladys, bitching to Bob about Sheila. Elton's Mum and Derf had come to stay in the Orangery for Christmas, and Sheila had criticized Gladys's housework. I didn't care for Gladys, but for some reason Elton never saw through her conniving ways. Gladys's comments about Sheila really irritated me, and I was in a foul mood as I stomped down the driveway. How dare Gladys talk about Elton's mother in that disrespectful way. After my stay with her, I was feeling very protective of Sheila. As it turned out, when I went past the Orangery, Sheila was at her front door, and without thinking of the consequences, I related what I had heard.

Maybe I expected Sheila to shrug it off. To my astonishment and my outright panic, she stormed into the house, raced up the stairs and barged into Elton's room. Elton was wearing his dressing gown, the one he always wears when he's been doing drugs. He had been on a coke binge the night before and was not feeling very well. All he wanted was peace and quiet and for his head not to hurt. The last thing he wanted was his mother squawking about the hired help. As far as he was concerned, she should be sorting it out with Gladys, not aggravating his bad mood. He snapped at her to leave his room, at which she must have nearly burst a blood vessel, warning him not to talk to her like that. Elton was in no mood for criticism and told her in no uncertain terms to get out. I was in my room and could hear the yelling; feeling responsible, I went down to the kitchen to Bob and Jenny. Soon after, Sheila burst through like a whirlwind, heading for the Orangery. Elton loped downstairs a few minutes later, looking sheepish.

'What happened?' I said feverishly, silently wishing I'd kept my big mouth shut.

'I just told Mum to get the fuck outta here,' Elton confessed to all and sundry. Bob whistled softly and rolled his eyes. I was wrestling with my conscience. Should I confess? I shut up, and hoped this whole thing would blow over.

Derf stormed into the room, looking set to murder Elton. His stepson just glared back. Derf swallowed a couple of times before he could trust himself to speak: 'Don't you ever speak to your mother like that again.' Elton attempted to dismiss the incident with a wave of his hand, but this only seemed to infuriate Derf further.

Elton tried a bluff, 'Oh, look, just get the hell out of here, Derf.'

Derf wasn't budging, he was there to lay down the law: 'I mean it Elton, you'd better start treating your mother with a bit of respect.'

Bob rose from his chair and threw in his tuppence worth: 'Derf, I think it'd be better if you left.'

Derf turned on Elton's assistant and said savagely: 'You shut up!' Bob sat down very quickly. Spreading oil on these troubled family waters could be a severe career risk.

With Bob in his place, Derf turned the attack back on his stepson: 'If you ever speak to her again like that, I'll tell the police what you bleedin' well keep shoving up your nose.'

'Well, go on then,' was Elton's furious retort.

It may have sounded like the bantering you hear between kids in a schoolyard, but these two were deadly serious. You only had to look at Elton, his face red, and his eyes threatening to pop out of their sockets. There had to be more to this than Elton being rude to his mother. It was a cathartic, pivotal moment looking for an excuse to happen. Elton had to cut the strings, and Sheila didn't want to let go. How could she? He couldn't even run his own household. Her pathetic, talented boy was wrecking his life with drugs and over-indulgence. She had tried so hard for him and couldn't desert him at this point. On the other hand she knew Elton had to work it out for himself. For loving mothers there's never a good time to let go, which is where stern fathers come in handy, if they are still around. Elton had Derf but what he really needed was Stan to put him right. Stan would know the right way to do it, for he and Elton shared many of the same traits, and we can all advise ourselves from a distance. But Stan wasn't there, and Elton had missed the transition from adolescence to manhood. Up to this point he had been playing the naughty boy and playing it very well, but life had forced him into a position where he had to take a stand. Sheila would not have thought so at the time, but her life was to become easier from there on in.

For a few minutes after Derf's dramatic exit we stood there speechless. Elton began to say something then swayed and fell into a dead faint. I grabbed him just before he crashed to the floor. Bob was out of his chair like a rocket. He grabbed a wet towel and pressed it against Elton's forehead and then looked over his shoulder at me, telling me to run upstairs to the bathroom to find a bottle of yellow pills, one of which he forced into his patient's mouth. I was in shock, but within minutes Elton was reassuring me that he was OK. 'I need these pills, Gaz,' he explained, 'because of all the drugs I've taken over the years. I have these attacks once in a while.'

Derf and Sheila left the estate in a huff, probably unaware of Elton's fainting spell. To this day, I think only they have known that I was the catalyst to this explosive family battle. Needless to say the incident flattened any planned festivities. Christmas lunch was a glum affair, with roast lamb and cool conversation – none of the turkey, ham and pudding I'd dreamt of in Australia. Gift-giving was a non-event. I proudly presented Elton and Bob with their gifts, but they had bought nothing for each other, nor for anyone in the house, including me.

It was a blessing that we were off to Montserrat the next day.

Work started almost immediately on an album that commenced life as *Restless* but eventually became *Breaking Hearts*. One of the first numbers, 'Sad Songs', had unanimous approval. Another No. 1 for sure.

This time Montserrat was an insane place, with crazy people doing crazy things. Like Elton flying in someone he fancied for a threesome, and, then, because he didn't have any cocaine on him, not feeling sleazy enough to fulfil his fantasy. Instead, the two headed for Elton's bedroom with its curtains drawn tight while I waited outside. Bored after half an hour of waiting, I went swimming instead. I also arranged some of my own adventures, like Reid's friend Paul and I going shopping, returning to Reid's villa while he was away, and finding ourselves in bed together.

At one stage Elton and I simultaneously had the hots for a new tape operator, a cute boy called Steve, who, as it turned out, was straight and not interested in our advances. Another time a crew member brought a loudmouth girl to the island, and she incurred Elton's wrath. He ordered the crew member to remove her and then felt sorry for her, allowing her to stay. She thanked him by threatening the crew member with rape charges, adding that she was going to sue Elton because the guy was in his employ. It was a threat she did not pursue.

The only sane thing that happened during those sessions was one dinner at George Martin's home. A lovely, quietly spoken man, we caught George in a relaxed mood, and he regaled us with fascinating stories about his days as an arranger with the Beatles.

He told us how they couldn't hunt down an authentic hand-operated steam organ for 'The Benefit of Mr Kite' so they acquired old tapes of Sousa marches, chopped them up with scissors, threw the pieces in the air and then glued the tape together. We were stunned to hear that EMI paid Martin the grand fee of £15 for arranging 'Eleanor Rigby' and £33 for doing the score to 'Within You Without You'. He told us how the sound of marching feet on 'Yellow Submarine' was made by filling a box with coal and rolling it from side to side. There were more stories than time to tell them, and Elton, an avid Beatles fan, was fascinated.

One of the developments at Montserrat I noted with pleasure was Renate's progress. Along with the other tape operators, she'd received a thank you on the credits of *Too Low For Zero*, and when Elton had to re-record a hit for *Top of the Pops*, he insisted that Renate handle the session. Now, for *Breaking Hearts*, the German girl had been promoted to the role of engineer.

During the second Montserrat trip, Renate kept a low profile. Her continual wearing of jeans and T-shirts led to some of the shallower crew members insinuating – with absolutely no evidence – that she was a lesbian. One night she arrived for dinner in a dress and everyone, including Elton, commented on her attractive appearance. The truth of the matter was that Renate wasn't very interested in relationships, she was married to her work.

After her promotion, it was inevitable that Renate and Elton would work closer together on this album. I noticed that they exchanged giggles, and, after dinner, the two of them would return to the studio to listen to the tapes. 'If I didn't know any better,' Nigel said one day, 'I'd swear there was something going on between those two.'

'Those two?' said another member of the band. 'Hardly likely!'

Renate and I spent time driving around the island on a jeep, and she told me how lonely it was to be in the music biz, mainly because relationships were so difficult to sustain. I later told Elton that Renate was the first woman whom I'd met that I thought I could really love.

During one of our drives, Renate asked me what I was doing after the recording sessions.

'Elton's touring Australia right after this, so I'm going with him,' I said.

Her eyes widened. 'That'll be nice. We're going to put the final touches to the album in Sydney, so I'm going along as well.'

'I hope you get some time off,' I said in all innocence. 'I want to show you around Sydney . . . it's a beautiful place.'

'Does anything exciting happen there, Gary?' she enquired sweetly.

'Sydney? If you know where to go, I suppose. But after you've been living in London, I think you'll probably find Sydney a bit dull. Nothing out of the ordinary for you, I reckon.'

8. I Wanna Kiss the Bride

If only the paparazzi lying in wait outside the hotel had known that Elton's ex was helping his bride-to-be choose her wedding gown!

THE QANTAS NIGHT flight from London to Sydney was thankfully routine, giving Elton, Bob and me the chance to relax. The plane was packed with raucous holiday makers, but First Class was serenity itself. Bob and Elton sipped Heineken beer while I toyed with a glass of juice. Conversation was never more than tired small talk.

After the Qantas cabin crew served trays of martinis, and salmon and caviar canapes, Elton burrowed into his recently acquired biography of Barbara Hutton, *Poor Little Rich Girl*. The way Hutton showered her friends with diamonds mirrored Elton's own torrid generosity to his friends and staff. Like the Appaloosa racehorse and a powerboat he presented to Reid for his 25th birthday, the Rolls for an American agent, a solid gold heart with a diamond in the middle for a publicist and the Pulsar and Cartier watches and Polaroid SX-70S for band members.

Elton's generosity flowed into his public persona, and he was so welcoming that complete strangers had no compulsion about coming over to chat and ask for autographs. After all, onstage he didn't mind doing anything for his audience – outrageous fashions that cost the earth, pounding his piano until his fingers bled or smashing his £100 piano benches for effect. But off-stage he'd learnt how to weave people graciously out of his life as soon as he desired. Before this flight, when fans spotted him browsing through the biography section of Heathrow Airport's bookstore, he signed their autographs and dispensed with them before they became a nuisance. And he did it with such charm that no one ever felt insulted.

The double serving of in-flight roast beef and Yorkshire pudding had me soporific and contemplative. What was to become of me after this Australian tour? Would I be allowed to stay on for the New Zealand leg as well? Or was I going to be given the heave-ho once we got to Sydney? What about my feelings towards Elton? We'd had a good time at Old Windsor. But I was starting to feel edgy about the way he insisted that I share his sexual favours with others, the encounters often spiked with cocaine for a greater thrill. Was I being edged out of the picture? If I was, would my ego accept that I was to be the latest in an endless series of meaningless relationships? When we started out, Elton had whispered, 'We'll be together forever.' I wasn't just a fling, surely? Didn't his threat to cancel the 1982 US tour unless I accompanied him mean something?

Before I could resolve my thoughts, the plane had touched down at Sydney's Mascot Airport, and Elton was clowning about and shouting in an Australian accent. He seemed to be happy to return to Australia, and I innocently assumed it was because it was one of his favourite countries. We rushed through customs and were limo'd to the compact Sebel Town House on Elizabeth Bay Road. The hotel catered for the showbiz set, so Elton was assured that every whim would be catered for and the odd indiscretion overlooked.

Despite the wet weather, I was delighted to be back in Australia. There was a youthful energy and innocence about the place that I didn't know I missed until I returned. I even started whistling to myself on the ride to the Sebel. Elton was quiet in the car, but as we swept up to the hotel entrance, he turned to me: 'Chook, I forgot to tell you. I've booked us into different rooms. There'll be so much activity going on in my room . . . meetings and interviews. It'll be easier for you not to have to put up with it.'

I thought his explanation ludicrous, but I shrugged it off. By this time I was used to his swinging moods. Anyway, I was back on home turf. I had enough friends in Sydney not to be at anybody's whim, and if things got claustrophobic at the Sebel, I could always stay with one of them. Still, the worries that had tormented me on the flight started to gnaw. Bob and Elton quickly checked in and, unusually, didn't wait for me. When I collected my room key, I glanced at the key tag: 'Mr A. N. Other'.

A little joke? No matter, I was indignant. As I made my way to the lift, I brooded. Hey, I wasn't even on a wage, merely expenses paid. Why should I be considered to be just A.N. Other addition to this entourage? It was almost as if Elton were planning something, starting with an insult that suggested that I didn't exist. If I was to be shuffled out of the scene, who had taken my place? Elton had not brought another boy with him. He certainly didn't have one on stand-by in Sydney. Maybe he'd brought me here to dump me where he'd found me – in Australia. A sort of complete cycle. How poetic. Much better form than when he bounced me in Los Angeles. As I started to unpack in Room 211, it occurred to me that mine was the room furthest from Elton, who was in the Presidential Suite about a dozen floors above.

I decided to forget about it, there wasn't time for brooding. Renate and I were to travel to EMI Studios in Kent Street to help mixing the *Breaking Hearts* album. I enjoyed being with Renate. She was a soft-spoken girl with a private nature and hardly noticeable in the hustle and bustle that surrounds a superstar. She liked it that way. In Montserrat, while staff and crew returned to their respective cabins after a hard day's recording, Renate would stay on at the studio, working alone. Because she kept to herself, the crew would jump to all sorts of conclusions.

In Sydney, Renate and I maintained the close informal

relationship that had started with those Moke rides around Montserrat. The fact that she'd told me how lonely working in the music biz could be and how difficult it was to have a relationship, especially for a woman, indicated how relaxed she felt with me. While Renate and I continued working happily together in the studio, Elton was busy preparing for the tour. Although officially not on staff, I had a Ford Fairlane at my disposal for errands had to be run, promotional material had to be coordinated, and cocaine had to be procured.

A day or two after I arrived in Sydney, my phone rang and a familiar voice said, 'How are you?' It was Mr Gay Sydney himself, Sean Roney, the young, blond and beautiful rent-boy who'd successfully stalked the redlight area of Kings Cross, Australia's centre for sex hire. A typical Sydney beach kid, Sean lived for nothing more than thrills and expensive fun, and his charms and great physique were his pass to that luxurious lifestyle.

I hadn't heard from him since my farewell party in Melbourne, but he dropped in to see me at the Sebel, as teasing and amusing as ever. Sean had the face of a poet and the daredevil humour of an Australian bushranger; the manners of a Sloane with the street sass of a kid who had to live off his wits. It didn't take me too long to melt into his arms. The next morning as we headed out of the hotel, Elton was standing in the foyer, talking to a journalist. His eyes flashed, although no one in the lobby would have suspected that he'd even noticed us. Sean muttered something about wanting to meet Elton. 'Oh, yeah, maybe when he's not so busy,' I muttered. All in good time, I thought to myself.

Sean and I spent our time tour-guiding the entourage around Sydney's beauty spots, boutiques and beaches. Eventually I did introduce Sean and Elton. Sean was star-struck and rabbited on about how he'd always loved Elton's music. Elton was nodding his head, but I knew he wasn't really listening. Behind Sean's back, Elton raised an eyebrow and nodded his approval. I knew exactly what was going through his mind. It was now a question of when, not if. The next morning I rang his suite. 'EJ, do you need me to hang out your wardrobe?'

'Why don't you come up, Chook?' he said, and I knew it had nothing to do with clothing.

When I entered his suite, Elton was hyper. He rambled on about how rehearsals were going, and how a reporter had asked him if it was true Elton and his 'mysterious Melbourne man' had gone through a marriage ceremony. I smiled vacuously and waited for him to get to the point. We both knew neither of us had the slightest interest in what he was saying. Finally he sat at the end of the bed and, pushing his specs back on his nose, asked if Sean and I would care to join him later for a threesome.

It was easier said than done. As a visiting superstar, Elton was under a personal spotlight, whether it was in his hotel, eating in a restaurant or wandering the streets. He was never alone, and things had to be done discreetly. If news leaked out, even innocently, it would be newspaper headlines. I rang Sean and set up the meeting. If Sean was impressed because Elton fancied him, he never showed it – he was so cool. Years of rent-boy work had him in control of his emotions.

That evening Elton faked a migraine and retired to his room, with the express orders that he was not to be disturbed, under any circumstances. He was looking forward to the pleasure of Sean's company and had already prepared his suite with champagne and cocaine. Sean arrived wearing a pair of tight blue jeans, accentuating his bulge, and Elton's stare was locked on to that infamous crutch. We sat around sipping the bubbly and slowly got wired, and I noticed Sean was careful not to touch drugs.

After three quarters of an hour of casual conversation, which predictably became more horny as the cocaine took effect, Elton ordered Sean to remove his clothes. As Sean stripped off his jeans, Elton gasped, and I couldn't blame him – years of swimming had honed Sean's body to perfection. There was not an ounce of fat and to say he was well hung would be a ludicrous understatement.

Elton soon tired of looking and joined in, while I videotaped the action, so Elton and I could later sit back and watch it for a giggle. An hour later, Elton did what he always does after he blows – went to sleep. It was left to me to pour Sean a final glass of champagne and to take him home. The next day, when I returned to my room from shopping, I noticed that the video camera and tapes (with last night's antics) were missing. I hastily went to Elton's room to tell him. Reid was there, discussing business. 'Yes, I took it,' said Reid. 'Because of the footage you took last night.' When I told him I'd already erased it and that one tape had all our Christmas footage, Reid handed over the tapes without question. I was amazed!

On the Friday night I went out for a Japanese meal with Chris Thomas, the talented producer who'd notched up a No. 1 with the Pretenders and who was helping to produce *Breaking Hearts*. He was a tall, awkward man, with a pleasant face and receding hairline, a workaholic who had little time for the groovy image of rock and roll: his clothes were shabby, and he always looked as if he'd dressed in the dark. Although his appearance didn't do a lot for me, I was impressed with his creative ideas. After dinner I returned to the Sebel, where the crew and staff were gathered to discuss the day's activities.

Heading for the bar, I tossed the car keys to the doorman and walked into the lounge. From the hush in the room I knew immediately something was a-buzz. There was none of the good-natured banter and camaraderie typical of our usual Friday-night drinks. Bad news? An accident? A sacking? Good news? It wasn't quite that, I figured. I felt uncomfortable. There was an excitement in the air, but it had an edge of threat. When I arrived, heads turned, eyes averted, conversation stalled. My mind recorded the next few minutes in slow motion and in great detail. I could see Elton look up, and then walk over to me. He put his lips against my ear: 'Don't be upset, Chook, I have asked Renate to marry me.'

A bolt of lightning crashed through my body and scorched my soul. It was nightmarish, like a drawn out death in a horror movie. Elton patted my arm and moved away. Senses reeling, I could see Renate approaching: 'I can understand how you feel,' she sympathized. She seemed as shocked as me. Earlier in the evening, Elton had asked her to accompany him to an Indian restaurant called the Mayur and popped the question.

I'd sometimes wondered how it would feel to drown. Right now, I had a pretty good idea. I was literally gasping for breath, my brain screaming 'Don't panic!', as it, with agonizing and infinite patience, searched for a point on which to anchor fresh hope and understanding. My body went into shock, the adrenalin pumping, blood vessels slamming shut, face whitening as the blood drained, my palms cold and sweaty. Even if you know you have to leave, your legs are numb. I could feel the spirit draining out of my heart. In that gut-wrenching sickening emptiness I remember thinking: I envy her – I love her – I fear for her. But I could never hate her. Through the haze I could hear her murmuring that she wanted me to help her choose her wedding dress.

Then it clicked. Montserrat! When Renate was suddenly promoted from tape operator to engineer. When I noticed him glancing at her over dinner. But who'd have guessed it? Yes, the two of them would disappear into the balmy night, but everyone figured they just wanted to hear the latest batch of recordings. Renate? Too quiet to be noticed in a showbiz crowd where the loudest and pushiest invariably gain attention. A no-contender where power games and mind tricks are essential to stay in the Number One spot. Not Renate, surely. Too aloof, too dedicated to her work, too much of an individual, too independent to need anyone's approval. Renate, the girl with no past.

I could appreciate why Elton had chosen her. Renate and I were like peas in a pod: introverted and enigmatic. Neither of us would threaten Elton's spotlight. Ironically, she and I had become close because we were so much alike, and ours was almost a sibling relationship. I'd once or twice joked to Elton that if I ever married a girl, it'd be someone like Renate. No, hang on, not someone like Renate. It would be Renate.

If what had just occurred was a shock to my system, there were more shocks to follow. John Reid came over and placed his arm around me. Wonders will never cease. 'Unbelievable,' he clucked. Maybe he was retrieving his knife from my back at the same time. Cluck! Cluck! There were clucks of sympathy around me. 'You poor love', Patti clucked. It was meant to be tender. But she couldn't stand around clucking at me all night. She was the tour publicist, after all, and she was determined to milk this for all it was worth. What time was it? Midnight. Good! She could still catch the newspapers' deadlines. Patti raced for the phones. Once she had relayed what had happened to the outside world, the spell in the Sebel bar was broken. The place was a hive of activity. I stood silent as people rushed about, laughing and giggling, or tending to their duties. What use was Yesterday's Man to them?

'Is it a publicity stunt?' asked the jaded media, while Elton sat in a luxury hotel bar, arm around his lady, surrounded by wildly jubilant people, with a smile that said, 'I'm so much in love, folks.' Not one of Elton's closest friends would believe he'd take the plunge into a hetero marriage. 'It must be a stunt,' was the common opinion.

I had to escape that night, and left the hotel to sit in the car with the radio playing loudly. Why was he doing it? To be unpredictable? Well, that was my Elton. To gain respectability? To gain approval from his Mum? Or was it that he was trying to come to terms with the feminine aspects of his personality? Was he using Renate to gain access to the shadowy recesses of his psyche? Could Renate be the key to his self love? If not, the odds would be that she, too, would fail and later be stacked in with the six-foot woman, the perfectionist mother, and Stan, his missing father. I had been filed elsewhere – under Temporary Remnants and Black Virgins.

Dazed and distraught I drove aimlessly through Sydney and into the countryside. Finally, the tears poured down my face so much I had to pull over. If ever I despised myself, it was tonight. As I sat in the car and howled, I cursed myself for my wretched lifestyle, for chasing a man who sang about love instead of living it.

The memories came flooding back. Trying gay sex when I was 16 and feeling bruised and confused. My parents finding out from an irate woman. The confrontation over the kitchen table. My father, unable to cope, giving me an ultimatum. 'You can either stay here and go to a psychiatrist. Or you pack your things and leave.' Moving out to live with a succession of friends and not seeing my family again for two years. Interestingly, as I raged over Elton's betrayal, my father was the one I turned to. 'Come home,' he said.

Elton John's marriage plans grew more bizarre by the hour. It was a surreal dream. It is not often that a homosexual man gets his ex to choose a wedding dress for his female bride. But that was precisely what I was doing the next morning. Elton was too busy, what with rehearsing at the Showgrounds for the tour and listening to final edits of tracks from the new album. Renate had no girlfriends in Sydney to confide in. I was the obvious – and only – choice.

The wedding was to take place four days after Elton proposed – Tuesday 14 February, St Valentine's Day. There was a bureaucratic hiccup because the State of New South Wales had a Marriage Act that required that a couple give 30 days' notice. That meant the wedding would have to be delayed by a month, until after the New Zealand tour. Elton threw up his arms in disgust and declared he'd hire a boat and marry outside territorial waters; however, Kevin Ritchie and Bob Halley had a special meeting with the Attorney-General, who was empowered to waive the rules.

Renate and I rushed around Sydney's wedding boutiques but couldn't find a thing. She was the type who usually slopped around in T-shirt and jeans and didn't have a clue as to what sort of wedding dress would suit the occasion. Unlike other girls I knew, Renate hadn't spent years dreaming and scheming about the day she'd walk up the aisle. She was the sort of person who wanted to live her life for the minute, to seize the moment rather than plan it.

Typically, Renate avoided anything ostentatious. I'd have imagined that an unknown girl marrying a worldwide celebrity, especially with TV cameras and British journalists flying in to cover the spectacle, would have wanted something glitzy. But not Renate: I was close enough to her at this point to know that it was not Elton's power or wealth that attracted her. It was his generosity, and his uncanny manner of making you feel special. Even if you didn't think it. Especially if you didn't think it.

I felt sorry for her because she had virtually no one to confide in, so I did the best I could under the circumstances. As we sat in the back of the limo driving around Sydney, she talked about how she loved Elton and how she might best respond to him in different situations. What would Elton expect of her? She didn't want him to be disappointed in any way. She was in a state of shock, although, apparently, they'd already discussed marriage earlier in Montserrat, when Elton had asked her what she thought of marriage and the sort of man her husband might be. But she'd thought nothing of it, for her it was just a casual conversation.

Last night's shock and hurt still wasn't too far from the surface, but I decided that I would take a positive approach. For her sake, at least. Be happy for her and be her friend. We arrived outside a small place in trendy Double Bay that was full of exquisite clothing, with price tags to match. I selected an off-the-rack job, a white silk (or off-white, really) with a low neckline. I held the dress out in front of me. Eureka! Renate agreed. The dress only cost about £1150. Damn cheap considering that the wedding and reception themselves cost close to £50,000. I remember thinking: if only the press knew that the ex-male lover chose the gown.

The bride-to-be knew that this was the dress she wanted, but it needed some alterations. She wanted Swiss lace covering the low neckline and Elton's wedding gift of a heart-shaped gold pendant set with 63 diamonds woven into the bodice. The shop owner's eyebrows raised melodramatically when I told her that the alterations had to be done in no more than two working days, but when I told her Renate was going to marry Elton John, the response was just as I expected. Suddenly nothing was a problem. The shop would stay open all weekend for the forthcoming Mrs E. John, and the owner talked herself into decorating the church as well.

Patti Mostyn, who was to be one of the bridesmaids, along with Betty Ritchie and Bernie Taupin's wife Toni, had already decided what they'd all be wearing. The material was flown down from Brisbane, and the dressmakers worked through the night. The morning after the wedding, Patti went on the mid-afternoon TV hour *The Mike Walsh Show* and described the frocks she'd decided upon as 'making us look like swordfishes, right out of Dynasty!' How true. Thank God she didn't dress Renate.

After we had chosen the dress, we returned to the Sebel for lunch – to discover that the EJ nuptials were the biggest thing to hit the planet as far as the Sydney newspapers were concerned. That morning the wedding announcement had bounced the death of Soviet premier Yuri Andropov right off the front pages. As we drove up to the hotel, a huge crowd had gathered outside hoping to catch a glimpse of this 'mysterious girl'. And as we jumped out of the limo, I heard someone yell, 'Look, there she is!', and immediately there were photographers everywhere.

The British press were certainly gunning for photos and gossip about Renate. They had been caught on the hop when the news was telephoned to England, and the *Sun* had rushed out a 'This is Elton's girl' story but, alas, ran a picture of the wrong girl standing next to Elton. This afternoon's flurry of shots were the first of Renate and were quickly transmitted back to London. The next issue of the *News of the World* managed to get the pictures right. There was one particular shot, taken inside the Sebel, that showed Renate walking in front, with me looking despondent in the background. It was published on front pages around the world. It summed up this whole situation – and close friends like Molly were in absolute hysterics about it. The caption could have read 'Every Bride Needs a Sister!'

After lunch, Renate and I tried to sidle off to do some more shopping but to Renate's annoyance Patti Mostyn insisted on joining us. No doubt Patti had been specifically asked by Elton to lend his prospective bride a hand, but Renate felt she could manage without her. Patti, in her bombastic fashion, and oblivious to Renate's feelings, indicated she was prepared to manage the whole show and excused her intrusive manner by emphasizing the obvious shortage of time.

By the time we returned to the Sebel in the evening, well-wishes were flooding in from the rich and famous: Rod Stewart, Yoko Ono and Sean Lennon, Kenny Rogers, Bryan Forbes and representatives and players from the Watford team. Boy George, whose 'Karma Chameleon' had just won the most popular single of the year award, took the opportunity to say: 'I hope it's love. If Elton got married to either a man or a woman it wouldn't bother me. I think he's past the stage of having to prove his sexuality to anyone.'

The papers were still beating-up the story, gleefully reporting every movement, shoving microphones into the faces of anyone who'd known Elton. His good friend Kiki Dee was stunned, while Bernie Taupin told one newspaper: 'I always knew that if Elton suddenly got a bee in his bonnet about wanting a family, it was likely to happen pretty suddenly.'

Obviously the press were oblivious to the bust-up between mother and son after the swearing incident at Woodside, but Sheila was quoted as saying she approved of her son's choice: 'She's 30, not some slip of a girl, which is what I first feared.' Despite this distant approval, the relationship between Renate and her mother-in-law never got past an oh-so-proper politeness. To overcome any embarrassment at the wedding, someone fed the press a story that Sheila and Derf were not attending because Derf had 'an eye problem'. The British papers tracked down Elton's biological father, Stan Dwight, in Wales. Stan moaned that everyone in the family was personally informed by the groom but he had to read about it in the papers. If Stan had been sitting by the phone waiting for his son to call he must have had a strong belief in miracles.

People magazine ran a fresh angle by speaking to Elton's first fiancée, Linda Woodrow. Angry at Elton's quips that their relationship had been an unmitigated disaster that put him off heterosexuality, Linda told the world that Elton was always an effeminate mother's boy and warned Renate not to expect satisfying sex or hope for the Big O because 'he's lousy in bed.' Still, Elton had practised since then, and he certainly improved over his time with me. But I think Linda's first comment still held ground.

The British press, and even elements of the public who'd turned away from Elton after he confessed to his bisexuality, were certainly impressed with his conversion to the straight and narrow. What a good old-fashioned romantic hero. Didn't he ring Renate's father in Germany and formally ask Poppa for his daughter's hand? Didn't the couple decide to continue to sleep in separate rooms until the knot was tied? Mind you, she wasn't English but, hey, his Mum approved, didn't she? And she's very English.

The press hit poor Bob Halley right in the neck, with the *Daily Express* reporting that Bob – 'he and his boss even wear His and His earrings, one each of a pair of diamond solitaires' – was refusing all calls to his room. I don't know how Bob took to the news of the marriage, because I didn't see him during those days leading to the wedding, but the castle was getting crowded, and this woman was a real contender.

I ducked the media. Not that it did me much good. Tabloid journalism's vile intrusion is its fascination, and I'd heard enough tales of photographers and journalists chasing celebrities down the street, into shops and even into toilets to know they would be ruthless if they decided they needed my story. It seemed inevitable that a journalist would decide on 'Elton's Melbourne Man' as an angle. Despite the fact I was registered as A.N. Other,

I was located. The house phone rang. It was a journo on the line, asking about Bob Halley's and my reaction to the marriage, plans for Elton's buck's turn, where the honeymoon was going to be, if I would be returning to stay with Elton in England and if Elton was going to give up performing after his marriage. I managed not to give anything away and told John Reid, who then had Reception screen all my calls.

Elton and I didn't converse immediately after the announcement, and I was feeling quite worthless anyway and preferred to be alone. Thankfully, over the next couple of days I was kept busy by entourage members asking me to purchase wedding presents. I'd buy what they wanted, hand over their gifts and return to my room where I'd watch TV and brood. I was aware that Elton's wedding meant that I might be out of the entourage, so I knew I needed to keep a sharp look out for another job.

It was on Monday, the day before the wedding, that Elton finally spoke to me. 'How's it going, Chook?' he muttered, averting his eyes as he always does when he's feeling guilty. 'Thanks for looking after Renate right now.' I nodded and walked off. Renate spent her wedding eve chatting with Pattie Nobler, head of AIR Studios in London, and I believe the groom had a quiet night entertaining members of his band in his room. I don't think Elton had a buck's turn; and if he did, I certainly wasn't expecting an invitation.

St Valentine's Day 1984 dawned miserable in Sydney. The skies were leaden, and the weather report ominously predicted rain. Despite the damp chill in the air, crowds were surging outside the Sebel by ten in the morning, with delivery vans carrying in the goodies providing the only entertainment. TV crews were positioned outside to provide an hourly update.

Preparations were well under way at the Sebel. The wedding reception area had an apricot colour theme, and platters of seafood, stuffed quail with honey, turkey, lemon chicken and loin of beef were being prepared in the kitchens. All this fine food was to be accompanied by fine wines. The wedding cake had five tiers and nine dozen bottles of Elton's favourite champagne – Roederer's Cristal at £80 a pop – were flown in, and some 1976 Château Latour and 1959 Puligny-Montrachet were also ordered.

Reid recommended that Elton should get Renate to sign a pre-nuptial agreement. Elton refused with a finality that Reid must have found exasperating. Although it is sometimes thought that Elton is manipulated by Reid, in the end it is Elton who always rules the day. When the chips are down, in personal matters, it is Elton who is in control, and Reid knows his place. Unable to win this debate, despite his carefully staged theatrics, Reid swept from the room, muttering under his breath. The singer was still in control of this song.

I kept low-profile, too upset to talk to anybody. Since the Big Announcement last Friday, no one had talked to me about coming to the wedding. Although Elton hadn't actually asked me not to come, there was no mention of hiring or buying clothes for me, as was the case for everybody else in the entourage. It was only when Molly flew in that morning from Melbourne that I thought I had a sounding board, but I could hardly edge in a word, for Molly was in a state of garrulous shock: 'It's all too bizarre, just too bizarre,' he mumbled.

After a while Molly pumped me for details about Renate but I told him that I couldn't tell him more than the sketchy details that everyone else knew. She was born to a wealthy German family; her father, Joachim Blauel, was a respected publisher in Munich; Renate had rebelled against the family by taking a job as a stewardess with Lufthansa before drifting to England, where she lived in a tiny £35-a-week flat in Kensington.

'But you spent time with her in Montserrat, you must know more than that!' Molly insisted.

I was becoming exasperated: 'Look, Molly, Renate was a girl who kept to herself. I know she plays a little bit of piano, I know she lives eternally in those jeans and T-shirts, and she told me that her ambition was to become a respected record producer.

She never liked talking about herself. When we did chat, she never mentioned her private life.'

'Does she love him?' Molly asked the question that was on everyone's minds, if not their lips.

'Yes, I think she does,' I declared, and I meant it.

Wedding time was nigh. Elton wore a white waistcoat, black pants, a striped silk shirt with a mauve bow tie, a boater with a mauve sash and a New Zealand orchid in his lapel. Once I would have been in his suite, helping him dress, listening to him crack jokes to disguise his nervousness. I'd have accompanied him to his car and driven with him to the church. Instead I watched the wedding on the TV set in my room.

Two buses ferried the guests, who included Olivia Newton John, Michael Parkinson and the Australian satirist Barry Humphries, to and from the ceremony. Neither the bride's nor the groom's parents attended. Kevin Ritchie, the Aussie promoter, gave away the bride. The buses ran from the Sebel to St Mark's Church in Darling Point, and TV cameras scanned the 500 fans who had been waiting behind police barricades for up to five hours on the tree-lined road outside the church.

At one point fans accidentally knocked over a wrought iron fence in the crush, throwing people on to the pavement below. A 22-year-old fan was carted to hospital with an injured leg after being trampled in the crowd. A woman and a child were treated on the scene for their minor injuries. It was becoming clear to the most disinterested observer that what was to have been a private and intimate commitment to a lifetime of togetherness was turning into a circus. I hoped Renate was impervious to the hype.

Light drizzle did not deter the on-lookers. 'Journalists and photographers from virtually every major magazine and newspaper flew into Sydney today to cover pop star Elton John's surprise marriage,' droned the TV commentator. 'It's reported that residents near the church have been offering vantage-points on their rooftops to the media and to fans – at £250 a time. Now that's what I call private enterprise.'

From the loneliness of my hotel room I watched the television broadcast of Elton's white six-door limo, bearing a pink balloon and arriving at 5.45 pm. The police cleared a path as TV crews pushed their way around the barricade in front of the church, and the crowd gave a hefty roar as Elton and his best men, Reid and Taupin, stepped from the car. Elton gave a slight wave before disappearing behind the huge wooden doors of the church. It was too much for me. I reached for the remote control and silenced the TV, preferring to stretch out on the bed. It was still light outside but the heavy curtains were drawn tight. The room was a tomb, the only noise was the low hum of the air conditioner.

The wedding, I was told later, was a traditional ceremony, with hymns like 'Song of Joy' and the '23rd Psalm' and a sermon from the Revd Wilder based on 'The Lord Is My Shepherd'. Apparently, as Renate arrived with her entourage 17 minutes after Elton, someone in the doctor's surgery opposite blasted out Elton's hit songs 'I Wanna Kiss the Bride' and 'I'm Still Standing'.

At that moment I was submerging myself in a hot bath, wondering whether I should drown. Elton's cruel betrayal was torturing my mind. Why had he used me like that? Was the marriage really to keep a promise to his mother, made many years ago, when he confessed the real nature of his sexuality to her, vowing that he'd still give her a grandchild? Was he punishing me?

Why was he pretending to the world he'd gone straight when a few days earlier he was having a male threesome in his room? How long was this deception going to last? Other famous bisexuals, like Freddie Mercury, had girlfriends quite happy to share with boys, but what was Renate going to do about this? Was I out of Elton's life for ever? And what had brought about this change towards me? He'd always told me I was more special than any of the other boys because I'd never used him. I knew how distressed he was when a former boyfriend, with whom he'd had a torrid affair, was accused of stealing a watch from Elton to give to his lover.

The phone rang. Bugger it, I thought, I'm not going to answer it. It continued to ring, so I slid one wet hand out of the bath, turned up the radio and went back to my pitiful wallowing. Whoever had been trying to ring through desisted. But a few minutes later there was a pounding on the door. Drop dead! I thought crossly, turning up the radio louder and immersing my head in the water.

About five minutes later I heard my front door open, and someone ran into my room and then into the bathroom. It was Molly. 'Oh, lovey, I thought you might have done something drastic' he gushed. 'Are you OK?' I was pleased that someone had bothered to check on me, and I was about to start unburdening myself, but a figure rustled in behind him. It was Renate, in full wedding regalia complete with sprigs of baby's breath in her hair. She looked divine. Elton would later tell a friend that when he'd turned to watch her walk up the aisle towards him, he almost burst into tears because she looked so magnificent.

'Hello, Gary,' she said smiling gently, and then handed me over her bouquet. 'This is for you.' Despite how rotten I felt, I couldn't help but smile. Renate gave me a quizzical look, her head cocked to one side: 'Why didn't you come to the church?' How could I tell her it was because I loved her – and him. Before I could think of a suitable fib, she reached for the flowers and returned to the living room, quietly placing her bouquet on top of the TV set. 'I'll leave these here for you, alright?' she called out. 'And come down to the reception – please.' She and Molly left.

I emerged from the tub and looked ruefully at the bouquet. Slowly pulling on my clothes, I switched on the TV, only to see a repeat of the wedding footage. Elton and Renate leaving the church; Renate looking hassled as the crowd moved in; Elton holding on to her and pushing his way into the limo; the photographers chasing for their shots, one falling over and breaking his leg. I turned the TV off. Did I really want to go to the reception? I had paranoid visions of guests turning *en masse* as I entered the reception room, roaring with laughter, pointing and jeering. Why should they? I wasn't the loser. No one had won. Not Elton or Renate. Despite what Elton might have thought, this marriage was not a destination, just a milestone in his sad search for self. It was tragic that Renate would have to take the brunt of the misery, for I knew Elton would merely distract himself or hide in drugs and booze.

The phone rang. Elton calling. 'Chook! Come on down!' he said. It was about 10.30 pm when I slipped into the ballroom, and at this stage most of the guests were leaving. There were flowers everywhere and a mountain of food remained on the table, but I certainly wasn't hungry. Elton's boater lay abandoned on the main table. Paranoia took over: I suspected people were giggling.

I certainly didn't want to be in this room, but as Renate and Elton had made it clear they harboured no resentment, how could I not reciprocate. They'd hurt me, sure, but they were still special people in my life, and if I didn't love them so much, I would have rejoiced – but I knew their union would be short-lived and unhappy. Intimacy was beyond Elton.

From what I gathered, the reception had been a sedate affair. There was none of the drunken revelry that was to mark later weddings of Rod Stewart and Slash of Guns 'n' Roses. Elton's party was an all class act, just a little light on soul. The 87 guests had returned from the church at about 7.30 pm and were ushered into a reception room for pre-dinner cocktails. Then, in a true Eltonian theatrical style, the dividing wall slid into the floor to reveal a ballroom dazzling with £3000 worth of white roses, carnations and lilies flown in from New Zealand. The Palm Court Orchestra played tunes such as 'Teddy Bear's Picnic', 'Washington Post', 'Love Song' and a selection from the repertoire of Scott Joplin and Strauss, all adding to an atmosphere of cultured dignity. It was like something from the pen of Scott Fitzgerald, with Elton as Gatsby.

As to be expected, Elton's speech had been quite amusing: 'This has been a magic night for me. I would like to thank the New South Wales government for letting the wedding go ahead – particularly as I told the Attorney-General I'd cancel the tour if he didn't give us permission!' Reid read out the telegrams, but Elton leapt to his feet for Michael Jackson's offering, mimicking

Michael's high-pitched voice as he read out: 'I had to set my hair on fire to make the front pages but you only had to go and get married!' Jackson was referring to an incident weeks earlier when he was filming a TV commercial, and a special effect device exploded at the wrong time. It set the star's hair on fire and Jackson arrived at hospital in tears.

In his more formal speech, the bridegroom confessed that after he'd proposed to Renate at the restaurant, he'd admitted that organizing the church and reception would be a scheduling nightmare. Renate replied: 'It isn't that unpleasant – it's like going to the dentist.' The guests cheered at that one. How were they, or she, to know that the honeymoon was destined to be something like an incomplete dental operation – raw nerves exposed but no filling.

The groom also recounted that as he and Renate emerged from the church as man and wife, someone in the crowd had yelled out: 'Good on you sport, you old poof. You finally made it!' Elton said he had called back: 'It just goes to show how wrong you all were!'

Those in charge had placed a grand piano in the ballroom just in case, but at midnight Elton told the guests he and his bride were retiring, quipping: 'I'm going off to play monopoly.' The couple moved through the room, chatting and smiling, when Elton spotted me. It had been a long day but he was energised. Bowling over he said: 'Come up to our room, we're all going up there.'

The party raged through the night with guests in the know wandering into another room for a quick snort of cocaine. Eventually only the loving couple and Bob, Molly and I remained. Lounging on the beds, we played cards and drank alcohol.

By 4 am, Molly had collapsed, so I deposited him in my room and returned to the Presidential Suite. By 6 am, I was partied out and staggered back to Room 116. When I left Elton and Renate, both looked very much the worse for wear; still dressed in their wedding gear, they looked like they had no intention of going to bed.

Later that morning I stirred when Molly woke to catch his flight to Melbourne, and we simultaneously caught sight of the bouquet of roses that Renate had placed on the TV set. The drooping flowers looked distinctly seedy. There was something comically poignant about it all. We both burst out laughing.

After breakfast I was about to go for a stroll when Elton appeared in the lobby. Looking most earnest, he took me aside and handed down the well-considered verdict: 'Sorry, Chook, you're not coming to New Zealand.' He explained that he was on his honeymoon and then added lamely: 'I want to watch a lot of cricket when I'm there.'

It was a wimpy and less than poetic way of saying, 'Goodbye, kiddo, you're off your pedestal. Next!' Our Elton was going to be totally reformed. Not unexpectedly, I was out. An important part of my life seemed to be over, and my melancholy intensified. I refused to allow Elton see my devastation and lied with mock cheer that it was no problem. Elton was pleased that I was going quietly.

A Sydney newspaper report suggested that the happy couple were about to buy a four-bedroom £350,000 apartment that occupied the entire eighteenth floor of President Towers. This luxury abode had a spectacular 360° view of the Sydney Opera House and Harbour Bridge, while the master bedroom overlooked St Mark's church. As far as the entourage were concerned, the real honeymoon was to take place after the tour, when Elton planned to take Renate to the South of France.

I said my goodbyes and started that long lonely 1000 kilometre Sydney to Melbourne drive. Elton had let me keep the Fairlane hire car for a week, and I preferred driving to flying. I stopped at tourist town Gundagai en route where I purchased a bedspread of sheep and calfskin as my belated wedding present to Elton and Renate. I gave it to them when they arrived in my home town, Melbourne, a week later.

About 13 hours after leaving Sydney I was home. Opening the door of my apartment and stepping into its darkness nearly broke my heart. The loneliness was palpable. Elton had trans-

ferred the curse of his life on to mine. Who could I trust? The
stillness in the room was a slap in the face, a cruel reminder of
my changed status. No room service. No well stocked bar. No
more limos. No more First Class travel. No luxurious
surroundings. No Elton. Welcome to the real world, kiddo.
Welcome home. Alone. Suddenly I felt very tired. The events of
the last week had taken their toll. Oh Renate, I hissed, you're
such a lucky thing.

Within two weeks the marriage had started to falter. Elton was
panicking and Renate had fled to England. Officially, of course,
the story was that she had decided to renovate Woodside – put
the stamp of the new mistress on the manor. Reports suggested
the marriage had been on the rocks before the couple cleared the
Heads. Elton and Renate denied all rumours, and the façade went
up. The publicists were set to their task.

I was to see Renate alone soon after the marriage for, when
she stopped over in Melbourne before flying back to the United
Kingdom, we spent some time together. She looked drained, and
even when I greeted her, I was disturbed by how unlike a new
bride she looked. She confided that, during the most intimate
moments with Elton, it was as if a shutter had come down
between them. Her new husband simply couldn't surrender
himself. He could give. Oh, yes, he could always give. But our
poor, talented, darling Elton could not receive. It was, is, his
tragedy.

In a way I'd anticipated these problems. For the last 12 years,
Elton John rock star had called the shots. When he had a fling,
he could always unload the intruder. He could retreat to his
bedroom any time he wanted. He had his privacy on tap: all he
had to do was to tell Bob or Reid to 'Get that person out of here,'
and it would be done.

But with Mrs Elton John that couldn't be done. He couldn't
tell her to vacate the bedroom at his whim. He couldn't tell her,
'I need my space.' He suddenly had to confront the realization

that hers was a true and strong femininity, a confident spirit. And he had not had to deal with this before. Survival instinct had driven him to choose her, but in the whole fanfare and theatre of being unpredictable Elton had not given any thought to the consequences of his marriage to Renate. True love has no purpose. It is a matter of being. It cannot be used to save one's self, no matter how important the star.

Having a woman in his life was to challenge Elton's preconceptions. He was going to be forced to confront himself, and he was not yet ready. So, wilting under the pressures of an intimate relationship, he resorted to his usual plea for 'private time'. The crowds who cheered at the ceremony must have envied him: rich, talented pop star finding the girl of his dreams and staging a marriage ceremony beyond their imagination – the razzmatazz, the publicity, the expense. Yet, at this point, the mother in his heart still ruled all powerful, and his absent father shaped his destiny. Perhaps the marriage was just a publicity stunt. Or the result of Elton's compulsive elated moods and wild metabolic swings. Whatever, it had certainly got to him, and he was out of control.

My feelings focused on the bride's dilemma. I felt upset when Renate told me the problems they were facing. My heart went out to her when she indicated that after two weeks the marriage had not been consummated. I felt sad and bitter about this whole wretched mess.

'We'll sort out our problems at Woodside,' Renate spoke bravely, 'we'll have a lot more time to ourselves to talk . . . I guess . . . no interruptions.'

I knew Elton too well. It wouldn't happen. But I nodded and said: 'Yeah, when you're alone you can discuss things.' Renate was another lamb to be slaughtered on the altar of Fame. Elton and I were attracted to each other because we were so alike as people. We reached for Renate at the same time. Now Renate and I were holding on to each other because we were the victims. Mind you, Elton was also a victim. Who wins? Well, there's John Reid and Bob and Patti Mostyn and the like. But the real beneficiaries are the millions of fans whose lives are filled with hope for the price of a song.

If there was one thing to smile about it was that, by now, Elton would have told Reid the marriage wasn't rocking along too well. And I could picture Reid's face, puffed in panic. The pre-nuptial agreement! She hadn't signed any goddamn pre-nuptial agreement.

9. Don't Let the Sun Go Down on Me

'This is from Elton. $200. For services rendered.'

ALTHOUGH THOSE WITHIN the inner sanctum were aware of the Johns' marital problems, it wouldn't leak to the British papers for another 18 months. The media was so engrossed in the 'fairy tale' romance and marriage that this deflected deflected the questions about Renate's sudden return to England. 'Prior commitments' was the official line, and the gullible media soaked it up.

In fact, by the time she returned to Woodside, both Renate and Elton had begun to realize the extent of the frightening emotional minefield that stretched before them. But they seemed determined to make a go of it. Renate found herself catapulted into a whirlwind of extravagance and inflated egos. After being an anonymous worker, it wasn't surprising that she enjoyed being rich and famous.

'It didn't take her long to get a taste for jewellery,' Elton said, joking about his bride's rapid adaptation to the pleasures of instant cash. But he really wasn't serious for he spared her nothing, and she remained relatively unspoilt. Like Elton at his best, Renate was kind, considerate and a lot of fun, and she seemed to see her powerful position as a means of helping others rather than a platform for her own ego. For instance, two weeks after the marriage, when I accompanied her to Melbourne Airport on her stopover between New Zealand and Woodside, I complained of a nagging toothache. Renate rummaged in her handbag and proffered a few hundred dollars to pay for some treatment. I protested no, but she sternly insisted I accept her generosity.

Everything Renate said convinced me she was devoted to Elton, that she loved him, thought endlessly of him, and that her only wish was to please him. Elton had a different perspective. As much as he loved Renate, he saw the marriage ceremony as a social initiation rite, allowing entry into another stratum of mature adult society. In particular, Elton craved acceptance from Watford's board members and supporters whom he thought considered their patron a big fat poof with too much money and no brains. A respectable marriage had other very special advantages for him for potentially it further opened royal doors. Of course not everyone with breeding and wealth lived on the straight and narrow, but the establishment didn't mind if it was one of their own. It was the outsiders who had to prove themselves, and a hint of scandal would wipe them from the list of the socially acceptable.

Elton referred to Renate as 'wifey' and spoke to interviewers about having children. Whenever they appeared in public, he would touch her affectionately, and the couple would exchange frequent loving glances. In interviews he would shower her with compliments.

After Renate's premature departure from the New Zealand tour, Elton and I saw each other a couple more times. When he rang, I would visit his hotel; and Elton flew me to Sydney to catch the last Australian show. But, for me, the rules had changed. He was now my ex, and as far as I could tell, he was determined to have Renate as his sole bedmate. I respected the new bride too much to damage their relationship in any way.

When Elton rejoined Renate at Woodside, he lavished gifts, flowers and stylish clothing on his new bride. Elton knew that the awkward transition from ex-employee to equal partner would take time and that it would be, at times, uncomfortable. But Elton helped Renate to adapt by supporting her in every possible way and made it clear to all and sundry that this woman was queen of his life. Both Reid and Halley were informed that Renate's wish was their command. No doubt Elton's henchmen were insecure but, given his protective mood, they knew that if they rocked the boat they would more than likely be breaststroking toward a different shore. Much better to tolerate the intruder and let time take its corrosive course.

Elton urged Renate to convert Woodside from an expensive and expansive museum to a home. However, apart from renovating the kitchen and introducing subtle changes to the master bedroom, Renate left Woodside as it was. Elton insisted that his wife should shape one of the mansion's bedrooms to her own taste, and so the queen's private chamber evolved. In defining her space, Renate installed her own, private telephone line and bought a computer system that helped while away the hours. Renate was slowly relaxing into an extravagant, hedonistic lifestyle but was having difficulty with the sheer scale of it all.

I rang Renate a couple of times after her arrival at Woodside and gained the impression that she found the house intimidating: 'I rarely use the squash court or cinema,' she confided. 'The two of us spend hours watching video movies together,' she giggled, 'and he's been buying heaps of movies, so I told him I'm going to catalogue them.' It was amazing how Renate and I reacted similarly to situations for when I first went to Woodside that was exactly my reaction to Elton's jumble. A little later on I rang for days without an answer and when I finally made contact she moaned, 'I've been to a health farm because I'm stacking on weight . . . I thought I loved chocolates but Elton's just as bad. When we're watching movies, we go through mountains of them.'

The first obvious sign that celebrity status was intruding was the number of times she changed her private telephone line number. Like Elton, Renate soon learnt that privacy was a precious commodity that the public treated with contempt. When she found that her phone number was in general circulation, or if someone was becoming a nuisance, Renate would simply dial for a new one. She was quickly learning the incommunicado game.

Later that year, Sheila and Derf came to Australia to visit my parents. From what Sheila told me, relations with her daughter-in-law were strained, and although she did not blame Renate for Elton's behaviour, she felt the girl could have persuaded him to look to his mother's feelings when making arrangements for the wedding. Elton had made no effort to introduce Renate to his mother before their marriage and held the event at a place and time that made it difficult for her and Derf to attend.

Sheila knew that after their confrontation, Elton was deliberately distancing himself from her, and that Renate was part of this imbroglio. Sheila had not forgiven Elton for the public – and humiliating – symbolic gesture of the long distance, short-notice, no-consultation wedding. It was an act of defiance for, despite her close involvement in his life, Elton had chosen to marry a girl who was a stranger to her.

But Sheila, the eternal optimist and doting mother, was eternally forgiving and as she had no personal argument with Renate, she did her best to establish a warm relationship with her. Unfortunately for Sheila, Renate was not the chatty type of daughter-in-law who would pop in for a gossip over a cup of tea or invite the rels over for a Sunday roast. She and Derf didn't go to Woodside that much any more.

By this time my involvement with my career had helped me overcome Elton's cruel deception. The computer market was booming in Australia, and buffs, like myself, who had learnt to master its software, were in demand. I worked in a local store selling computers. At around the same time, a software distribution firm called Imagineering was rapidly expanding. As my experience grew so did my reputation, and in late 1984 I was poached by Imagineering and was to be transferred within months to their head office in Sydney. Elton's parents arrived in February 1985 to stay with my parents and went cruising on a houseboat at Lake Eildon for two weeks. I stayed with them for a week-end before leaving for Sydney to take up my new job.

I shared a flat in Elizabeth Bay on Sydney harbour with singer Alison Jiar. It was 1985, and things were rolling along nicely for me. Elton was also travelling well. His album later that year, *Ice on Fire*, saw him reunited with original arranger, Gus Dudgeon, and Elton had hit the charts again – in a big way. 'Nikita' reached No. 3 in Britain and No. 7 in the United States. Those who knew him were whispering that the loneliness expressed in the lyrical, mournful ballad, 'Nikita', alluded to his marriage.

Ice on Fire also featured a duet with George Michael on the Culture Club track 'Wrap Her Up'. George and Elton had developed a close friendship. George had always idolized Elton's songwriting, and, fittingly, in March 1985 Elton presented an Ivor Novello award for Best Songwriter (for 'Careless Whisper') to a tearful George. Elton publicly acclaimed George as the 'Paul McCartney of his generation'.

George and Elton had met in France six months earlier. The pair immediately hit it off for not only did they have great respect for each other's work but they also had had similar childhoods. They had both grown up feeling lonely and unattractive, and had been indulged by their mothers. In George's case, his mother tried to compensate for his father's long absences. George's father worked long and hard, as is the migrant tradition, and his success was the base from which his children could more easily ascend the social ladder. Elton's father was also absent, but for very different reasons. Both performers constructed an outrageous public persona and chose catchy, marketable names before becoming multi-millionaires at a young age. George Michael had not even celebrated his 21st birthday before his personal fortune was estimated at nearly US$58 million. And when it came to looks, both were chocolate fanatics who had to work hard to keep their weight down.

The two men had business ties as well. They shared a publicist, Gary Farrow, who had started out as a record plugger at Elton's Rocket Records and went on to build an impressive clientele that included David Bowie, Paul Young and Bob Geldof. Like Elton, George ended up in court with Dick James Music: the publisher claimed 'Last Christmas' had a similar melody to Barry Manilow's 'Can't Smile Without You'. George won the case.

The Elton/George involvement came at a time when George had outgrown his professional partnership in Wham! with Andrew Ridgeley. George knew that he needed to develop into, and be perceived as, a 'mature performer', and Ridgeley's playboy antics were proving to be a liability. When the offer came to sing on an Elton John track, to George it was a dream come true, and it helped his image enormously. On 13 July 1985, Elton and George teamed up again, this time for the star-studded Live Aid project. There was an Australian concert, held in Luna Park, Sydney, with a bill of local acts, headlined by INXS, that coincided with the two Live Aid mega-concerts held at London's Wembley and Philadelphia's RKF Stadium.

Having been upset by the TV news footage of starving Africans, I headed for Luna Park. It was time for me to pay my dues and to support the cause by attending in person. And I must admit, I thought it would be a good concert. As I approached the gate, Molly Meldrum, the concert's compère, spotted me and invited me to join him. 'This is Crystal, he used to be with Elton,' was the way Molly introduced me around. I thought someone might be tempted to tip me up to check my 'use-by' date.

George Michael's fortunes changed because of that night. After a set with Wham!, George was introduced and accompanied on piano by Elton. George sang an Elton super-hit 'Don't Let the Sun Go Down on Me', and Ridgeley and Kiki Dee provided backing vocals. Until then Elton's career had been apolitical, but Live Aid provided him with the impetus, and the platform, to make powerful statements. He tapped into the charity circuit, and the fundraisers were pleased to accept his voluntary services.

Like patrons of old, Elton and his management had come to realize the multiple benefits of being involved in charity work. It was fairly simple really. As well as ensuring worthwhile causes received funds, superstars could be publicly redeemed for all previous sins – real or imagined. The charity stamp can even validate lousy performances, and the cost is minimal. Expenses can be generously estimated and written off against the year's overall income, and the free and benevolent publicity generated by the event more than pays for the time, effort and expense involved in these projects. It's a win-win situation. Of course there is also the boost to the performer's ego: magnanimous gestures at a universal level can be very satisfying.

Elton's advisers have learnt this PR lesson well. Whenever under media scrutiny, they wait for a lull in the battle and throw a tax-effective charity performance, knowing that the last slice of publicity is the image that remains. Elton's relatively unsuccessful 1993 Australian tour was a classic. Prior to and during the tour Elton had received publicity over his previous encounters with me, then just before he was scheduled to leave the country he threw an AIDS charity concert, which was nationally televised and restored his good image. Elton also appeared on a high-rating Saturday night show, *Hey, Hey, Its Saturday*, to promote the same cause, and I was amused to see a round and jolly John Reid beaming from the tube that Saturday night, squeaky clean with a grin from ear to ear. I was almost tempted to wave back but we're not on speaking terms any more.

After that first 1985 Live Aid Concert, Elton's and George Michael's careers started to criss-cross. Six months later Elton and Wham! found themselves sharing the same stage. This time it was at the annual British Phonographic Industry awards when they were presented with special trophies for outstanding merit. Elton received his, belatedly, for taking British pop to Russia. That feat was accomplished six years earlier in 1979. Wham! received an award for an innovative tour of China.

The presentations were made by the British Government's icon of conservatism, Norman Tebbit, whose bureaucrats had actively stifled the arts for years. They were now promoting popular music because the industry's export earnings were substantial, and the Tory party needed to foster the youth vote. After the awards Elton felt he had been manipulated by the Conservative's PR machine and, on returning to his hotel room, he smashed his trophy in disgust.

A few months after that, Elton played piano on a remix of 'Wham! Rap', which was included on Wham!'s final EP. During the month of its release, Elton and his white grand piano made a surprise appearance when Wham! played their farewell performance at Wembley Stadium on Saturday, 28 June 1986, before 72,000 distraught fans. Elton emerged as McDonald's mascot clown, Ronald McDonald, and sang 'Candle in the Wind' with George. He later reappeared decked out in a fetching pink mohican and a drape coat, and joined in on 'I'm Your Man' with Duran Duran's Simon Le Bon.

Temperatures soared into the nineties that day, but Elton was prepared for the heat. According to the *Sun* our boy kept cool in the comfort of a 60-foot air-conditioned mobile caravan complete with well-stocked bar, synthetic lawn and a portable child's pool. Apparently, although the pool was miniature, it was popular. Backstage, Elton mingled with guests like Le Bon and his wife Yasmin; members of Frankie Goes To Hollywood; Rod Stewart; Gary Kemp of Spandau Ballet; Paula Yates; designer Jasper Conran; and Patsy Kensit.

Elton and George Michael's careers bonded in other ways. Both became ardent AIDS research fundraisers, and around the same time they began traumatic run-ins with some of the British tabloids.

As the battle escalated journalists tried to suggest that a friendship based on mutual admiration for musical talent was something more, although they never proved otherwise. One paper offered up to £50,000 for a story on George's sex life, and another insinuated that he lived in mortal fear of contracting

AIDS. This rumour was based on George's revelation that he had not had an AIDS test.

By 1986 the British tabloids had focused on something that even casual friends of Elton and Renate had been whispering about for some time: the marriage wasn't working. The media became aware because of the tell-tale signs evident in every marriage break-up. The couple were hardly seen together in public except for official functions such as a music award show or a Watford gathering – and the marriage hadn't yet reached its second year. There were also snide remarks circulating about Elton's 'gay' past.

When the solemn and soberly dressed Johns arrived at Prince Andrew's and Sarah Ferguson's wedding, the papers built another twist in the tale. Elton was friendly with both Andrew and Fergie, and he attended Andrew's buck's turn at the Guards Polo Club. That was the night Fergie and Lady Di attempted to gatecrash the bawdy event dressed as policewomen and were affectionately jeered at by Andy and his inebriated guests. Elton had a fond regard for Andrew and Fergie and as a wedding gift recorded a special version of 'Song To Guy'. What the papers bought into the relationship was the claim that the royal newly-weds had been 'coaxing' the Johns to 'give their marriage a second chance'.

Elton's marriage niggled at the public's sense of propriety, and the alliance was always of interest. On a French TV pro-gramme, *Truth Game,* Elton agreed to answer any question. He circled enquiries about his 'happy' marriage, turning 40 and even one about wedlock, covering up his homosexuality with profes-sional aplomb. When one caller sneered, 'I remember seeing you on a beach in St Tropez, you were surrounded by beautiful boys,' Elton quickly turned it to his advantage. 'Before the caller saw me with a beautiful boy, and now I'm with a beautiful woman.' It was the perfect answer – glib, funny and evasive.

During a US tour, which followed the French broadcast, Elton continually claimed that marital rifts were a British media fantasy. As if to prove a point, his next album, *Leather Jackets,* contained

a track written by Renate under her nom de plume, Lady Choc
Ice, the character Elton assumed when his cynical sense of
humour dictated a patrician tone. Still, he showed his appreci-
ation of Renate's support by conspicuously thanking her on the
sleeve credits for being 'a continuous source of inspiration'.

But in November 1986, when Elton arrived in Australia to
tour, Renate was conspicuously absent. Elton and I had been out
of touch for almost a year at this stage, and the last time we had
spoken was when Sheila and Derf had visited Australia in January
1986 to holiday with my parents. Elton had, through his parents,
sent me a beautiful Japanese black designer sweater that cost
about £500, a white silk shirt and a pair of bright red Doc Martens
that were three sizes too big. There was a brief message attached
to the package: 'Hope all is well, love Elton.' Short but very
sweet. There was no mention of Renate in the greeting, and as
the gift was unexpected, I rang to thank Elton for the thought as
much as for the items.

During that year Elton had thrown himself into a tight touring
and recording schedule, taking a rain-check on his personal life.
For my part, I had left my computer job in Sydney and returned
to Melbourne, moving in temporarily with my sister Deborah.

My working life took a different direction when I landed a job
with Australian dancer Tony Battuccio, working as an assistant at
his dance school. I then worked for producer David Wilson who
had established a company specializing in fashion parades and
promotional functions and events. By the time Elton returned to
Australia, I'd moved out of my sister's place and settled into a flat
in the Melbourne bayside suburb of Elwood. In a positive frame
of mind, I'd returned to my original computer company.

Elton's arrival in Sydney was, as usual, on all the Australian
TV and radio news. Publicist Patti Mostyn never missed a beat
and made sure the media was impressed by the inclusion of the
Melbourne Symphony Orchestra on this tour. Elton projected a
more avant-garde, European image this time and a Melbourne
newspaper photo showed him sporting a ponytail pulled tightly
back. The ever present cap continued to protect the star's balding

Above: With Elton at
Bernie Taupin's LA
home. Private
moments were always
hard to come by for us
as a couple.

Right: One stormy
moment was the time
that Elton shaved his
eyebrows in protest
at my desire to return
to Australia without
him. For some days
afterwards he pushed
his hat low over his
forehead and wore
sunglasses.

Above: On holiday in Hawaii, where Elton and his new man, Hugh Williams, had invited me to celebrate Elton's recovery from his addictions to drugs and alcohol.

Left: Inside the exclusive Sebel Town House in Sydney, this shot of a despondent me with a smiling Renate was published as a world exclusive on front pages around the world. It was taken when Elton first made his shock announcement that he and Renate were to marry.

Above: Renate and I after the wedding reception. Following the marriage, she had given me her bridal bouquet of red roses.

Above: Elton in his library at Woodside. Business associates were usually taken there, where apart from enjoying its bar and pool table, selected guests would sometimes be invited to lines of cocaine.

Right: On my arrival at Woodside, Elton took me on a guided tour. One of our first ports of call was the kennels, to make friends with Elton's dogs.

Opposite left: Despite his outrageous performance costumes, Elton projected the dour persona of a serious artist. No one would easily believe that he liked goofing around.

Right: Elton clowning as Groucho Marx for me and my parents. Mum and Dad had entertained us for dinner, and now it was his turn to return the favour. Often Elton would slip into false dowager-duchess accents or play impish practical jokes.

Above: In LA, posing on the gleaming new white Mercedes sports convertible that Elton had hired for me and Cameron to see the sights. In it we cruised down Sunset Boulevard and discovered that Mercs were a dime a dozen in Hollywood.

Left: On tour in Stockholm, I am wearing the pink Christian Dior dressing gown that Elton had given me when I first went to Woodside. Elton's mum, Sheila, could hardly contain her giggles when I had swanned into the kitchen in the robe.

Right: My bedroom at Woodside, complete with TV and stereo system, which Elton had had filled with hundreds of red roses especially for my arrival.

Above: With my
father, Peter, at my
Commercial Pilot's
graduation in 1988.
For some years we
were estranged, but
ultimately we've grown
closer.

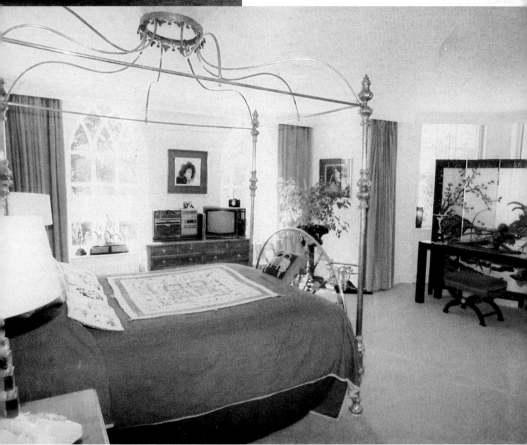

1982: The annual party at Woodside for players and families of Elton's beloved Watford Football Club. Elton used to hoist the Club flag to let people know he was in residence, much like the Union Jack marked Her Majesty's presence at nearby Windsor Castle.

pate from public scrutiny. After reading all the tour's promo hype at work, I took a break from computer duties and paintboxed on the computer screen a CD with the words 'Elton John – Tour De Force', and added the message.

'Welcome back to Australia, hope you have a nice stay.' I keyed in my work phone number, printed it out and faxed the greeting to the Sebel Hotel in Sydney.

Within two hours, Elton was on the phone, in high spirits. He was due in Melbourne soon, and we'd catch up then. A few days later he arrived and called me virtually minutes after he'd checked into his Melbourne hotel. He had no wife in tow and was back at the Hilton, a hotel that he said gave him more privacy.

When we were alone in his suite that evening Elton confessed that his relationship with Renate was on the rocks. He said it in such a matter-of-fact way that Renate already seemed to be contained within his past, consigned there as an interesting, much loved memory, available for reflection if not discussion. When he mentioned her, Elton was sincere in his admiration and always spoke well of her: 'She's really great to put up with me,' he would say in typical self-deprecating style.

It was obvious that Elton wasn't happy or healthy, but although his face was pudgy, and he looked miserable, he was wildly enthusiastic about the upcoming tour – especially because his 27 shows around Australia were designed to coincide with the visiting English cricket team's matches. A diet of cricket wasn't Elton's only unusual request for he had only agreed to do the MSO dates if James Newton-Howell, the famed conductor, would arrange his compositions.

Elton wanted me to fly to Sydney for the last show, right before Christmas, which ABC (the government-run television network) was going to broadcast live and national. It would also be recorded for a subsequent live album and video release.

The early shows received rave reviews from Australian critics. Elton's mixture of high drama, high camp and top rock 'n' roll seemed to hit the spot. For the opening set, Elton performed with a 13-piece band, sported a fright wig and wore a black suit with huge white stars that flashed under the spotlights. 'Funeral For a Friend' gave way for highlights like 'Rocket Man', which Elton transformed into a blues with brass interjections; during 'The Bitch is Back' Elton playfully indicated that the tough girl was him; there was a lovely moment during 'Benny & The Jets' when Elton lay on the floor under the piano, and, as the classical composer Mozart had done centuries earlier, Elton played perfectly. During the show he had undergone an extraordinary metamorphosis, appearing in 18th-century pink satin as an 80s Mozart, complete with wig, white make-up and beauty spot.

It was hard to imagine that Elton selected the Mozart character at random, for the two musicians had a lot in common. Both were inventive composers and pianists of remarkable and enduring talent who were patronized by royalty, and both were considered by established society as immature and outrageous rebels, whose torrid emotional lives energized their compositions and performances. Some close to Elton would say that his choice of character was appropriate for less complimentary reasons. Mozart's sense of recklessness and emotional intensity could be a cross that others had to bear; however, this is of little concern to audiences whose reward is the legacy that music geniuses such as he and Elton leave in their wake.

But why did Elton wait until now to make known his interest in Mozart? It seemed that as middle age approached Elton had become more aware of his own mortality and felt a need to define the breadth of his talent and the musicality of his work. What other choice than to draw the comparison by engaging a symphony orchestra? The Melbourne Symphony was chosen for the task, and it was brilliant in realizing Elton's dream. The concerts revealed the exquisite poignancy of Elton's melodies and provided a depth and range that fully explored the musicality, emotion and energy of his complex compositions.

This innovative, ambitious classical approach showcased Elton's unique theatrical style and musical abilities and demon- strated that despite an outrageous image, he was a consummate artist who could adapt to, and be comfortable in any musical company. Being a Melbourne boy, I have always taken some pride in the fact that, as a schoolboy, one of Elton's influential music teachers, a stooped character called Bent, came from my home town. Mr Bent would have been well-pleased with his protégé's performance in front of the prestigious Melbourne Symphony.

For those who had attended the rehearsals, it was no surprise that the South Australian and first two Western Australian shows were outstanding successes. But no one excepting Elton could have anticipated that it would all of a sudden stop there. In all but a literal sense, the wheels fell right off Elton's act. Sitting in his dressing room before the third Perth concert, Elton realized he was in trouble: he had lost his voice. The next show was cancelled and a doctor advised the anxious star not to speak for four days. Despite his concern, Elton avoided panic among the troops by resorting to humour, using his small blackboard for sight gags and contorting his face as he gulped soothing mixtures of honey and lemon. Never at a loss for something to do, Elton made productive use of his forced recreation by relaxing at cricket matches.

When oceans separated Elton and Renate, the errant husband could more freely indulge his sleazy ways, and I became suspicious when, on this tour, Elton enlisted the services of a young guy to assist with stage costumes. Knowing Elton, I felt the lad would have had talents that extended well beyond the zipper. It looked like marriage had lost its hold, and my suspicion was confirmed when Elton, soon after he arrived in Melbourne, casually asked if I knew anyone who might be interested in joining us for a threesome. If I wanted to be back on the social list, I had no doubt as to my instructions.

At that time, I was living close to Melbourne's redlight area and had come to know two 18-year-old street hustlers, Stephen and Mick. Mick and I became good friends, and he visited me at home, sometimes with Stephen in tow, and they would regale me with tales of tricks they had serviced, laughing about how effeminate types would beg these tough-looking guys to 'treat-em mean'. This was a role they relished for the boys loved aggression, the rougher the better. Normally I would be wary of this sort of rough trade, but there was a sense of recklessness and adventure about the boys that was very appealing, and I was in need of friendship. In time, Mick and I started going to bed.

When Elton sounded me out about a threesome, I took the unlikely pair to the first Melbourne show, gathering our tickets at the gate and slipping into the dressing-room area through a back door. Elton instantly took a shine to Mick who looked terrific in tight T-shirt and jeans, with the hint of a tattoo peeking out under his sleeve. 'He'll do me, Chook,' Elton said, licking the edges of his lips. But although Mick passed muster, unfortunately Stephen's social etiquette wasn't considered up to scratch, and his eyes looked psycho.

An hour after the show, Elton had cleared his suite of well-wishers, and as planned, Mick and I took the elevator to the top floor. As was usual in these circumstances, Elton had showered and was naked under his towelling dressing gown. From there on in the action took on a familiar pattern. We sipped champagne, loosening-up our guest attraction who soon progressed from the bubbly to brandy to beer and back again.

At this point, just prior to the sexual athletics, Elton slipped into the bathroom and snorted the two obligatory white lines and returned, telling us to undress. It was a short session, and Elton ejaculated before any extra games could be played. No polaroids tonight. In his long-honoured custom, the exhausted star rolled over and mumbled how tired he was, before suggesting that we should leave. Not so much as a thank-you. Without a word, Mick and I cleaned ourselves, dressed and left. On the way home, I passed over a wad of cash, $200 (£100) to the still intoxicated Mick. He took the money, and we headed off to finish what Elton had started.

• • •

Because of his throat problem, Elton returned to Melbourne for an extended stay over Christmas. This time, to keep himself amused, he selected a tanned blond Sydney surfer – nominally a tour helper. The kid was straight but seemed quite excited about the glamour of touring with a superstar, and I'm not sure of his duties except that he seemed to do a lot of shopping with Elton's money. His other main pastime seemed to be perving on girls. Still, of a night, the boy could usually be found in Elton's suite. The maid who had to tidy up the boy's room had very little work to do each morning. He became known as 'the latest ELF [Elton's Little Fuck].'

Elton was very keen that the ELF and I became acquainted, so he encouraged me to join them both on clubbing jaunts where talk inevitably focused on hot sex. On one occasion Elton suggested that ELF sleep over in my bed, but nothing eventuated. Another time Bob and I were commissioned to drive ELF to Torquay, a picturesque and popular surf beach about an hour out of Melbourne. We had orders to buy the boy a surfboard and to wait until he tired of riding the waves. The board was an early Christmas present, Elton had announced before we left. Presents like this, and holiday trips, were Elton's way of saying thanks. It was a little bit more dignified than dishing out cash.

Christmas Day was fast approaching, and judging by past experience Elton would not be in a good mood. However, I invited him to have Christmas lunch at my place, but he had other plans. During the tour he had taken a shine to Melbourne Symphony's first violinist, Robert John, and had accepted an invitation to the musician's home for Christmas Day dinner. So he spent the day with Robert – and with the violinist's wife and children.

Poor Elton. When it comes to romance he always seems to lead with his chin. He sets himself up to lose, attempting the near impossible, yet he knows how much even a hint of rejection angers him. There is more than a touch of masochism and self-abuse about this penchant for punishment. And here he was doing it again, for it was obvious to everyone, except Elton, that Robert certainly wasn't overawed by Elton's stardom or compellingly attracted to Elton's personality – well, not enough to stray from the straight life. Elton seemed to read sensitivity and softness as indications of homosexuality, and it ain't necessarily so.

One night, when Elton was whining about this unrequited love, I asked the obvious: 'Does Robert know you fancy him?'

'I told him I loved him, and I wanted him,' Elton snapped. 'Could I get any more direct than that?' I guess you couldn't. At times like that, No, usually means, No.

Elton's legendary excesses peaked during tours and this Aussie tour was no exception. Each of the 88 members of the Melbourne Symphony was presented with a £500 Cartier watch, and English cricketer Ian Botham, Elton's sports idol, received a Cartier bag containing a groin protector. Patti Mostyn received an expensive piece of jewellery in consideration for her outstanding publicity efforts. I'd received my present a few days earlier. A CD player, an autographed copy of *Leather Jacket* and £1750 in cash.

Elton had never been to my place, nor had I ever spoken about it, but he wanted me to use the money to buy some furniture for my flat. I was quite taken aback. He had rung my mother to find out what I really wanted. How thoughtful, I mused. Next day, Patti Mostyn took me aside and asked earnestly: 'Gary, Elton's asked Bob to give him about $3000 [£1500] in cash ... do you know what that was for?' I stared at her aghast. What the hell did it have to do with her?

'No, I don't know anything about that' I said coldly.

With the New Year concerts approaching, Elton had to face the reality of his throat problems, but when the tour hit Sydney he foolishly ignored his condition, and his voice rapidly deteriorated. After the third night of coughing up blood, Elton's doctor insisted he see a throat specialist. The tour entourage were at the Sebel bar when Elton returned from the consultation. His face was ashen, and he looked scared. The doctors thought it could be throat cancer. Elton was understandably devastated. That was just the start. The next few days were pandemonium, though Elton put on a brave public face: 'I'm not worried.' To his closest friends, he would sob and admit, 'You wouldn't believe how scared I am.'

Even in this crisis it was extraordinary how Elton's professionalism shone through. The question was should he proceed with the final show, which was to be telecast to the nation, or should he heed his doctor's advice and take a complete rest from performing? The first option carried an additional, albeit less deadly, risk in that the telecast was to be live, and Elton knew he would not be singing anywhere near his best. Yet, despite this, he put his ego behind him and went ahead, offering the best he had to give. I thought he was remarkably brave, and the circumstances brought out his noblest and most endearing qualities. He need not have worried about the effect on his reputation for in terms of its emotional impact and musical integrity, that concert was equal to the best of the tour. Elton had made sure that if this was to be his swan-song, it would be a boomer.

After the concert Elton flew to Canberra to see Dr John Tonkin, Australia's foremost ear, nose and throat surgeon. The prognosis was nodules near his voice box. If they were cancerous, Elton would not even speak properly again, let alone sing. The tension that surrounded Elton and his friends was electric, but all the publicity was low key. As it turned out, after an operation in Sydney to remove the nodules, a biopsy revealed the lumps to be benign, which was a relief all round.

While Elton was recuperating, cards and bouquets flooded in from all over the world – including well wishes from the Duke and Duchess of York and the Prince and Princess of Wales. Having noted how life-threatening illnesses have changed the way people perceive things, I was looking for any change in Elton's behaviour. In particular I was interested to see how he would now treat his wife. The media realized that Renate had not flown to her ailing husband's side. They could allow for the fact that the two didn't spend Christmas together, what with professional engagements and travel as the barriers. But not to be there when Elton might have a terminal illness? That was unforgivable.

The gossip was that Elton had complained to Renate about her absence, claiming it was bad for his image. According to the buzz, she had refused to comply with Elton's requests because for the last few months he had been cutting her out of his life. Hadn't they spent a mere three days together in the last four months? Why should she live his lie any longer? According to reports, the pair had a heated argument – and Elton decided there and then to initiate a divorce.

Naturally the 'forsaken husband–angry wife' line was preferred by the British tabloids. The *Sunday People*, as early as January 1987, reported that the marriage was over, and that Elton's refusal to forgo male companions was to blame. However, a most inventive counter-tale circulated, which claimed that, rather than divorcing, the couple were so in love they were about to enjoy a second honeymoon on a luxury yacht, with – wink, wink – a mirrored ceiling in the bedroom. Renate's media relations adviser even made a formal announcement that Elton's wife was to fly from LA to Sydney on 22 January to meet with her husband prior to embarking on the love cruise. In fact, Renate flew to Britain and continued to produce a record featuring Sylvia Griffin, former singer with Kiss the Pink.

The tabloids were starting to take offence at the continual and hollow denials that the Johns' marital rift was turning into a gulf. These corny announcements were an insult even to their intelligence, so the journos increased their vigilance and took to the Johns like hounds on the scent of a fox. To make the point that Elton wasn't on his promised love cruise with Renate, the press published a photo of him cruising Sydney Harbour with longtime friend, Peter Iken of Warner Brothers Records. Iken, who could often be found in Sydney, was the character that Elton deposited me with when he dumped me in LA back in 1982. Iken was not gay, but the pic of Elton and male friend was splashed across front pages. Wink, wink. But anyone who really knew the pair would realize they were hardly each other's type.

Much worse publicity was yet to come. There was a story out

about a Brisbane ex-cop who went on trial for seducing boys. Apparently the cop had attempted to impress his victims by telling them he was a friend of Elton John. No proof existed that Elton even knew the guy. Whatever the reality, the cop story was just the dirt the tabloids needed to juice up their allegations. My poor Elton, if only he knew that the torment had just started and that his past was about to sink its claws in deep and long. The heavy artillery was about a month away.

The phone jangled. My clock radio was showing midnight. I'd sent Elton a card for his 40th birthday a few days earlier, on 25 March 1987. John Reid had thrown a party at his new ten-bedroom Georgian house for his client and friend. There were 350 guests, including ex-Beatles George Harrison and Ringo Starr, Eric Clapton, Phil Collins, Bob Geldof, Britt Eckland, designer Zandra Rhodes, actor John Mills, Hazel O'Connor, pop entrepreneurs Richard Branson and Mickie Most, the Watford team and the Duke and Duchess of York. Reid had Elton's present, an £80,000 Ferrari Testarossa sports car, gift-wrapped in pink ribbons.

Renate wasn't there but during his thank-you speech Elton made her apologies: she had the flu. You could imagine the press reaction next morning, all in unison, 'Oh, yeah!' As if to prove his point, and to convey a sense of everlasting bliss, Elton flourished an antique diamond and ruby watch, apparently Renate's gift to him. The audience looked on ruefully. In usual flamboyant fashion, the party concluded with a fireworks display that illuminated Reid's mansion and most of the surrounding district.

But the call to me that night was not to thank me for the card. Elton sounded distraught, his words tumbling over one another. I managed to decipher what he was saying: I was on the front page of that morning's *Sun*. But, I protested, I hadn't spoken to anyone. Elton said the British press had just turned on him recently, and this was just part of it. The fake scoop revealed we had gone through a marriage ceremony when we first met.

Elton didn't know what was going on. The press had been good to him over these years, but now he was on their hit-list. They were digging up the dirt, raking up allegations about boys and sex and what not. He wanted me to be careful, because they would try to approach me.

I had no doubt that Elton was genuinely amazed at the hiding they were dishing out and assured him I wouldn't say anything. Nevertheless he worried for me and suggested I should leave Melbourne for a while, which I really couldn't manage, having just got back from Sydney. But he'd made his point: the heat was on for him in England, and he didn't want me involved.

After briefly recounting what had gone down, he asked me if I was still interested in being a pilot. He'd really hit the spot. It was still my life's dream. So he suggested I do a course somewhere out of town, at his expense. Then I would be happy and out of harm's way.

The story that started Elton's massive media trial was the invention of a mischievous 19-year-old London rent boy called Steven Hardy. A month earlier, Hardy had walked into the *Sun*'s offices and recounted a lurid story of sex and cocaine orgies with Elton at the Finchampstead, Berkshire home of Rod Stewart's one-time manager, Billy Gaff. Hardy's salacious story had the newshounds drooling. The rent boy alleged he had procured young lads for Gaff's parties and that these orgies had sometimes run for four days. Hardy also claimed each prostitute was paid £100 and offered limitless quantities of cocaine. Then he built Elton into the plot.

Hardy claimed Elton loved his boys to be tattooed punks or skinheads and that he 'begged' them to indulge him in his bondage fantasies. To add authenticity, Steve said Elton had fantasized about screwing him while he was tied to a tree deep in the woods. And, to add a bit of domestic spice, Steve said that these orgies took place in the early part of 1986 – at a time when Elton told the world he was happily married to Renate. Some of the paper's journalists and lawyers were incredulous, and as Hardy was receiving £2000 for his revelations, he could hardly be considered an unbiased witness. The non-believers advised the *Sun*'s executives to run some fact-checks before proceeding. It was eventually decided that Hardy would be referred to as Graham X, and the story hit the streets on 25 February 1987, with banner headlines blaring ELTON IN VICE BOYS SCANDAL. After the news hit Britain's TV and radio news bulletins it was soon echoed around the world. And on that very day the *Sun* was issued immediately with the first of many writs from Elton's lawyers. The battle was on.

Next day, to show their disdain for Elton's legal manoeuvres, the *Sun* dished up a variation on the same theme, headlined ELTON'S KINKY KICKS. The subhead read, 'The Story They're Suing Over'. This time they added details, including allegations such as how Elton would slice his cocaine with an American Express Gold Card and snort the drug through £50 notes. At a more personal level they added Hardy's claim that, without drugs, Elton's sex life couldn't reach lift-off.

Elton continued the legal assault. Six more writs arrowed their way to the *Sun*'s office, but the paper continued to hammer home allegation after allegation. Elton was panicking for, although rock stars saw a dusting of disgrace as a means of maintaining a fashionably rebellious profile, a full-blown scandal could destroy one's career. There are plenty of examples, but the classic case was Jerry Lee Lewis. He was railroaded out of Britain when it was discovered that his new wife was his 13-year-old cousin. Marriage to a younger relative was a common occurrence in Deep South, USA, but definitely not acceptable in London. Jerry's run of hits ceased in the UK. But Elton was not to suffer Lewis's fate for, within days of its release, the *Sun*'s web of scandal started to unravel.

It was a rival newspaper, the *Daily Mirror*, that came to the rescue. These competing journos successfully sought an account of Elton's movements from the man himself and compared it with rent-boy Hardy's scurrilous tale for discrepancies. Of course Hardy had painted himself in as attractive a light as a self-proclaimed pimp possibly can, and it was a romantic tale. He claimed he needed the money to buy an engagement ring for, of all people, his favourite girl. Apparently deep in self-loathing for his salacious past, Hardy was short of cash; he couldn't afford a ring and was forced to swallow his pride and forgo his dignity for the sake of true love. So, according to Hardy, for the very last time in his short but colourful life, he would procure two rent boys for Elton and Gaff. Hardy was very clear about the day this dirty deed was done – 30 April 1986.

It hadn't happened. With dignified glee, Elton told the press he was in New York on that day, accompanied by Bob Halley, and that he stayed at the Carlyle Hotel, where he lunched with an old friend, Tony King, and later discussed costumes with his designer. The *Daily Mirror* verified Elton's claim by contacting British Airways who informed the paper that Elton and Bob had returned to England on 1 May. A New York car-hire firm also confirmed that Elton was an ocean away from the scene of the alleged incident. Mr Hardy, and the *Sun*, were dumped well and truly in it.

The next day, the *Daily Mirror* launched the first of a series of articles rubbishing its arch-rival's claims, and Billy Gaff was bought into the fracas, claiming that he could prove he was in the Philippines on the day of the alleged incident. Elton then sued the *Sun* for £20 million, specifically denying the orgies with under-aged boys.

It was stand-off time. Elton was not lily-white, so it required courage to take on the newspaper. A lot of other rock stars felt that in these circumstances the safest course was to ignore the reports and hope it would blow over. It was a technique that the royals had successfully used for many decades. But Elton was concerned that these allegations would not only put him on trial but also damage people around him, including Renate and me. Elton could also see a successful prosecution preventing future involvement with Watford and the royal family, so failure to prove his innocence could have dire consequences.

Elton's management told a London magazine of the star's more altruistic objective: 'Elton hopes that he might be able to do something to improve journalistic standards in this country. When the legal action is over, he will be going to the Press Council to try and make sure this sort of thing doesn't happen again.'

The case became as much a test of patience as courage. The *Sun*'s tactic was to pile on fresh allegations, hoping that there would be enough substance in one of them to frighten Elton off. For example, they claimed to have three photos of Elton in bed with a young male, for which they'd paid £10,000. They announced they would only print two because the third was: 'Simply too disgusting to print in a family newspaper.'

It was about this time that Mystery Men came into great demand and the *Sun* had a queue of willing pretenders. A 'Malcolm M' claimed to have been at a 'five-day gay sex and cocaine orgy with Elton John'. 'John D' said he had supplied cocaine to Elton and saw him tear the plastic bags with his teeth because he was 'that desperate', and unfounded rumours of Renate's lesbian activities were added to the mix. Every type of rumour was fair game, and they even brought animals into the act. At one stage, Elton was condemned as a cruel animal owner who cut his Rottweiler dogs' vocal chords to create 'silent assassins'. And there was a little bit of Hollywood's *Goodfellas* written into the story with informants supposedly receiving Mafia-style death threats. If you believed it all, Elton made Vlad the Impaler pale into insignificance.

The well-publicized farce reached monumental proportions when spies were assigned to follow Elton to a Los Angeles hotel hoping to catch him with boys. No luck. And, Watergate style, a bug was secreted by unknown agents in Elton's LA hotel room. Again to no avail. In desperation, the *Sun* is reported to have hired someone to locate witnesses who were willing to testify against Elton, but every single witness failed under the interrogation of the *Sun*'s own journalists.

At one stage, when the battle was raging fierce, a *Sun* reporter saw Elton at a club and had the temerity to pressure him for a quote. Tiny But Tough John Reid was waiting in the wings and grabbed the offending scribe by the neck, whacked his head against a pillar, thumped him around the ears and ejected him from the club.

Score: three stitches and a blood-stained shirt for the *Sun* man. An assault charge and a £150 fine for the midget bouncer, Reid, who mumbled sheepishly to the judge that he was very sorry, but he'd had a few drinks.

The incident also earnt Reid a scolding from his star client. As Elton pointed out, Reid's antics reflected very poorly on his employer and needless to say, the *Sun*'s headlines read: ELTON THUG FINED.

The first Elton *v.* the *Sun* trial was a circus. For a start, Elton's lawyers explained that their client did not own Rottweilers but German Shepherds. Secondly, all the dogs had healthy barks. Apparently the story was filed after a reporter had visited Woodside, spotted the dogs and pulled faces. No response so he figured they were 'silent assassins'. The dogs probably thought the reporter was a drunk left over from a Woodside party.

It was a bit of a hoot, but the debunking had serious implications. Once it was established that the *Sun*'s reporting was shoddy, the paper was on the back-foot and defending vigorously. As you can imagine, those around Elton breathed a sigh of relief as public opinion seemed to be turning his way. Regardless of the outcome, though, Elton still wanted to make quite sure that no one could get to me and rang a few days after that first harassed midnight call. He still sounded edgy. His first question was about the pilots' course. Had I found out how much it would cost? It was obvious what was on his mind – bundle Gary out of the way at all costs. But I saw it as an opportunity and had well and truly completed my homework. It came to about $22,000 (£11,000) over nine months, with cost of living, repayments for my car and things like fuel and food, an extra $8,000 (£4,000). He agreed immediately to wire me $30,000 (£15,000). I was dumbstruck, but after regaining my breath, I asked him how things were in London. Elton's reply was extremely aggressive: it was all as bad as ever, and Renate was getting it in the neck too. He felt really protective toward her.

As a result of the London scandal my name appeared in the Melbourne papers, and I thought I had better make mention of it to Elton. A journo wanted my reaction on the rent boys, but I had told them no comment. Elton moaned as he told me to be careful.

With the money from Elton on its way I was able to make my move, and the next day I quit work and donated my furniture to friends. Once again I was relocating at Elton's behest, but this time it was as much to my advantage as his. Making the most of the available time, I rang my former flatmate Ross, who'd moved to Queensland a year before with a new love. They'd since split up, and Ross now lived alone and was eager that I spend some time with him before I started the pilots' course in Cessnock, central New South Wales. On the day before I drove to see Ross in Queensland, Elton rang to check I had received the money and to wish me all the best. He was obviously feeling beleaguered and pretty keen to know that I was well and truly tucked out of sight and out of mind.

My 14 months at the Pilot Academy was probably the happiest period in my life, for I thoroughly enjoyed the company of my fellow students and was fortunate in that the four of us who shared a small dorm were compatible. We came to be the best of friends, hanging out together and urging each other to achieve as best we could. This was one moment in my life when I felt that I really belonged, and it was reinforced when my friends gave me the honour of representing them as their Flight Captain. My social life improved as well for I started a relationship with a student by the name of Simon. We slept together a couple of times but we both knew there was no future in our relationship for Simon wanted a female wife in his life. But our friendship endured.

Meanwhile, back in England, Elton was going through hell. He would later admit that it was 'the worst year in my life', a time when he locked himself away, nursing a dark depression and not able to face the world: 'It was a nightmare. I think it escalated because I wouldn't drop the case and kept issuing them with writs. But it made me enormously miserable and unhappy. When I went into the studio to do the new album, I thought, Christ, I hope I don't do a Marianne Faithfull – her last album was slit your wrists time. I think they [the media] did it to demoralize me, and it really worked. If I hadn't said in 1976 that I was bisexual, maybe it would have been a big deal. But it wasn't news to anybody. The story they printed initially just wasn't true. I can't believe it's not against the law in this country to pay people to tell lies about you. And you can't do anything about it.

'It's a matter of principle for me, being lucky enough to be in the position where I can afford to do it [i.e. to sue], whereas most people in this country haven't got a dog's chance.'

Elton confided that he would spend his days crying or compensate for his feelings of inadequacy by eating masses of ice cream. As well as the sugar hits he also ripped into the grog – vodka martinis and red wine were a favourite. Anything to postpone reality. And the allegations were taking their toll on his family for his Mum and Derf fled to Spain, Sheila claiming: 'I am too humiliated to live in England.'

When the *Sun's* sex scandals stories broke, Renate returned to Woodside, no doubt to console Elton. He celebrated by asking Princess Margaret's furniture designer son, Viscount Linley, to design and construct a double bed – at the cost of £75,000. Elton's PR machine made sure the press were well exposed to this grandoise gesture. However, Elton's greatest fears about his public credibility were becoming realities as he and those around him rapidly lost favour. For example, a series of TV ads for Cadbury's chocolate bars featuring Elton were dropped, and it's said that the scandal destroyed his royal buddies' plans of having him awarded the Order of the British Empire (OBE). Yet there was great public support for Elton throughout his media beat-up, and he was genuinely appreciative of any warmth that the public extended to him. There was also plenty of publicized support from those who knew him at closer quarters and benefited from his interest and his work – the Watford team, the music industry and his fans. Elton received thousands of letters and replied to each one.

At one stage Elton decided that for his own well-being he had better concentrate on his career, so he toured China with Watford and released the *Live In Australia* album. It successfully took his mind off his troubles, and this showed in his improved demeanour and health. By November 1987 the feud with the *Sun* was over. Elton's accuser, Hardy, confessed to the *Daily Mirror* that his allegations were all lies; that he'd done it for the money, and that he'd never even met Elton: 'I've never been to one of his concerts or bought one of his records. In fact, I hate his music.' The *Sun* had obviously abused the freedom of the press, and a year after Hardy's statement the newspaper paid Elton £1 million in damages. On hearing that he had outlasted his tormentors, Elton burst into tears.

More important to Elton than the money was that he had also achieved a moral victory. In the wake of the settlement the British tabloids pulled in the reins and became more cautious about feeding off gossip. Celebs under unfounded attack could now refer to Elton's precedent and not feel obliged to grit their teeth and bear unfair treatment. He had changed the rules, and it wasn't a minor victory.

There is an addendum to this tale. Speaking to *Q* magazine in the spring of 1995, Elton was asked if he had ever paid for sex. He replied, 'Yes,' before lapsing into silence. When the journalist commented that it was surprising that no one had asked him that question at the time of the rent-boy fiasco, Elton's answer was: 'Well, it never went to court.'

Christmas 1987 I received a card from Elton and Renate, and it indicated that Elton was once again in good spirits. It showed Renate sitting on a couch wrapping presents, while asking her husband what he had on for Christmas. Behind her was Elton, dressed as a Christmas tree, complete with blinking lights.

While all this public collapse and resurrection was occurring,

I was tucked away in central New South Wales practising how to put aeroplanes safely up and quietly down. My graduation from the flying academy was to be held in February 1988, and I had written to Elton and Renate some months earlier, telling them that they were welcome to join me in New South Wales for the proudest day of my life. I received no answer. If I had known what was going on, that the marriage was over in all but name. I wouldn't have been disappointed by the lack of response. I was really out of touch, for by this time Renate had left Woodside – permanently.

Some months earlier, before the problems with the *Sun*, the couple had separated for a few weeks with Renate moving into a £300,000 flat in London, which Elton had bought and decorated for his ever more distant wife. I was saddened when I finally read about their separation for I had always hoped that their marriage would work. But I knew that Elton was truly gay and that it must have been heartbreaking for Renate to know her inconstant husband was having flings with men. No spouse could bear that pressure for long.

Elton, though, was denying his marriage problems and beavering away on a new album in London. During April 1988 he was expected to join Ian Botham, the famed English batsman, on a well-publicized charity tramp for leukemia research. Botham was to follow Hannibal's ancient route through the French Alps where, in 250 BC, the northern African general's forces boldly invaded Italy on elephants. However, Botham, unfortunately, failed to cross the pass, but only because the event was cancelled. Elton went on to a contingency plan, the less stressful, if lower profile, option, sunbaking with George Michael at Hilton Village in Hawaii, where George was on tour at the time.

I knew my life needed a drastic change in direction. I now had my pilot's licence, but the Australian aviation industry was in disarray around the time of my graduation, and there were few enough jobs around for experienced airline pilots, let alone a rookie like me. I'd moved to Sydney, and after sharing a hotel room with Bill Gibbs, an entrepreneur from my early days in the

Melbourne gay scene, I felt disillusioned enough with life to know I needed another challenge, a positive goal. It was time to stop being a victim, to take control, and if I had to lose, to lose in my own way.

This emerging decision to improve my lot unfortunately coincided with devastating news from home. Dad wrote to tell me that he and Mum were separating. Mum had twigged to Dad's philandering and decided to settle in the warmer climes of Perth, well away from Casanova. It was all too much for me – the only stable relationship I knew had evaporated. Despite our problems, my parents were my last refuge in times of crisis for, no matter what I suffered, I believed that they would always be there for me. It was no longer so. I now had no base, nowhere to build from, no home. It was like a death, and the grief was overwhelming. I felt there was no way out, and I started to become unhinged.

It was irrational, but I felt that, as with Elton, I had invested my essence in that family partnership, and all the meaning I had given it was worthless. My parents behaviour seemed so illogical, so unnecessary. Why now, after all those years of togetherness? I believed that in some way I was to blame. Elton was gone. My family was fragmented. All I had left inside was a gut-wrenching black void – and this void was me. My life really fell apart.

Bingeing on cocaine and ecstasy numbed the emotional and spiritual pain, but within six months I was a drug-dependent wreck. However, there was now a purpose in life – to get more drugs. Wallowing in despair, I abused myself terribly and had become what I despised – a hollow-eyed parasite, preying on the lonely, endlessly visiting my pain on the next generation of eager, aimless victims. I came to realize that my only release would be my premature death. Either that or jump off the roller-coaster there and then. One day I decided to leave the ride and to rejoin the living.

With this resolved I had to review my options – head for Africa where a pilot's job awaited, or try my luck in the computer world in America or Europe. But home beckoned. I needed to touch base. On the car trip to Melbourne I decided that for my own sanity Elton was out of my life for good. I would no longer orbit his star.

10. The Last Goodbye

'I love you a lot (heaps). God bless.
Elton.'

ELTON HAS A penchant for purging his soul in
public, and the impending divorce was no
exception. The most obvious public indicator of his
mood was the much publicized auction at the
family home, Woodside. The official reason for the
auction was that Elton was disposing of Woodside and moving
further into the country. He had told the media that Woodside
resembled a goods warehouse, crammed with expensive junk,
some still in crates. He said he felt 'suffocated', however, most
assumed it wasn't the physical junk that was cutting his air
supply.

Perhaps Elton thought the emotional baggage would
disappear with the other remnants. Whatever his motives, the
date for the auction was set, and Sotheby's were instructed to sell
everything that wasn't nailed down. Priceless lamps, antiques,
paintings, jukeboxes, stage costumes, personal wear, jewellery,
gold discs and luggage. The auction of some 2000 lots started on
6 September 1988 and ran for four days.

For a garage sale it had spectacular dimensions. Some items
were toured through New York, Sydney, Tokyo and Los Angeles,
and such was Elton's desperation to clear the residue of his past

that he had to be dissuaded from some very poor business decisions by the auctioneers.

Sotheby's advised that Elton retain 14 cars, the £75,000 bed in the master bedroom, a number of rare paintings, his massive collection of records and original Goon scripts. Things of sentimental value got the chop – a programme autographed by Elvis Presley, a set of John Lennon lithographs, platinum awards for his records, the suit he wore onstage at the legendary Dodger Stadium appearances and even the huge boots he wore as the Pinball Wizard in *Tommy*. All discarded. It must have looked ominous to Renate.

Elton definitely wasn't in a family frame of mind, for even if it did occur to him, he didn't offer any of these mementos to Sheila and Derf, who, at this stage, were still enjoying their self-imposed Spanish exile. Sheila was not one to let her pride prevent participation, however, and she arranged for a proxy buyer to grab some sentimental favourites from the pile.

Throughout the auction promotion Elton never lost sight of the fact that his name would add innumerable dollars to the price of every item. But his obsession to acquire had not really been harnessed, for in between posing with sale items for PR shots, and regularly explaining why he had to be rid of possessions, he slipped out to another auction and paid £44,000 for two works by Russian artists Igor and Svetlana Kopystianski.

More than 600 people attended Sotheby's rooms, eagerly purchasing memorabilia and priceless art. Telephone bids flowed in from all over the world. The sense of controlled establishment power, fostered by Sotheby's to attract a wealthy clientele and high bidders, generated an elitist atmosphere, in which pin-stripers paid in excess of triple the estimated value of some items. For example, a diamond and onyx Cartier watch, which sold for £25,300 to a Japanese department store, went for 12 times its reserve price. A director of Doc Marten cheerily paid £11,000 for the *Tommy* boots – they had only been valued at £1800. To cap it off, at the end of the auction Sotheby's staff brought in the *Elton John Sale* banners that, moments before, had been fluttering outside the building. They raised another £550. The auction was a huge success: expected return, £3 million, an actual return, £14.8 million.

Corporate reminders of Elton's past also headed for the scrapheap. Rocket Records ceased recruiting new acts and existed merely to issue Elton's releases. Even more surprising, his active involvement with Watford came to an end. It took a while to unload the club, and it was only after a couple of unsuccessful tries that he finally sold his majority shares to London millionaire entrepreneur Jack Petchey. He did, however, accept the honorary title of Life President. He still rings the club every day and speaks frequently to the club's manager, Glenn Roeder, but admits: 'I don't go as much as I'd like.'

Elton was in a belligerent mood, and the name of his next album, *Reg Strikes Back*, also suggests a yearning for pre-stardom days. Elton John needed to revisit Reg Dwight, his alter ego, the boy prodigy who always felt out of place. Little Reg had been left behind somewhere along the track and didn't want to be neglected – he was an important part of Elton's life. All that consciously remained of Elton's childhood was the confusion and the unhappiness: he had no idea who or where Reg was. But he was tucked away inside Elton's mind; his anger still burnt bright.

Elton had decided symbolically to wipe the slate and create a new persona, a new character, a new him – as much for his own sake as for his public. David Bowie had gone down a similar track, but in a more premeditated and controlled way. Elton was more spontaneous. Gone was the outrageous, flamboyant, larger than life caricature. This Elton took himself seriously: bank teller look-alike, subdued glasses, Nehru cap. Physical training was in earnest, and he shed two stone. It was a sort of a Clark Kent impersonation. Leading to Super what? For whom?

The man rated by the *Sunday Times Magazine* that year as the 75th richest man in Britain, with a fortune estimated at £42 million, was on a search for self and in doing so was publicly expunging his past. Elton was 41. He had tried it all. He was coming clean. This was the stuff of Orson Wells and *Citizen*

Kane, it was how and why the twig that was Reg was bent to become the man the world knows as Elton. Yet an investigation into all of this seemed beyond the interest of the tabloids. It was as important as life itself to Elton, but no one else really seemed to care.

Elton's management team were naturally very sensitive to his mid-life adjustment. They carefully monitored each and every rumour, and when a paper ran a lightweight story stating that the star was planning to move to Florida, John Reid complained. The counter was that if Elton had stayed in Britain during his nightmare with the tabloids, why would he want to leave now? That was enough logic to keep the press at bay. The lid was to go on as tight as possible – leave him alone, let him sort it out. Transformation time.

Not surprisingly, in this time of crisis, the one thing that Elton clung to desperately was his music. Other rock stars had turned their hand to creative recreations such as painting or challenged themselves with a new music style such as jazz or rap. Others found a new manager, producer or record company. Or just fresh ventures. But Elton's music was all he could proudly say he had conquered, and he wasn't quite ready for real change, to reform himself altogether.

During this period the tentatively maturing Elton retained his business associates and threw himself into what was really a repetition of earlier exercises – another album. However, in developing his new persona, Elton had touched upon the clue to his new direction. He needed to quieten down, to be more in touch with his senses and look to his own needs. An overly sophisticated, unnatural lifestyle had disconnected him from the things that keep the feet of ordinary mortals on solid ground. Elton was afloat, drifting aimlessly in a cloud-soft, surreal world of excessive luxury and services.

The drawbridge of opportunity was down at this point, inviting Elton to enter the refuge, a different and unknown domain. The bridge only stayed down for a brief period, and Elton faltered and missed his chance. Instead, he satisfied himself with the reaction to *Reg Strikes Back*. It pacified him in a familiar if not totally fulfilling way, for despite the *Sun*'s damage to his reputation, his following stuck by him; the album went Top 20 in the UK and the USA. 'I Don't Wanna Go On With You Like That' peaked at No. 2 in America.

Still searching for something to complement his constant diet of musical success, Elton turned to films. He first agreed to, and then bowed out of, Ken Russell's adaptation of D.H. Lawrence's *The Rainbow*. Later his name was connected to a movie on Liberace, but nothing eventuated. He wrote a song for Bonnie Tyler that appeared on a record version of Dylan Thomas's *Under Milk Wood* and played piano on records for Jon Bon Jovi, George Harrison and Olivia Newton-John. He even featured in a duet with Aretha Franklin for a track on her album.

Almost frantic at times, Elton was pushing the edges, but he didn't know in which direction. When on tour, he threw himself into manic performances with such gusto that he collapsed from exhaustion a couple of times and on two occasions was forced to break his time-honoured creed of 'The Show Must Go On'. In Paris, Elton was sternly ordered by doctors to take a rest before continuing on his tour to Australia, New Zealand and Japan.

All this activity peaked in 1990 in yet another chart-topping success. His double-A side 'Sacrifice' and 'Healing Hands', which had been issued as separate singles a year earlier, had flopped. Then the unexpected happened. When re-released they went to No. 1 in Britain, giving Elton his first solo single UK chart topper. It had taken two decades. Elton was enraptured. For all his overseas success, his inability to peak in his home market must have been a disappointment that sapped his confidence. No doubt Elton rationalized this phenomenon as a 'prophet not being recognized in his own country', but it had played on his mind and had surfaced some years earlier when he appeared on *Wogan*. His host had asked if he ever felt sad that his success and astonishing achievements did not include a No. 1 in Britain. Elton had replied No, but on reflection added that it would have been nice, but he didn't expect to achieve the same sort of success at home.

Elton may have feared that the spate of scandals in the late 1980s would adversely affect his career, but it was not to be the case. And he was pleasantly surprised when, in late 1990, *Sleeping with the Past*, which had been a Top 10 hit some years earlier, zoomed back into the charts to provide him with his first No. 1 album in Britain for 13 years. Some time later, *The Very Best of Elton John*, a selection of his hits from earlier years, also topped the charts. To his own amazement, the early 90s were proving to be as commercially satisfying as his successes of 15 years earlier. No small achievement in the harsh world of pop. There was only one conclusion any observer could make, that 'over time, cream rises'.

But it wasn't only commercial success and personal glory that motivated Elton in the early 90s. He had gained a social conscience. So what pleased him most about the five-week stay at the top and sales of 600,000 copies of 'Sacrifice'/'Healing Hands' was that he could donate the substantial royalties to AIDS research.

The money from the single, as well as from the sales of the follow-up 'Club At the End of the Street', raised £328,000 for various AIDS charities. But in the same way that he had the courage in 1976 to become one of the first superstars to admit to being bisexual, Elton copped the bigots' flak. For irrational but very emotive reasons, there were those who thought that Elton's publicized behaviour indicated he was more likely to promote the spread of AIDS than prevent its transmission. Elton ignored the insinuations and continued his support of AIDS research unabated. His stance was that if you promote seatbelts, it doesn't mean you promote crashes. The same goes for AIDS. In the 90s, he took the lead in expressing his support for AIDS research and expressed deep and sincere compassion for its victims. He also felt and showed sympathy for the grieving families and friends.

In the 80s being gay, or even being perceived as having

bisexual proclivities, was still hush-hush in the entertainment world, including the land of the royals. There were a few brave souls such as Boy George who, at the peak of success with Culture Club, admitted to having an affair with a drummer in earlier days. And you could sense a relaxation of Victorian standards when Holly Johnson of Frankie Goes To Hollywood quipped that there was a definite difference in taste between white and black penises.

Gay culture was being exposed, one way or another, right around the world, and there was no hiding, no shyness acceptable to the gay militant groups. If the high profile homos weren't game to come out, who else would? So like it or lump it, the closet door of rich and famous gays was coming off its hinges, and the guys exposing the vulnerables weren't bigoted red-necks, they were the Sisters themselves. In American soaps, which seem to set the moral codes for much of the Western world, it was only as recently as 1987 that actor Billy Crystal played the first gay character who wasn't a mincing poof. But it took another four years before the heterosexual Tom Hanks would take the plunge and appear in *Philadelphia*, the film about an HIV-positive lawyer who lost his job as a result of his illness. When that movie became a box-office smash and Hanks received an Academy Award for best actor, suddenly Hollywood found the 'courage' to work on no less than 16 AIDS related movies in one year.

In the early 90s I discovered that being gay no longer meant being treated as different or seeing myself as life's victim. I'd come to understand that when working with straights, admitting to being gay didn't automatically lead to sniggering. People now seem to understand that sexual preference is just that – no more and no less. Not a big deal. Not an issue. Just life.

When AIDS reached epidemic proportions, the compassionate Elton was among the first celebrities to offer his services to help fund research into a cure, drumming-up both financial and moral support. He played benefits, donated royalties and used his celebrity status to canvas the issue. 'Sure the AIDS problem worries me,' he told *Woman's Own,* 'it should worry everyone.' In that interview Elton remarked that he was terrified of becoming infected and had a blood test every six months.

In what appeared to be a sincere gesture, even though it proved to be a PR coup, Elton took an avuncular interest in an American child AIDS victim, Ryan White. Ryan's family had been ostracized by their Indianapolis neighbours, and Elton visited the boy, stayed to comfort the family, paid for the funeral when the child died and was a pallbearer.

The boy's positive spirit in the face of adversity had hit Elton hard. He realized he had no reason to feel sorry for himself, and this recognition started him on his path to overcoming his addictions. He keeps a photo of himself from around that time, looking overweight and with expressionless eyes. He remembers seeing footage of Ryan's funeral and being startled by how old and fat he looked. 'I had to change because I was frightened,' he told an American journalist. 'I didn't want to die angry and bitter and sad, and that's what I had become . . . physically ugly, spiritually ugly . . . a slob, a pig.'

By early 1990 my life had regained its balance, and my socializing was such that AIDS was not any sort of a threat. I was happy enough, for I'd landed back on my feet and was enjoying working for a number of computer firms. On my return to Melbourne a year earlier, I'd found my family still coping with our parents' divorce. Having left home at 16 I hadn't really expected it to affect me so dramatically. But by now I had accepted the situation. However, I was still very much aware that the family home, as a fallback position, no longer existed.

When I arrived in Melbourne in 1989 I stayed with my elder sister, Sue, sharing a bedroom with her children, Brea and Karl. It was a loving atmosphere, and the sheer normality of it all made it easy to forgo the drugs that had devastated me in Sydney. When clean as a whistle, I moved in to Sky Farm in Yara Glen on the outskirts of Melbourne with Dad and his new partner, Gail, to a degree I joined in their life together. I needed to connect with Dad again and to come to terms with his new lady, an independently minded woman. This sort of contact really throws you for a while, especially when you haven't been around during the breakdown. To show good grace and approval of the new arrangements, I designed a logo for the Victorian Animals Aid Trust that Gail managed and started a Trust newsletter.

At this point Elton had been physically out of my life for nearly three years, and I thought I had overcome withdrawal symptoms. However, when I read that he was going to tour Australia again in 1990, my heart raced, and my breathing quickened. No, I said to myself, I am not going to get involved – NO!

As the tour promotion material began to filter into town, people who hadn't spoken to me for years suddenly rediscovered me, asking if I could score them some free tickets. It was then that I realized how closely people identified me with Elton, and here I was trying to forget him. I was determined to let the tour go by, to pay absolutely no attention to it at all. Elton had not written or called for almost a year, and I had cut my ties with his family. Prior to that I would ring Sheila in Minorca about every six months and also give his grandmother at Woodside a call – just to say hello. But I had dropped them all, and Elton was definitely out.

I wasn't even aware that my ex had arrived in Melbourne until I overheard two girls sitting next to me in a train chattering about what to wear to his concert at the Tennis Centre that night. So what? I thought, trying to convince myself I wasn't interested. Who cares? The next morning, while loading a machine at the local laundromat, my mobile phone buzzed. It was Sheila.

'Gary! Where are you?' she said excitedly.

'I'm in Yarra Glen, doing my laundry.' It seemed incongruous, washing my dirty linen and discussing it at the same time, but there it was. Elton's Mum was chasing up her son's old lovers.

'Elton's frantic. He's wondering why you haven't called . . . asking everybody where you are.'

'Well, I don't know Sheila. I just thought I wouldn't . . .' my voice trailing off.

'Oh, Gary, don't be so silly. He's been asking, "Has Gary rung, has he come around?"' Sheila was very persistent. She surely wouldn't set me up. It had to be genuine. Or was it just my determination slipping away?

Almost despite myself, I felt a glow – Elton was actually thinking about me, he was making an effort to see me. He wanted me to go to the show that night. I wasn't sure. I hedged. Sheila probably thought I was being shy. In fact I was worried about my survival. I had promised myself that I wouldn't risk it again. 'Oh, Gary, come along . . . I want to see you, too.' That personal plea was the clincher.

By the time I drove back to Sky Farm, Sheila had called Dad and asked him along as well. Gail was also invited but graciously declined. 'You don't want to go and see Elton John?' Dad moaned incredulously.

Gail didn't miss a beat: 'Oh, for heaven's sake, he's only a pop singer.' Absolute sacrilege! If Elton's Mum had heard that she would have dropped dead in her tracks.

I arrived at the show to find Dad already ensconced in Sheila and Derf's room, cracking jokes and exchanging gossip. The three of them really did get on well. What was also nice was that with Renate gone, Sheila had drifted back into her son's life. Elton had taken the initiative. He had contacted his mother in Spain, all sins were forgiven; he had invited her and Derf to join him on tour. The prodigal had returned. All was well with Sheila. That night, after half an hour of chit-chat, she took us to Elton's suite. There were about 15 people present, mingling and having drinks before the show. Apart from the usual Patti Mostyn–Molly Meldrum team, there was touring Scottish comedian Billy Connolly and MTV Australia's host, Richard Wilkins.

Elton happened to be walking past the door as we slipped in. He saw me and boomed out joyfully: 'Chook!' A bear-like hug. 'So good to see you again.' He slapped me on the back. 'Mad bastard!'

Elton was maintaining his *nouveau* colonial clerk-Nehru jacket image and looked neat and a lot slimmer than I remembered. While the other guests chatted among themselves, he gave me his full attention, wanting to know what I'd been up to and how my work was going. Then he led me into his bedroom to show me a stack of CDs he'd bought that day. 'You've got to come up to Sydney, Chook,' Elton implored, throwing his arms about enthusiastically, and only occasionally stopping mid-wave to push his glasses back up his nose: 'There's this boy called Hugh Williams ... he's the love of my life ... he's just wonderful.' Surely Elton hadn't invited me to tell me about his new lover who awaited him in Sydney. That wasn't Elton's style. Everything with a purpose.

From the main room, we heard Bob Halley's pre-show warning: it was time to hit the road. Elton grabbed my arm; he wanted me to ride with him in the limo. It was the first time I'd seen any of his motorcades receive a police escort. Two bikes in front, a patrol car behind, lights flashing and the occasional siren screeching as we approached intersections, where the cops had stopped all traffic. As the motorcade flew up the side road to the Tennis Centre, fans waved. A couple of guys sported large Elton John specs. I mused on the strangeness of my situation. The previous day I had been on a train determined not to see Elton again. Now I was in a motorcade with a police escort. What would happen tomorrow?

As we jumped out of the limo near the back stage area, you could sense the crowd's excitement – it was tangible, volatile. Elton looked to the fans crowded near the embankment and waved. Someone threw a rose. After accompanying the star to the show, I joined my group of friends, by now stacked into good seats, which Elton had generously provided me with. As he walked onstage, the high-pitched scream reverberated throughout the building, the frightening energy of it hitting you somewhere deep in the gut. Even if a performer was feeling low at the point of entrance, this sort of ovation could lift him through the roof. It was the audience's contribution, and it was always welcomed. After the gig my mates insisted that we hit the clubs, so I made my apologies to Elton and left.

Next morning, while driving in the countryside with friends, a call came through on my mobile. 'Just rang to say goodbye, Chook . . . I leave today . . . See you at the Sebel . . . I really want you to meet Hugh.'

'Yes, Elton,' I said, 'I'm looking forward to it.' Everyone in the car tuned into the conversation – they were wary for me; some of them had helped restore my crushed spirit after Elton's traumatic dismissals and didn't want to see me hurt again.

After he rang off, one of the more curious asked: 'Who on earth is Hugh, Gary?'

'Elton's new boyfriend,' I said quietly.

There was a stunned silence in the car, then someone, amazed at Elton's effrontery, repeated what I had said, emphasizing each word: 'Elton wants his ex-boyfriend to meet his current boyfriend!'

I kept my thoughts to myself. Maybe he thinks I've got over him, I mused, watching the countryside warming to the late morning light. Or maybe he hopes the three of us will get on well and become an item . . . maybe that's what I really hope.

Whatever my reservations, I headed for Sydney, and on checking into the Sebel, I received a note from Elton. He and Hugh were busy – they could see me that evening. Having dined with members of Elton's entourage, I was heading back to my room when the star and Hugh stepped out of the lift. One look at Hugh, and I knew we would be friends. Elton's new lover wasn't anything like I'd expected. A dark haired American boy from Atlanta, decisive and a little stocky – not the blond, surfing pretty boy that Elton usually panted over. Most un-ELF-like. We exchanged a few polite words before Elton announced he was tired and that we should catch up the following day.

The next morning at 8 am, the phone rang, and, bleary-eyed, I muttered a gruff greeting. It was Elton. He wanted me to meet them – just Hugh and him – downstairs for breakfast. I dressed hurriedly and made my way to the dining-room.

The waiters, hovering at a discreet distance, observed us giggling over scrambled eggs and toast like schoolboys on a camp holiday, and it was evident that the three of us were getting along famously. Elton, clearly over the moon that Hugh and I were compatible, encouraged this truly gay mood; it was clear to me, and I know to him, which way things were heading. Breakfast came to a conclusion, and the waiter cleared the table. My ex, feeling that he had mastered a difficult situation, indicated his attitude when he decided to pour us all a cup of coffee: he had business to attend to, so why didn't I give Hugh the all-Aussie guided tour of Sydney?

Hugh and I had a great afternoon. We nosed our hire car around the tourist spots – the Opera House, the Harbour Bridge, then down to the Rocks area, where we had a seafood lunch at a favourite restaurant. Unknown to Hugh, it was the place where Renate and I had lunched, six years earlier, on the frantic day that she and I had rushed around town looking for the perfect wedding dress. As the day wore on, Hugh insisted we visit a bar at Darling Harbour, and I broke my no-alcohol rule, knocking back a few Caluhas and milk. Hugh stuck to chilled Australian beer, and as the afternoon wore on our façade of propriety crumbled, revealing a strong and mutual sexual attraction. It was equally obvious that I was becoming very drunk, very quickly.

We staggered back to the Sebel at 5 pm. I went off to take a bath before the concert, mystified at how the hotel walls could move without making any noise. The next thing I remember, I was lying on the bed, and the phone was ringing. It was Hugh, wondering where on earth I'd been. Oh, my head ached, and my mouth was so dry. They'd been calling and calling and hadn't got an answer. It was 7 pm, and Hugh was at the concert hall. I must have passed out. Hugh sent the car to pick me up. When I arrived Elton was onstage, and my indiscretion had become public knowledge; you would have thought it was the funniest thing the entourage had heard about in years. 'Prim and proper Gary, who'd have thought!' Sheila gently chided, with a maternal and knowing grin on her face. Even John Reid cracked a smile.

That evening everyone gathered in Elton's suite, and, towards the end of the night, Elton pulled me aside to ask me what I thought of Hugh. As I enthused, 'Great ... really cute,' I was waiting for it: 'Well, he thinks you're very cute too, Gary ... he told me so ... so why don't we have a threesome?' This time I didn't mind. I had the hots for Hugh, and I wanted to please Elton – satisfaction all round.

A soirée was planned to coincide with the end of the tour, so that Elton could relax without worrying. There would be no more concerts, so he could get drunk, rip into the cocaine and sleaze the night away. For me, the Monday night date meant two days of frustration: I couldn't wait to place myself in the hands of that gorgeous Hugh.

He and I spent the whole of Sunday sightseeing, and we both played coy. Obviously Elton had spoken to him about the threesome, but neither of us broached the topic. On that Monday evening the tour party dined at the Rocks before trailing its way back to the Sebel. Sheila, Derf and Sheila's sister Winny, who was also visiting Sydney, had returned from a harbour cruise kindly provided by the NSW police. Sun and sea air had them exhausted, and they soon hit the sack. Like three schoolboys sneaking behind the gym for a smoke, Elton, Hugh and I made our way into the Presidential Suite. We had all been drinking and were fired-up.

'All right, let's get to it!' Elton took control. Later, the three of us went to sleep cuddling each other, and in the morning we awoke to find our three bodies still entangled. 'Breakfast anybody?' Elton said cheerfully, extricating himself from the tumble of torsos and limbs. But it clearly wasn't over for Hugh and me.

Tuesday morning, when Hugh and I went shopping, what was understood needed no statements – just time. 'I wanna get you some mudpacks, Gary,' Hugh said, making a lame excuse for going into the local pharmacy. I laughed uncontrollably. Along with the facials he purchased a packet of condoms, and without another word we returned to my room for the hottest sex I'd ever enjoyed.

My experiences with Elton had me shunning sentimental attachments, but there was no lessening of sexual interest or pleasure. Rooting without the romance was a breeze – it's easier to get your rocks off with a body when the romance is limited to sensual pleasure. All fun, no responsibility. In fact, my capacity to enjoy sensual experience had increased when I decided to detach body from self. And my senses were in full rage when I was near Hugh.

An hour later the session finished as abruptly as it had begun. Hugh looked at me and said guiltily: 'I gotta go.' In his eyes we had broken unwritten rules, wandered beyond Elton's unspoken sanctions. Hugh felt he had betrayed his lover. I, on the other hand, shrugged it off – we were just finishing what Elton had started. When I saw Hugh later in the day, he seemed to have come to terms with our afternoon affair. No guilt, no furtiveness. No doubt he had laid off the blame by confessing to Elton. The star appeared magnanimous, all was forgiven – but you could bet someone would pay.

I could sense a gradual change in Elton. His mood and the situation reminded me of how he had treated me in Los Angeles the first time he had dumped me. That débâcle had been prompted by the arrival of my young Australian visitor. Elton had encouraged that liaison, flying the boy in from Melbourne. It looked as if, once again, I was to suffer the same fate. Elton had to be in control – no show without Punch.

Elton's perfunctory goodbye the next day, as he packed for his flight out of Australia, was a clear indication that the offended prima donna had cast me back into the shadow. 'We'll ring soon,' Hugh called as I left.

'I bet you won't!' I replied in a matter-of-fact way. I knew what to expect from the churlish Elton, the radiant star who tempted fate then recoiled from the outcome. I wasn't far wrong for, as it turned out, it would be another year before I'd hear from either of them, although unbeknown to me, they were going through a hell of their own.

Elton had flitted into my life, gained a little excitement, shown that he still had me an emotional prisoner and slammed the door. Any time he wanted a threesome down-under, there was good old Crystal. Use me up and spit me out. I should have learnt by this stage, toughened myself for the predictable fall, but each time my emotions churned, and I felt as vulnerable as before.

On the way back from our last dinner at the Rocks on Monday night, we'd come across a homeless woman lying on the footpath. I quietly approached her, slipped some money into her hands before rejoining the group. Sheila had noticed my gesture: 'Gary, you have a very good heart.'

Elton must have noticed and said: 'Your time will come, Chook . . . you'll meet someone, and your life will fall into order.' He obviously knew how lonely I really was, he knew how much I loved him, and yet he always treated me so harshly. It really upset me terribly. Even those words, clearly spoken in praise of me, indicated that I was not to be the one. So why didn't he leave me alone?

There was nothing for it but to put some order into my own life. Get tough. And it would be easier without a perpetual habit known as Elton. On the other side of the world, at the same time, Elton was about to experience some critical changes of his own. Reality had caught up with image.

On returning to London after the Australian success, Elton and Hugh really got stuck into the high life. Hugh was the first to realize he was heading down the never-ending track and pulled the pin. In May of that year, he told Elton that he was checking into a detox centre. Elton's fractious response to his lover's statement was predictable, and one that I'd heard before: 'If you can't sort out your own problems . . . fuck off then!' Elton would later admit that, at that time, he thought anyone who couldn't cope was weak.

But Elton, despite his bravado, pined for Hugh and soon flew to visit him in an Arizona clinic. Unfortunately the visit ended in screaming rows, and Elton returned to his London house, shattered because he thought his relationship with Hugh was finished. He took his rage out on the furniture and tore his lover's photographs to shreds. 'I stayed in my room and cried,' he said in an interview, 'but eventually I realized how much I cared about this person and how much I admired him for doing it.' Elton would admonish himself, drawing on Hugh as a role model: 'He's tried to do something for himself [while] here you are sitting here – fat, haven't washed for two weeks, vomit all over your dressing gown.'

Despite the artiste's high drama, Hugh's withdrawal eventually had its positive effect, and it wasn't long before, cap in hand, Elton returned to Arizona. It looked as if Elton was about to seek solace in the wisdom of another culture, outside the class-ridden conservative society that had bred his neuroses. I personally wondered if a cure outside the culture that had produced him would be of any lasting value.

Seeing that Elton was prepared to seek help, Hugh suggested they approach a counsellor to discuss their relationship. The advice they were given was to compile a list of complaints about each other and then review them in the counsellor's presence. They faced each other with their demands, and, according to reports, Hugh and Elton shook with trepidation as they exchanged lists. Hugh was worried that Elton would storm from the room in anger; but, no, Elton was there to win Hugh back, and it really was no time for games. Out it came: Hugh was angry with Elton for his drinking, drugs, promiscuity – and bulimia!

Elton was stunned. He expected the other complaints but didn't realize that Hugh – or I, for that matter – knew about the bulimia. What he didn't realize was that although he used to lock himself away and throw up in private, I could always smell the vomit on his fingers. So could Hugh – and it certainly wasn't a turn-on.

To the relief of all present Elton didn't over-react and stayed to present Hugh with his list of irritating traits. His list was short, however, and a sceptic would say a little contrived, after all he was there to win Hugh back: 'Hugh does not put his compact discs away neatly.'

Elton may well have been underplaying Hugh's weaknesses for effect, but he appreciated the simplicity and honesty of Hugh's observations. It was then that the veil of self-deceit began to lift, and Elton really decided to seek help. He went initially to Los Angeles, where, to his amazement, he found that the first two places he approached refused to treat him. These clinics wouldn't accept patients who needed treatment for drugs and bulimia.

'I finally decide to get help . . . and no one will help me?' he later complained. It was a frightening predicament, for he had thought his condition and treatment quite mundane. Now he was beginning to appreciate the extent of his psychological illness.

Eventually doctors helped him locate a sympathetic hospital in Chicago, where he checked into the Parkside Lutheran on 29 July 1990. Elton had decided that he wanted to walk out of that hospital with his badly fractured dignity restored. With cases like his, the treatment was to break down the patient's inflated ego by returning to the basics of life: to force the person to live outside his or her head and to stay in touch with the body; to strip the person down, allowing rebuilding into someone capable of self-love. Elton's self-centred existence had to come to a close.

For the first time since his teenage years, Elton's talent and wealth could no longer shield him from reality. There was no Sheila or John Reid to protect him from his own excesses. He was on his own. This confrontation with reality was so brutal that he faltered on several occasions: 'I tried to run away twice because authority figures told me what to do,' he recounted in an interview some time later. 'I didn't like that . . . but it was one of the things I had to learn – to listen.

'I packed my suitcase on the first two Saturdays, and I sat on the sidewalk and cried . . . I asked myself where I was going to run . . . "Do you go back and take more drugs and kill yourself, or do you go to another centre because you didn't quite like the way someone spoke to you here?"' He concluded by saying: 'In the end, I knew there was no choice . . . I realized this was my last chance.'

The therapy included writing a farewell letter to cocaine, and, for Elton, this was to be an eloquent and passionate outpouring of bitterness toward the narcotic's hold on his life. The prose tells of how the alluring white powder enslaved him, of how he had been so hooked that he'd sent staff out in cars to try and score. Like alcohol, the drug has a seductive attraction – an appetite for it is very easy to gain and excruciatingly painful to lose. In the lonely hours of pre-dawn light Mistress Cocaine calls you back – 'without me you are alone' – and before the sun rises, she has you again. Elton later told me that when he showed this letter to Bernie Taupin, his friend burst into tears.

This was do-or-die time for Elton, and his career had to take a back seat. Despite the fact that he would lose income, and it was likely that his popularity would fade, he decided to take a year's break from the punishing schedules and madcap life that he had endured over the previous years. No recording sessions. No touring. In fact, this radical decision was an indication that the therapy was working.

The star had come to realize that he could lose his way when the ebb and flow of his moods clashed with the demands of his high-profile lifestyle. He realized, too, how his erratic behaviour had devastated those closest to him, including me. Although he could not change the past, Elton told friends that he intended to spend that year trying to compensate for the damage he had caused others.

After checking himself out of the Chicago hospital, Elton returned to London intent on coping by himself. He bought what was by his standards a modest London apartment, adopted an old terrier, which he named Thomas, from a lost dogs' home and did things for himself. This was a novel experience for him. Spoilt by a doting mother, he had essentially gone from Sheila's home to a flat he shared with others to a series of mansions where staff rallied to his bidding.

Renovations being undertaken at Woodside gave the star some respite from his memories of the self-indulged monster that once lurked in its attic. When he finally returned there, it was to a place that breathed subtlety and sophistication, a far cry from the litter of a fragmented past. Yesterday, including Renate, had been obliterated entirely, and now the mansion could well have belonged to a conservative country squire. A large ornamental lake had been created in the garden, and the kitchen was totally restyled.

Elton attended to a lot of neglected aspects of his life during this time. He reviewed his diet, excluding white flour and refined sugar, and went to numerous Alcoholics Anonymous (AA) meetings. Now he was able to talk about his fears to those who understood and received hugs instead of condemnation and gratuitous advice. Elton knew the fragility of his grasp on reality and that, to hold to the straight and narrow, he had to speak to his AA sponsor every day. The outside world no longer held him a prisoner of fame, and he would freely wander around London with Thomas.

Elton's closest business associates were astonished at this change. He seemed so happy. The demons seemed to have been exorcised. The dark clouds had disappeared. This really was quite an extraordinary effort and showed Elton's incredible recuperative abilities and will to survive. There are many rock stars who have reached a similar crisis point and who now rest in well-marked graves.

In December 1990, Elton appeared on British TV, on the *Jonathan Ross Show*. He'd lost two stone and looked great. A fedora perched jauntily on his head, he looked casual-chic in a green jacket, chatting happily – and frankly – about his turbulent past. He beamed with the confidence of someone who had won the hardest battle of his life – to deal honestly with himself and to acknowledge the hurt he'd caused others.

'I used to get depressed,' he admitted to Ross, 'and I'd overeat and overdrink, and it used to get ridiculous. Because I'd always wanted too much. Whenever I had a hit record, or met someone,

I was never happy with just that. I always wanted more. I never gave myself time to stop and smell the roses. Well, now I'm going to stop, and . . . I just want to smell a few roses.'

A few days after Christmas 1990, I received a Christmas card in the mail from Hugh and Elton. Although signed by both of them and wishing festive cheer, on the back of the card in Hugh's writing was the message, 'Gary, call me!' A telephone number invited an immediate response. Did I really need more of this? I'd heard nothing from Elton that year. My birthday card to him in March had never been acknowledged. He hadn't remembered mine six months later.

But the temptation proved too strong, and two days later I dialled the number. Hugh was delighted to hear from me. He'd been trying to contact me all over the place but without success. He had lots to tell me, but in particular mentioned that he and Elton were going to holiday in Hawaii in February and wanted me to join them, along with some other people. He sounded genuine, but I was hesitant. Why wasn't Elton asking me himself? Coolly I told him I'd think about it. I was still waivering when Hugh rang the next evening, but though he refused to take no for an answer, I told him I wasn't keen.

Two days later, London calling, Elton on the line: he really wanted to see me. I felt myself weaken and give in. I took a freelance job to typeset a Melbourne doctor's book, a guide to prescribed drugs, to earn spending money for a month's holiday in a luxury resort, though Elton was paying my fare.

My flight to Hawaii was a nightmare. Elton's office in LA had only booked me a one-way ticket. At Honolulu, the customs officials, extremely suspicious of one-way ticket holders, only let me through when I showed them my travellers' cheques and casually dropped Elton's name in conversation. Then it was over to the island of Maui on a smaller plane, where Elton and Hugh picked me up from the airport in a snappy white BMW convertible. There were hugs all around.

On the drive to the Four Seasons Resort, where Elton was booked in as Kenneth King and Hugh as Howard Hughes, the two regaled me with tales about their experiences in detox clinics. Hugh recalled how they weren't allowed to communicate with the outside world. He kept thinking of Elton but couldn't talk to him. And Elton had to scrub floors and do his own washing – something he hadn't done for a long time.

It transpired that the Maui holiday was to celebrate their survival in all ways – including as a couple. Also in the party were four guys whom Hugh and Elton had met while in rehab – Shane, Greg, Rick and another fellow called Hugh. Apart from myself there were two others who were not in rehab, who accompanied the group. Patch, who was Hugh's housemate from Atlanta, and Eric, who arrived two weeks into the holiday and worked in the Versace shop in LA where Elton regularly bought his clothes. I'm not sure who instigated my inclusion, and I felt a bit uncomfortable about it. Was it Hugh wanting to continue our relationship? I thought so when we indulged in touching each other up during a sauna, but it never led anywhere.

Was Elton wanting to atone for his past mis-treatment of me? Or did he still relish the idea of the three of us ending up in the cot together? Sure enough, when I started a brief fling with Kevin, a friend of one of Elton's guests, Elton's immediate reaction was to lick his lips and fantasize about a foursome. But Kevin, a well-travelled salesman from New York, who had decided to visit us while on a business trip to Hawaii and who was not impressed by celebrity, firmly turned the star down. Elton was offended, but I was enraptured. Kevin cared enough about a relationship with me not to allow it to develop into something sleazy. We still keep in contact.

Since detox Elton had become confident, more relaxed and less prone to mood swings and, despite my better judgement, that lovable nature kept me drawn to him, flickering like a moth to a flame. There was more openness to him, and he seemed pleased that he could cope without nannies like Reid and Halley. The fact that he'd lost a lot of weight gave him a much needed shot of self-esteem, and for once in his life he actually seemed to relish being outdoors, in the sunshine.

We started to enjoy long conversations again, and now Elton actually listened to my hopes and dreams. To provide me with happy memories he even bought me a video camera, and at the end of the holiday I blew the last of my money buying him and Hugh a present for their anniversary – a collection of their favourite geko lizards. It was smiles all round.

'I'm just lucky to be alive,' Elton told me one afternoon, 'you should have seen me just before I cleaned up . . . I simply had no pride left. Towards the end, I'd be up three days on drugs, sleep for two days and eat for another three. That went on for six months.'

'Was it an easy decision to clean up?' It seemed a silly question after I said it, but it drew a very revealing response:

'No, because I honestly thought I could beat it. I guess I never thought I had a problem. You can kid yourself when you go down for breakfast and demolish a couple of serves of bacon, sausages and eggs. Then you go through tubs of ice cream and huge blocks of chocolate. Even as you're eating lunch, you're dying to finish it so you can throw up and come back and have another lunch.

'But when you get to that pathetic stage – when you've got vomit on your bathrobe from throwing up, dozens of empty bottles around you, and you're actually on your knees checking out the carpet to see if there's any cocaine there, then you can't hide it any more.'

Elton survived the ordeal because Hugh had undertaken a similar journey, and they could discuss their experiences from a common perspective. The cathartic process of collapse and restoration had a great effect on Hugh, whose personality seemed transformed. He was supremely confident in his manner, and more sure of his relationship with Elton than ever before. It was most evident in the way the two of them made their decisions – jointly and equally. On this trip they discussed buying a million-dollar apartment in Atlanta – to use on their trips there.

In a New Zealand TV interview, Elton admitted that the relationship with Hugh was working because Hugh was now direct, telling Elton exactly what he was feeling. In the past, the star admitted he'd always wanted to dominate. He said the power gave him a sense of security for, deep-down, he really trusted nobody. He revealed that in the past, he'd see it as rejection if his lover wanted to go off on his own, as a signal that he didn't want to be with him.

Hugh also pushed Elton into doing the simple things that made him enjoy life more. 'I'd been to Paris many times,' Elton recounted, 'but it was when I went with Hugh that I visited the Eiffel Tower for the first time. Before that I could never see the point.'

Hugh's influence became obvious on holiday, for he encouraged Elton to be involved in all our activities, not just those that involved food and sex. Being with a group made this easier, for there was a range of input. The eight of us hung around together during our month in Maui and came to know each other very well. All but two of the others were on Co-dependency treatments, and the only time I'd feel a bit out of it was when the Co-deps would gather in a room, introduce themselves as if they had not met before and talk about their weaknesses and how they were dealing with them.

In these sessions Elton would bleed his soul, expressing sorrow for the way he treated his mother, wife and friends. These quasi-religious, formalized, AA-type meetings were important for them. Once, when we were returning from a day trip on the Hana highway, with its 50 miles of winding roads and 54 one-lane bridges, the rented four-wheel drive overheated. We tried several times to go a few extra miles when it had cooled down, but before long the vehicle overheated again, and we were forced to stop by the roadside. As luck would have it, phones were scarce and other motorists none too helpful, although some did promise to send help back to us. If only they'd realized who was in the car I'm sure assistance would have been no problem – maybe it was Elton's fluorescent-pink track suit that fooled them, who knows? We all soon tired of waiting, and someone grabbed a blanket from the vehicle and laid it out by the roadside. We had an AA meeting there and then. At these encounters they always discussed the positive, what they wanted to do with their lives – the negatives were accepted but never dwelt upon.

Over that month we all spent so much time together we even started dressing in a similar fashion. It was freaky when you look back at the photos. White T-shirts and cream jeans seemed to be in vogue.

On the first week, when I slipped into one of the stores to buy some sunglasses, the girl behind the counter said:

'Hey, did you know Elton John is on the island?'

'Elton John? Really?' I said, feigning ignorance.

'Yeah, he's got half a dozen boys with him. I think they're his doctors. That's what I'm told anyway.'

That's the stuff legends are made of – roadside consultations.

One of the party, a Canadian lawyer, was embarrassed about his gay tendencies. Humour was the best way of dealing with these anxieties, so Elton decided to play a practical joke on him, something right over the top. In a fit of inspiration he decided that we would dress as drag queens in order to cause embarrassment to the lawyer. The intention was to do the dirty deed the following night, at dinner in the resort's restaurant. After that, everything else would seem small-fry.

When it came to these jokes, Elton never did anything by halves, so the pranksters headed off to the shops to buy wigs, dresses and high-heeled shoes, giggling like kids on a school excursion. Elton even arranged for a make-up artist to visit their rooms. I was to play the patsy. Fortunately no dress-ups for me.

At about 7.30 pm, I went to the guy's room. Then, together, we went to knock on Elton's door, to accompany him to dinner. There was, of course, no answer. I suggested they'd already left for the restaurant, so we made our way downstairs. The lawyer didn't notice the half a dozen security guys we passed on the way, speaking into their CBs. Elton and the others were being informed of our every step.

The hotel's management, as much to protect other guests from our outrageous behaviour as to provide us with privacy, had sectioned off an area of the dining-room for our use. As we waited, the lawyer and I nibbled impatiently on our bread rolls. Out of the corner of my eye, I could see a sprawling gaggle of cheap-looking tarts in garish dresses and fright wigs creep in through the kitchen, obscenely mincing their way toward us. The lawyer turned just as the gushing group enveloped him. His eyes boggled.

Elton and his queens squealed and jumped about the embarrassed man, who could only respond by covering his eyes with his hands. Elton slid alongside him and, pouting his red-smeared lips, put his arm around his victim. I caught the whole thing on my video camera. It was incredibly funny to watch.

After a scrumptious dinner, and heaps of fun and banter, it was time to leave. The hotel management had asked us to go back out through the kitchen, as they didn't want us to embarrass the other diners. You couldn't blame them with their guests paying a minimum of US$350 per night. Looking at these tarts, the shock would be worse than the embarrassment.

Elton wasn't going to have any part of the management's plan, though, and haughtily throwing his head back, charged off towards the public entrance.

The girls, giggling all the more because they tried to behave themselves, straggled through the sedate restaurant like a pack of old dears heading home from a big night out at the pub. I thought the head waiter was going to pass out, but as Elton and his party were spending about £50,000 for their stay, nothing was said.

In the foyer the tarts really camped it up madly. One pulled his skirt up to show his jocks. Another rolled on the floor giggling helplessly. Then Elton spotted the grand marble staircase that led to the swimming pool. Time for a bit of voguing.

'Over there, over there,' he squealed, making sure everyone knew their place on the makeshift catwalk. I was instructed to record it all on camera.

It's astounding how wearing a dress can transform a personality. The posturing and hip wiggling could have, with a good stretch of the imagination, been out of a Paris parade. Well, maybe not. Some of the girls got a little over-excited and ran back time and time again, prancing about like half-drunk trannies at a karaoke night. Elton, not to be outdone, slid down the banisters screeching like a banshee, and finally, out of voice and party-tricks, the group headed back to the lifts. As the doors closed, Elton couldn't resist pulling up his skirt for the camera. Of course he had nothing on underneath.

The whole night was a harmless hoot, and once back in our rooms, undressing was as much fun as dressing-up. Still revved, the giggling party boys eased and squeezed each other out of their dresses and kicked off uncomfortable high heels. Wigs went in all directions.

Then Elton suggested scaling Haleakala, the world's largest dormant volcano, to catch the sunrise. Although one of the most beautiful sights in the world, the bad news was that we would have to start the trek at 4 am. So we stayed up all night, watching *The Wizard of Oz*, of all things, and then set off in the early hours, stumbling and cursing in the darkness. Thank God the hotel thoughtfully provided us with blankets and thermoses of black coffee.

As it turned out, Elton's timing was askew. We beat the sun by a full two hours. Sitting about in the freezing darkness made me think that time had created night as a punishment and sleep as a gift. However, it was worth the wait. The sunrise was spectacular, but next time Elton gets to write the travel brochure, not schedule the trips.

One Sunday afternoon, as we headed off to various swimming and sunbaking sites, Elton told us over breakfast to be back there by 3 pm on the button. He wouldn't tell us why. It was to be a big surprise. It turned out that New Kids On The Block were playing that night on the main island of Oahu, and, as a treat for the eight of us, Elton had hired a 737 to fly us over to catch the show. Imagine a Boeing 737 with fewer than ten passengers aboard, when they normally carry around 115 people. Room to spare! We all took turns sitting in every seat on the plane, just for the hell of it.

New Kids On The Block, then at their peak of teen hysteria appeal, were pleased to meet Elton. He was old enough to be their father, but he looked like a rock star in black slacks, black shirt with huge white designs down the sleeve and black cap. The young musos crowded around, laughing and bantering, and gave us stacks of T-shirts and caps. They even asked Elton for his autograph.

We then went into the auditorium to catch the show with an audience of mostly 14-year-old girls. My ears can tell you that the kids paid good money to scream their way right through their concert. However, the New Kids put on a good performance: their choreography, in particular, was most impressive. After that we headed for a gay bar and went dancing. As everyone in our party, aside from Patch and me, was on AA courses, it was soft drinks all round.

The holiday mode rocked on – scuba diving at Kaanapali and Kapalua, checking out the restaurants and clubs and exploring the volcanic rocks. At one stage I decided to hire an aircraft for an acrobatic flight and told the others I'd buzz the hotel: I almost made it down the quick way when another plane headed straight for me.

There were a few down moments, but not many. Every now and again memories of the old times would filter through, and Elton would become maudlin. One night in particular, while at a restaurant, we chatted with a PR lady whom Elton had met by chance at an AA Co-dependency meeting. He invited her to our farewell dinner, and she had broached the subject of food and, in particular, marzipan.

'When I was married, Renate and I would binge on marzipan and chocolate,' Elton recollected. 'She would buy whole blocks of it . . . then she'd eat 5 lb of chocolates.'

'But she was never heavy, though,' she said, thinking Elton was either exaggerating or joking.

The month soon flashed by. It was great fun, and I really enjoyed myself, but the time was fast approaching for us to leave, and people started talking about their plans for the future. Elton was returning to America to start recording again, and he intended to help Hugh establish a chain of ice-cream parlours. I was hoping they would suggest I come over to LA, but it was not to be.

One night when Hugh was talking about his venture, I'd become so stressed by listening to them working out their future without me, that I blurted out how much I'd love to work in America with them. Hugh thought it was a great idea. So did Elton, who promised to follow it up after they got back. When they left a day ahead of me, our goodbye was a quick hug and a 'we'll ring you'. Nothing sentimental said, but Elton had given me a farewell card.

I returned to Australia. No phone calls. After six weeks I rang Elton, who told me evasively that they were still looking into the possibility of getting me a job with them. It'd be great to have me there, he enthused. A month later, it was the same answer, but less enthusiasm. Six weeks later, there was still no call. I rang Elton and Hugh. The phone number had been changed.

Later in the year, around Christmas, when the design company I was working for went broke, I took the plunge and rang John Reid in England. I told him I was unemployed and could he do something for me? I really wanted to live in London. In what seemed a genuine and obliging tone, he said it was too close to Christmas to do anything, as all the companies were shutting for the festivities, but that he'd ring in late January. I never heard from Reid. Or Elton. Or Hugh. It dawned on me that I'd been wiped. Elton might have been trying to change his life and come to grips with his unhappiness, but some things didn't change. If he wasn't using you, you were off the agenda. C'est la vie.

Next to my bed was a photo of me, bronzed and happy, which he'd given me on our last day together in Hawaii. Scrawled over it was: 'To Gary, all our love. Elton and Hugh.'

And when I wanted to remember the best of times, I'd pull out the card Elton had handed me as we'd said goodbye in Hawaii. It was dated 25 February 1991 and ended:

'I pray that you find some happiness when you go back to Oz. If you reach out, people will help. It's very hard to do – it took me 43 years to ask for help. But I'm so happy now. I want you to be happy too.

I love you a lot (heaps). God bless. Elton.'

11. Finale
Nobody Wins

'They [the tabloids] can say I'm a fat old cunt, they can say I'm an untalented bastard, they can call me a poof, but they mustn't tell lies about me.' Elton to *Q* magazine, April 1995.

HOW I LOVED Elton, as much for his weaknesses as his genius, for it was his vulnerability that allowed my inclusion in his life. Me, the reluctant lover to a star. No matter how absurd a notion that seems, it is my reality.

With the wisdom of hindsight, I can see how and why Elton and I went wrong. He needed to find an innocence that had to be spoilt, to be controlled, unconquerably alluring and, most important, sweeter in promise than life. Someone that he might have been. It was an illusion, a fantasy promising that there would always be more to be found. So he returned to me, again and again. Despite boys, men and wife, mother and mansions, health and wealth, success and adoration. Or because of them?

It was not that I consciously pursued Elton. In fact, I spent most of our time together worrying that I might be expelled from the empire. But he needed me. I had become part of his psyche, the 'boy' friend, the 'man child' he could shape into a better version of himself, a private and perfect person, to return to Dwight and start again.

Each time he came to me, I gave myself. Each time, I fell short of the mark because I was not perfect. I was like him – and each meeting became more desperate than the last. I was his chance to make it right. And once he had me in his presence, representing all the things Dwight could not be, he would punish me, denigrate me, humiliate me. Somehow I instinctively understood his need, and, despite the pain, I kept coming back for more. This was my love.

As with any relationship, ours had been the collective container of the needs of each of us. It wasn't a one-way exchange, for we both fumbled through distracting rituals of sensuality to find ourselves. But whether the match would ever have worked – well, I doubt it. The seeds of our destruction had been planted well before we met in that Brisbane hotel room. He was a victim, and I was the victim's victim. Puppets of our past, we each looked to be cherished, and rejected affection in our search to find it. It's a no-win formula.

Looking back from 1995, Elton John's career has held up well. Fellow musicians continue to hail him as one of the great songwriters of our time. Pop star, Howard Jones suggested that young couples who were too embarrassed to propose to each other could just as well play any of Elton's ballads. Billy Joel invited him to play 21 shows around America in July 1994 on a duet tour playfully called *The Piano Men Tour*. Joel, who often plays Elton songs during soundcheck and burst into 'Your Song' at a Long Island show earlier in the year, made sure that the two of them would jam on each other's songs.

Even the hard rock fraternity are seeing through the old outrageous costumes and balladeer reputation to come to grips with his music. Much of this has to do with the fact that Axl Rose of Guns 'n' Roses hailed him as a major influence in his music and duetted with him on 'Bohemian Rhapsody' at Freddie

Mercury's tribute concert in London.

In the 90s, another generation have looked closely at Elton's work and dismissed preconceptions of him as a buffoon playing sissy songs. There's something irresistible about a figure who, at a time when the leaders of 90s rock seem negative about life and almost hostile to their fame, Elton has the enthusiasm and talent to realize his own musical fantasies. There's been a growing interest in revisiting Elton's mid-70s albums like *Rock of the Westies*, which he made when he started to take cocaine. *Blue Moves*, the double album from 1976, which was rejected for being too dark and humourless, is being reassessed by some critics as a compelling piece of work.

John Reid admitted that he was petrified when Elton started working on his 1992 album *The One* because it was the first album Elton had completed while sober for a very long time. The title track was a flashback to the genius of earlier days, but too many other cuts were paddling shallow water. Still, that fitted right into the conservative 'if it rhymes, recycle it' attitude of the early 90s, and the album charted.

According to interviews, Elton's current ambitions are to work with people he admires, like Sting, Bonnie Raitt and Eric Clapton. When asked to look back at his career, he says:

'I'm just really happy to have survived so long. I'm happy after all this time to be as enthusiastic as I still am. I probably worked too hard, and there was a time when I felt burnt out, not fresh any more.

'I take each day as it comes now. I don't have any professional ambitions left. The ideas just seem to arrive now when they need to arrive.'

But the smartest move Elton made in 1994 was to become involved with *The Lion King*, Walt Disney's full-length animated film. Its use of state-of-the-art computer technology gives its visuals a sense of epic spectacle that is perfect for the storyline, based in the African bush. The movie was a box-office smash and has provided Elton – who wrote the music for the soundtrack to Tim Rice's lyrics – a universal hit with 'Can You Feel the Love

Tonight'. It was to consolidate yet another Elton John record – he is the only artist to score a Top 40 hit on the American charts for 25 consecutive years. Until a few years before this release, only Elvis Presley achieved that milestone.

Tim Rice, spinning from the mega-success of *Aladdin*, was asked by the Disney corporation to choose an artist to work with him on *The Lion King* soundtrack, and he said: 'Elton John'. He then added, 'You won't get him because he's either too expensive or too busy.' As it turned out, Elton was available. He was hired and in a tape on the making of the film says the compositions came to him quickly. The rest is history. *Lion King* quickly outsold *Aladdin* and is tipped to become the biggest-selling home video in America.

As soon as he started on the work, Elton was instantly acclaimed 'a genius' by arranger and digital synthesizer pioneer, Hans Zimmer. It seems Elton provided him with everything he needed to make the tracks come alive. The soundtrack for *Lion King* shows that as maturity comes, Elton's voice is taking on a new depth and strength. 'Can You Feel the Love Tonight' has a richness to it that provided the song with guaranteed chart-topping success.

Elton continues to work tirelessly for AIDS. He champions new performers like RuPaul and was the first of the 'old guard' to tip his hat to the arrival of Nirvana and the new breed of popular-music stars that followed in their wake. And looking back to his own youth, he understands and acknowledges that 90s kids need their own heroes, and he always encourages the next generation to pursue their own identity, to define their own place in time. At one award ceremony, Elton announced he was grateful to be asked to appear, but said he would have preferred it if younger acts had also been invited.

At the 1995 BRIT awards, he was honoured with an Outstanding Contribution to Popular Music award, presented by Sting before a studio cross to Rod Stewart. Elton and his old buddy teased each other referring to their nicknames, Phyllis and Sharon. Some of the best 90s acts performed but, without a doubt, Elton stole the show when he closed with a three-song set, concluding with 'I'm Still Standing', an obvious dig at his critics.

The award paved the way for his current album *Made In England* (his 40th), the title indicating that it was written and recorded entirely in the UK, something Elton had not done for a long time. Many of the songs like 'Please' and 'Pain' looked back at his 16 blurred years of emotional turmoil. 'Man' hinted it wasn't only the female of the species who struggle to come to terms with their sexual identity, while 'Belfast', complete with pipes and strings, was a rare Elton John political statement. Under the guidance of producer Greg Penny, the album touched on all those aspects that kept the traditional EJ fan happy – tear-jerking ballads, uptempo songs that were more clever than raunchy, superb musicianship – although generally the reviews suggested that while Elton and Bernie retained their flair, neither matched the cutting-edge inventiveness and freshness of 90s composers. Originally it was to be called *Blessed*, my favourite track on the album. It would seem that Bernie has also taken stock of his life, with lyrics that reflect all the craziness.

Elton made peace with Sheila and Derf, who returned from Spain in 1991 to live near him in Berkshire. They accompanied him to Los Angeles to the 67th Academy Awards in March 1995. Elton and lyricist Tim Rice were nominated for three of the songs from *The Lion King*: 'Can You Feel the Love Tonight?', 'Circle of Life' and 'Hakuna Matata', only the second time in the history of the awards that three songs from the same movie had been nominated. Elton performed 'Can You Feel the Love Tonight?' before good friend Sylvester Stallone announced it had won the Oscar for Best Original Song.

None of the millions of people watching the show would have guessed how devastated Elton was by a recent bereavement. His beloved grandmother, Ivy, had passed away the week before. On accepting the Oscar he thanked the Academy, his parents, his current companion David, and John

Reid and then dedicated the Oscar to Ivy, mentioning that she had been responsible for sitting him down at the piano at the age of three. During my days at Woodside, she and I had become very close; at times she was my only companion, and I loved her dearly. After the awards, Elton hosted a $7000-a-head AIDS benefit party.

As far as Elton's love life goes, Hugh has long faded from the picture. In April 1995, after keeping their affair a secret for two years, Elton revealed that his current love, 32-year-old David Furnish, had left his highly paid job with a London advertising agency to move in with him. Elton has shed a lot of the friends with whom he once took drugs and avoids the night-clubs he would once go to at five in the morning to score. He seems determined to cling to his clean lifestyle, realizing there is always the possibility of a relapse.

'But I don't have any fear in my life on a day-to-day basis,' he told Robert Hilburn of the *Los Angeles Times*, 'except in a relationship you have to work things out.' If only he had been that aware when I first met him, but life's not like that.

'Since I've been sober,' Elton said, 'I've been through deaths, been through the end of a relationship . . . things that I could never cope with before. I am so much more confident . . . so much easier to be around. I'm not afraid of confrontation. It's still hard for me to say no, but I have to learn.'

To arrive at this state of affairs, Elton attended over 1350 counselling sessions and had therapy groups in his house, some of which began at 6 am. He hasn't taken drugs since 1990 and, after three years of Alcoholics Anonymous meetings, does not drink any more. As part of his therapy, he continues to confront his past as honestly as possible. In his first major interview with the British media for four years, in February 1995 with *New Musical Express* (*NME*), he revealed he never voted, was intensely patriotic and was so desperate about his weight that he underwent a series of injections of lambs' urine. He almost shook his head when contemplating the days when he would complain if the colour of a private plane or hotel-room furniture weren't to

his liking and demand instant change. He was no less forthcoming about past excesses.

'I would not eat for three or four days because I'd be doing
coke and then I'd sleep for two days, then I'd get up and I'd be
starving hungry,' he told *NME*. 'So I'd have three or four pots of
cockles, then I'd have three bacon sandwiches and then a pint of
Häagen-Dazs vanilla ice-cream. So then I'd go and throw up, then
I'd do the whole lot again. I'd throw up and it would be all down
my dressing gown, there was no shame in anything I did.'

In other interviews around this time, he talked of trying
heroin once and throwing up, and of how life became a haze of
cocaine, alcohol and marijuana. How he would have a snort
every four minutes. If he went out for dinner, he would wolf
down the meal, sink half a dozen Martinis in rapid succession and
rush back to his hotel room within half an hour, because he knew
there was a gram of coke there. How he would have seizures
when he took cocaine, but this would not deter him from having
a snort ten minutes later. How angry he was because the cocaine
took control to the extent that he broke his all important rule
about live performances – never play a concert stoned. How he
tried to figure out the amount he spent on the white powder over
the years and gave up, too scared to know the truth.

Despite his fulsome admissions, Elton remains prickly about
what is written about him. In November 1993 he was awarded
£350,000 in libel damages after the *Sunday Mirror* claimed he'd
been spotted at a party at John Reid's, taking a bite out of a
seafood canapé and then spitting it out into a napkin. He had not
attended the gathering.

Elton's attitude is to enjoy life as much as possible and to be
generous. At the back of his mind, there is still the relief that he
escaped becoming entrapped like Elvis Presley. He can see the
irony in the comparison. It had been 'Heartbreak Hotel' that had
made him fall in love with rock 'n' roll as a child. In 1977, when
he met Presley a few minutes before a show in Washington, Elton
walked away with tears in his eyes because the King's situation
seemed so pathetic. Yet just ten years later, some of Elton's own

friends and associates were tearfully walking away from him for the same reason. They did try and help him, he says, arguing with him and taking his drugs away. He just wouldn't listen.

He obviously thought marriage would solve his problems. It didn't. He admits he got married 'for the wrong reasons', that he'd tried to find happiness with a woman because his male relationships didn't seem to be working. While he still declares Renate is one of the 'classiest' human beings in the world, they no longer see each other.

Elton is now worth £110 million, making him the 92nd richest person in Britain; the spending demons still, however, seem to be hovering. His car collection numbers 15, including a £400,000 V6 Jaguar, and, according to press reports, he has built a 'castle' for his Shetland ponies at Woodside, while a room in his house in Atlanta is decorated entirely in Cornish seashells. He still holidays with 40 suitcases and buys three copies of every new album release so he can keep one in each of his houses.

The French magazine *Voici* reported in June 1994 that Elton had spent £21,000 for a day by the sea with eight friends. This included hire of a 12-seat luxury helicopter, which took the party to St Tropez (£12,000), a Bentley and Mercedes to transport them to the beach (£4000), the hire of Coco Beach for two hours (£1500), a standby suite in the nearby Byblos Hotel in case he or one of his guests wanted a shower (£500), a round of shopping that included shirts and an antique watch (£2000), a motorboat to take the exhausted group 500 metres to the main quay (£500) and then a helicopter back to Cap Ferrat, where a suite cost about £700.

The sleazy side of Elton's personal life is no longer of much interest to the tabloids. He has robbed them of the dirt by speaking regularly and honestly about his bad old days. It's the perfect PR ploy: 'The biggest mistake I made was taking drugs, but I've learnt from it. It's got me to a point in my life where I'm very happy. Maybe I had to go through that experience to find myself personally.

'It was a long road . . . I wouldn't advise anyone and say,

"Don't do that" or "Do that", it's up to each individual. I couldn't take just one, I had to have so much it didn't help matters at all. I regret that.

'But, you know, you can't dwell in the past. You can't have too many regrets because all you have is today . . . and today I'm happy. I don't do drugs or drink any more. I'm glad I don't. It's made my life much easier to deal with.'

In some senses his attitude has changed, but he is still self-centred and the 'I's dominate his language. He's found a way to unload his emotional baggage, and the star is back in orbit; the universe, his universe is OK. I suffered personal hell, but I'm pleased he's feeling good.

You might wonder how this trauma between us could come about. How could two intelligent human beings – logical, sensitive, settled in their sexuality, strong in their convictions, able to analyze and dissect – fall in and out of lust and love in a torturous, obsessive tangle that runs for over a decade? If you doubt the intensity, just recall the events. Yet even after Elton's therapy, the end of our relationship and his clutching for 'a new life', he fails to understand the extent to which he devastated me and how he affects my life.

When I started to write this book, Elton's circle of friends and associates began to ostracize me. Molly Meldrum is one who cuts me off. So do some of our mutual friends. Not all though. A lot of my gay friends who've come to terms with their victimization because of 'the system' understand it's a tale that has to be recounted.

When Elton tours Australia in 1993, I am interviewed by *Woman's Day* magazine and Channel 9's *A Current Affair*. Elton, who is usually honest with the media about his past problems, can't – or won't – come to grips with the gulf between us. His lawyers unsuccessfully attempt to stop *A Current Affair* from running the interview with me. The producers offer him the opportunity to reply. He refuses. So the Channel run parts of a TV New Zealand interview. It's a contrived piece of denial and PR media manipulation. Confronted with my revelations, Elton says:

'It's very hard to live with someone like me because I'm such a dominant personality, and because you have to deal with Elton John business people around and stuff like that.'

Elton claims that 'Gary was always well treated.' Then he admits, 'I was very unpredictable, no one knew from one minute how I was going to be. I hurt a lot of people that I loved.' Remorse without action is a bit thin, but no one bothers to make the point.

Real Life, the main rival to *A Current Affair*, fights back in the ratings war with a suitably inflated, soppy piece, in which Elton's media training comes to the fore. The interviewer is chosen because he is safe: the themes covered are predictable – Elton's new life, the old lows, young Ryan White's courage in the face of AIDS and the compassion of Ryan's family towards those who hounded them: 'They had simple dignity, which was everything I wanted and which I was a million miles from.'

To draw attention away from the main issues my story raises, Elton wanders down another track. He says he doesn't care what people think of his £15,000 hair transplant because it is not a wig. He enjoys washing and shampooing it. Hardly mind-blowing comment from a middle-aged millionaire whose songs have influenced people all over the world for more than 20 years. But it's trivia time with a purpose. Elton knows most people couldn't care less about his hair, as bad as it looked, but it distracts from the meatier issues.

'I've been to Australia so many times, and this is the first time I'll be sober,' he admits, grinning broadly, and the interviewer almost wets his pants. According to most reports, next time the star had better come drunk because his last Australian tour was highly forgettable – it certainly lost him a lot of repeat business. God bless *The Lion King*, though, for that success has given him another burst in the southern hemisphere.

Elton seemed to spend most of his time in Australia in 1993 attempting to salvage his image. His reaction to my interviews is feigned nonchalance – I'm disappointed but, it doesn't really bother me. The PR machine has trained him well, and he avoids mentioning my name. I am a mirage that Elton is anxiously waiting to watch vanish.

My sincere wish is that he can successfully plumb the depths where Reggie Dwight waits, and that both are for ever happy, one with the other. For when he's on the up curve, Elton is the nicest person I've ever met, and when the demons depart, Elton, oh, my Elton, an angel sings.